TWICE
A
SOLDIER

TWICE
A
SOLDIER:

One American's
Life & War Stories

RUSSELL BABCOCK

with Glen Sharp

– 27 Rivers Press –

New York – London

Published by 27 Rivers Press

***

Communication may be directed to TwiceASoldier1961@gmail.com

***

***

***

Cover design by Crystal Gibbon

***

In-Publication Data Keywords: American military history; Vietnam War; Delta, Colorado; Fort Riley, Kansas; South Korea; Tennessee; 101st Airborne Division; Biography and Memoir; Hue, Vietnam; Tet Offensive

ISBN-13: 978-1546977780
ISBN-10: 1546977783

I dedicate this book in memory of

My mother, Naomi Irene Babcock

And my sister, Donna Jean Cooper

TABLE OF CONTENTS

INTRODUCTION

The officers checking the new recruits at Fort Carson, Colorado, that February day in 1990 didn't know what to make of me. Their paperwork said Russell Babcock was 35 years old, but one look at the man in the flesh told them otherwise.

I was actually 48. The recruiter lied about my age for the military's computer system to accept me for my requested post there at Fort Carson.

It was the second time I enlisted in the Army. The rest of the story was in the hard silver Samsonite briefcase that I'd originally bought while at Fort Carson in 1971: enlistment papers; leave papers; financial and insurance statements; certificates for my three Purple Hearts, Bronze Star and Silver Star; a letter of appreciation from President Nixon.

A lot of water had passed under the bridge from my joining the Army in 1961, at age 19, to my deployment to Vietnam to my military exit in 1973. Most of that water collected in my military 201 File, so I thought a nice briefcase would come in handy to keep it all together.

Little did I know that my briefcase would come in handy again nearly twenty years later, when I decided to re-join.

I won't feed you a line about how I joined both times out of love for my country, though I do love my country. The fact is that the first time I enlisted was after an enjoyable summer harvesting crops, and I didn't know what I was going to do during the winter. The second time was after a far-flung series of jobs made me realize I could make just as much money working for Uncle Sam while giving my life some structure.

A look through my briefcase straightened out the personnel specialist at Fort Carson. My military record exempted me from age restrictions. But, the question on the minds of my new cohorts was: Can this old man survive training?

***

I initially wanted to set down my story for my family, but I feel anyone entering the Army or wanting to know about the Vietnam War or wondering what life was like before the internet may find interest in it.

I was a grunt in Vietnam, stayed a grunt in National Guard and Army Reserve service, and remained a grunt when I rejoined the Army. By the time I retired from the Army at age 56, I was probably one of the oldest grunts still marching.

This story is told from my point of view as boots on the ground in war and as a working man in peace, sometimes living high and sometimes scraping by, but always doing it my way.

Chapter One
Colorado Boy

The Pacific Northwest was the end of the trail for many of the old pioneers crossing America, but it's where my trail begins.

My dad, Leroy Babcock, and my mom, Irene, were living in Wenatchee, Washington, when I was born January 14, 1942. They had a stormy relationship. I don't know what brought them together in the first place, but it wasn't enough to keep them together for very long at a time.

Though Mom's first name was Naomi, she preferred to be called by her middle name, Irene. Born in Greensburg, Kansas, in 1919, she enjoyed doing hobbies that were common to many farm families: quilting, rug making, embroidering and making ceramics, and would sell and give away her finished projects. She could cook, too. Mom was a woman who was big in heart and body. Everybody who knew her loved her.

Dad was a different story. He was a scrapper, and the mood to fight followed him home too often. I never knew much about him because he wasn't around much and rarely talked to me aside from scolding. I have never cared to find out what became of him after he left us for good.

Shortly after my birth, during one of my parents' spats, Mom and I moved to Delta, Colorado, where her family lived. Nearer to Utah than Denver, Delta is on the western slope of the Continental Divide, in the fork of the Gunnison and Uncompahgre rivers. It was a former fur trading post that grew into a small town. On the north side of town, there was still an old cottonwood tree that had been the meeting place of the settlers and the Indians. Farmers in the area benefited from good soil.

Grandpa Walter and Grandma Logan, Uncle Fred and Aunt Louie Logan, and Uncle Howard and Aunt Lucille Logan had lived in Delta for years. Grandpa and Uncle Howard had brick houses next door to each other. Uncle Fred lived a block away in a log house.

I don't recall where Mom and I stayed, but she would say that after I was done eating I would climb down from my high chair and throw my plate out the door.

In spring 1946, Mom and I moved to Helena, Montana, where Dad was working construction. We stayed in tents on a site where a bridge was being built. There was a mess tent where everyone would eat meals. This tent had an old-style refrigerator that in those days was just called an ice box. Some mornings the ice box would be raided by a brown bear that lived in the nearby woods. He would leave the ice box lid open and drop a trail of food on his way home. This went on for several weeks until, finally, the construction workers hunted down the bear, and filled the ice box with his meat. The meat of older bears has a strong smell, and I still remember it seventy years later.

One day while Dad was working, a telephone pole rolled over his right foot, smashing his big toe. You would think a co-worker would have been around to take him to the doctor, but evidently not. He was unable to drive the jeep by himself and Mom didn't know how, but together they managed to get to the doctor's office, and he received treatment and his foot healed.

When winter set in, we moved from the wilderness to a basement apartment in town, but I may have been better off left behind.

Before the world became touchy-feely, you could ask people if they remembered a childhood whipping, and they would tell you about it like it were yesterday. The worst whipping I ever got was over a five-cent candy bar. The neighbor woman asked me if I'd like to go to the store with her and her daughter. I got permission and went along. The woman bought her daughter and me a candy bar apiece. When Dad saw my candy bar, he asked if I stole it. When I said no, he whipped my butt with his leather razor strap. He marched me down to the store, where the clerk verified the neighbor lady bought the candy. He marched me back home and whipped me again. Then he took me to the neighbor lady's house, and asked her if I'd begged for the candy bar. She said no, but when we got home he whipped me a third time for good measure.

Another day, the neighbor girl and I decided to throw rocks at tin cans in the yard. I thought the safest place to stand would be behind her. I was wrong. She didn't know how to throw rocks. She wound her arm around and released the rock behind her back and into my eye. My black eye ended that game.

***

I started school in fall 1948. That winter was so cold it seemed the plumber had to come to the house nearly every day to thaw the water pipes. One day while walking to school, I grew so cold I couldn't move. An older girl grabbed my coat and dragged me on to class.

Our apartment had a single wood-and-coal stove for cooking and heating. Mom was lighting it with kerosene one day when the kerosene can caught fire. She hurried to the door to toss it out, and as she did I walked in and some flaming liquid fell on my head. I spent the next week in the hospital. Not long after, I spent another week in the hospital getting my tonsils removed, but at least that time I was given ice cream for every meal.

One bright spot in our time in Montana was the birth of my sister Donna, on February 10, 1948, which was Mom's birthday too. They would always have fun celebrating their birthdays together.

Another bright spot was the gift of a bicycle from my mom. I recall riding my bike up and down a street and seeing a boy with a slingshot shooting rocks at me and at windows. He wasn't very good, and missed me. When he dropped his slingshot in a bush and bent over looking for it, I rode past and kicked him in the butt, knocking him down. That put an end to his game.

The end of my childhood in Montana came when Mom moved Donna and me back to Delta, Colorado. She and Dad called it quits for good. Sad to say, I wasn't sorry to be rid of him.

We moved into a wooden four-room house that sat across a field from Uncle Fred's. I ran around the neighborhood with his son Dwayne. One evening we went walking and didn't come back until shortly after dark. Uncle Fred whipped Dwayne for being out late, and then came to our house wanting to whip me for keeping Dwayne out. Mom talked him out of it, but she ended up whipping me herself.

During a visit to Grandpa's house, my sister Donna and I went next door to Uncle Howard's so we could play with our cousin Wanda in a tent Howard put up in the yard. Howard happened to walk out of the house as I was holding a stick a few inches over Wanda's head. He and I locked eyes. In that instant, I knew he thought I was going to hit his daughter and that I needed to start running. The chase was on. I raced around his house, into Grandpa's yard and around that house and back around to Howard's before he caught me. Of course, he whipped me.

***

When school started, I walked. My path went along Third Street to the top of a hill, left down a trail, across Fourth Street, over a bridge crossing a creek, and then another block to school.

Kids played marbles in those days, mostly boys but sometimes girls. We'd chalk a circle on the pavement, put some marbles in it, and then use a thumb to launch a larger marble into the group to knock marbles out of the circle. Whoever knocks out the most marbles is the winner.

Among my friends were Lloyd Robert, whose dad owned a funeral home; Sky Fairlamb, whose dad and uncle were lawyers; Charles Fiedler, whose dad was a farmer; Danny Blaine, whose dad was a banker; and Reggie Jordan, whose dad was a fireman. I also remember Charlene Apple, Lloyd Armour, Mary Bones, Steve Crocker, Jerry Crim, Richard Jones, second-grade teacher Mrs. Thompson, and third-grade teachers Mrs. Winters, Mrs. Sidebottom and Mrs. Aschenbremmer.

I recall the school day started at 8:30 a.m. and we had two ten-minute recesses to play in the morning, a forty-five-minute break at noon to eat and play, and two more ten-minute recesses in the afternoon. We also took a half-hour nap on rugs after lunch. For class work and studies the teacher would pass out pages for us to copy the alphabet and numbers. We also got to color pictures. For recess, we could slide, swing, play kickball, run, use the big round slide, swing sets, saw horses, or baseball field. Heck, we even played cowboys and Indians without worrying about offending anyone.

In second grade, some of the girls joined the Brownies and the boys joined the Cub Scouts, including me. Mom bought me a blue cap, yellow-and-blue scarf and a blue shirt. Sky Fairlamb was in my den, and we'd go to his house for meetings because it was so big – three floors! It was at the corner of Fourth and Fifth streets, across from a store.

During fall of our third grade year, we were excited to take a field trip from Delta to Olathe, Colorado, on the last passenger train before the line shut down for winter.

***

After third grade, Mom moved us two miles outside town onto High Garnet Lane, into a four-room wooden house on Louis Shelby's 40-acre farm, where we stayed until I graduated high school in 1961. It had two bedrooms, a living room and kitchen. We did farm work in exchange for some room and board; Mom also received welfare checks.

I recall two things that happened soon after moving. Our previous house on Charles Street burned down, and I broke my arm. In the Shelby yard was an old set of bed springs, and somehow I fell on them, bending and breaking my right wrist. I wore a cast for six weeks.

Wearing that cast was no fun when trying to adjust to farm life. Yes, Donna and I had room to run around and play with the Shelby kids without being whipped, but we also had serious chores to do.

Our house didn't have running water. It had a cistern outside, and we dropped a bucket on a rope to pull up water to haul inside for drinking, washing dishes and bathing. When we wanted to take a bath, we'd heat the water in pots on the wood-burning stove then pour it into a big, round metal washtub. Once a month I was lowered into the cistern to scrub it clean. I also had to chop wood and carry it and coal into the house.

Delta, Colorado, where I was raised.
From top: Old Days, Middle Days, Nowadays.

As you probably guessed, our toilet was outside too. It was an old wooden outhouse that was mighty cold during Colorado winters.

About a hundred feet of fenced area separated our house from the Shelby home. Sometimes Louis kept pigs in the pen. Louis and his wife Hazel had two girls and two boys: Nancy, Catherine, Roy and Ray. Their family home was a three-bedroom cinder block with living room, kitchen and back porch. The acreage included a silo, a corral with a stream running through it, and a barn with a haystack.

The corral ran downhill, and in summer we kids would grab the cows' tails and let them drag us through the grass like we were skiing. Once, the Ellis brothers, who lived on a farm down the road, were both hanging onto our cows' tails and the cows ran toward each other. We gritted our teeth at the thought of the coming collision, but the cows turned away at the last second. One of the boys lost his grip and fell on his knees. The other brother tripped over him, and rolled behind another cow that kicked him in the head. The kick just missed his temple, which could have killed him. As it was, Mr. Shelby rushed him to the hospital. We never rode the cow tails again.

***

Colorado has a dry climate, very little moisture in the air. It may have changed, but I recall the weather service in Colorado measuring the temperature in degrees Celsius, instead of Fahrenheit like in other states. In the winter, on a clear day with no wind, the temperature would be 16 degrees Fahrenheit and we would play in T- shirts. We ice skated on ponds and rode tire inner tubes down snowy hills.

We had a lot of fun making a sled that could slide from the front or back and spin around. We took the runners off a broken sled, nailed each runner to a two-by-four then nailed the two-by-fours to one-by-twelve boards, which we connected with crossbars. We bent water pipes at the front and back to connect the runners. One day we were out sledding and Catherine Shelby, who was in a dress, said she wanted to ride. She made me promise not to make a U-turn, for fear of flying off. I promised, but when we got about three-quarters of the way down I made a U-turn back up the hill. She went down that iced hill on her panty butt. Boy was she mad. She chased me around for a good five minutes.

With no money to spare on buying toys, we made our own toy boats and cars out of wood. We also made archer's bows with sticks and string, and arrows with cattail stocks.

On the first of the month, Mom got her welfare check. She and Donna and I would walk two miles to town for groceries at Safeway. Mom would buy two ten-pound bags of sugar, twenty pounds of flour, a ten-pound bag of beans, and various canned goods. When we were done shopping, mom would call a taxi, load everything in the trunk, and home we went.

Mom would make light dough bread. She'd mix flour, sugar and yeast, let the dough rise then smash it into balls. These would rise up into buns. Some of the dough Mom flattened the dough into strips, on which she spread a mix of butter, sugar and cinnamon. Then she rolled the strips and let the dough rise again. Donna and I couldn't wait for these cinnamon rolls to come out of the oven.

In the fall, mom would do a lot of food canning. The Antelope Hill Orchards, about fifteen miles from us, grew sweet cherries and sour cherries, apples, pears and peaches. Because the farmers irrigated the peaches, they would grow up to five inches around and when we bit into them the juice would run down our chins. Mom would buy a couple of bushels of cull fruit, the fruit left after the packing shed sorted the best and shipped it out of state. Mom would also buy corn, beans and tomatoes for canning.

Back home, we all helped with the canning. We stoked the fire in the wood-burning stove, and Mom would put a big pan of water on it. When the water reached boiling, we dropped the peaches in for a couple of minutes then removed them to peel the skins. Then Mom would slice up the peaches for cooking in a big pot, after which she would put them in glass jars and put the lids on the jars. The last step was putting the jars in a pressure cooker to seal the lids.

The next house down the road from the Shelby farm belonged to the family of a boy in my class named Steve Crocker. After his little brother died, the family's brown-and-white dog Sandy wouldn't stay home. Sandy kept running to our yard. Eventually, the Crockers just let us keep her. If Mom left her basket of peaches in the yard, Sandy would grab one and eat it.

Our country road continued past the home of my first grade teacher Mrs. Anderson. We passed it every day in the school bus, which was driven by a man named Floyd, who was the driver for years.

My sixth grade teachers were Mr. Phillips and Mrs. Crumpacker, who taught two of my aunts before me then later my cousins Wanda and Dwayne and my sister Donna. She said Donna was a better student than me. Another sixth grade teacher was Miss Fettinger, who had a grey Plymouth car and kept the backseat loaded with boxes. She lived north of town with a lot of cats and kittens. She didn't mind if kids stopped by the house to see the cats.

I remember that sixth-grade year we had a half-day of school before Christmas, and one of the classes put on a play with grade school principal Mrs. Dixon singing holiday songs. Then in spring, at the end of the school year, we had a little graduation ceremony. The ceremony was the last one the school held; maybe the teachers decided it was too much trouble.

***

Junior high signaled it was time to start growing up. My classmates and I had to adjust to no recess in the morning and afternoon, just forty-five minutes to eat lunch and play. But we did have physical education class to use up any extra energy. The junior high school was built onto the south end of the high school building, and we had lockers just like the high-schoolers and different teachers for each class. I still remember some things from Colorado history class.

I was about twelve years old and therefore old enough to work on different farms around town after school and during the summer. I cleaned out ditches, plowed fields, and pitched or bucked hay. I bucked fifty-pound bales of hay from the ground into wagons pulled either by horses or tractors. When the farmers drove the wagons where they wanted, I then bucked the hay off the wagons to the haystacks. It was hard work, but the money helped my family and the exercise toughened me. Another bonus was learning to drive on the farmers' tractors or trucks.

Mom was a terrific, strong woman who raised my sister and me by herself. She taught me how to cook, and I've never gone hungry.

Some days I would eat four or five times: I would eat at home, stop by the neighbors' and be invited to eat there, eat lunch at school or home, eat later in the day if I was somewhere else and they were eating, then I would go home and eat supper.

***

I started high school during the fall of 1958, the ninth grade. I took gym, math, English, agriculture and possibly other subjects. I went out for basketball but didn't make the team. In the spring I successfully went out for track and field. Uncle Howard gave me his old track shoes, maybe the nicest thing he ever did for me. I competed in the mile run and the quarter-mile relay, and sometimes other events, and lettered in track. Another school activity I enjoyed was the Future Farmers of America. My fellow members elected me reporter all four years of high school, though I don't know how because my writing is bad, my spelling is worse, and my grammar … well, forget it.

During freshman year, my first class after lunch was English in room 109 with Miss Innis. We dissected sentences into nouns, pronouns and whatever else, and it nearly bored me to death.

Sophomore year classes included biology, gym, agriculture and more English. A cruel twist of fate placed me in English again right after lunch and again in Room 109 with Miss Innis. I took every opportunity to miss class or clown around.

One day the Red Cross was giving some kind of test. Mom signed my permission slip for it and Miss Innis said I could skip class. When my friend Kenny Sanders and I returned from the Red Cross test, Miss Innis sent me to the principal's office. Vice Principal Wigham asked me if I had taken Chinese, because I was sure failing English.

At that moment, I knew I was going to fail English and have to repeat it if I didn't get out of Miss Innis's class. Action was needed.

One afternoon I started throwing spit wads all over the classroom. Miss Innis didn't say anything, though. The next day I started throwing spit wads again, but this time Miss Innis took me to the principal's office. I was then transferred to Mrs. Baker's class, where I passed English. After we were out of each other's hair, Miss Innis and I became good friends.

There was a week or so that a wild urge took hold of me to skip some classes. I played baseball with different gym classes in the mornings and go to my agriculture class in the afternoons. Someone turned me in. During agriculture class, I was told to report to Vice Principal Wigham. He suspended me for several days. Mom didn't find out about that for a long time.

***

Outside of harvest season, I took a job working at a service station after school. Most stations in those days were full service, so I would pump gas for customers. A gallon of gas cost twenty-five cents. While the gas tank was filling, I would check the oil and water, and wash the windows and windshields at no additional cost, though customers sometimes tipped me. I also washed cars and changed oil and tires.

One evening when I got off duty, my friends Kenny Sanders and Charlie Dixon picked me up for a trip to a little bar in Hotchkiss, twenty miles away. In the 1950s and 1960s, Colorado allowed sixteen-year-olds to drink beer and eighteen-year-olds to drink hard liquor. We were in this bar drinking beer, and I hadn't eaten all day so it didn't take much for me to get drunk. The waitress bet me bottles of beer over games of pinball and pool, and I won enough beers until all I saw was colored lights. When we ate some fries and I got sick, they took me home. At my house, I stepped out of the car and fell to the ground. Kenny took me in to my room. When I lay down I had to put my foot on the floor to keep the bed from turning. The next morning Mom asked me how Kenny had gotten in and out without falling over her groceries and boxes that were on the floor.

***

We made more mischief in the Future Farmers of America when initiating new members. We blindfolded the candidates and seated them in chairs in the agriculture classroom. The teacher, Mr. Shaw, would read an offense and ask if a candidate was guilty. Someone standing behind a candidate would stick him with a pin, causing him to jump up. When Mr. Shaw would say "guilty," the blindfolded candidate would be led to the bathroom and made to kneel next to the toilet and retrieve an old candy bar that we left floating in the bowl. Not knowing it was a candy bar, the candidates would be grossed out.

That wasn't the end for them, though. We also made candidates drink from a jar of Sulphur water, which smells like bad eggs, and then eat raw eggs. We told them we'd wipe off their mouths, and we did so with Kotex tampons that we'd doctored with red food coloring.

Finally, we gave them pills that we told them would settle their stomachs, but the pills would actually turn their pee blue. When the candidates went to the bathroom the next morning, the sight scared the hell out of them.

***

One of the boys in my agriculture class, Keith Perchavel, lived a mile past the end of the bus route, so far out they still used kerosene lamps due to lack of electricity. He rode a horse to another farm then got on the school bus. I worked for his family one summer, during which time Keith had a girl cousin visit from Kansas for month. While I was mending fences one day, she was firing a BB gun. She asked me what would happen if she fired at a fence pole. I told her the BB would go back up the barrel of the gun, which it did when we fired the BB gun from one inch from the board post. When I turned my back, I heard her cursing a blue streak. She had fired the BB gun standing five feet away from the post, and the BB had come back and hit her in the chest.

***

During a couple of summers, I helped our neighbor Glen Dawding lay out land claims for potential uranium mining.

Glen, his wife, sons Gary and Dale and a daughter lived in a two-story house on a hill. They were Mormons, and were involved with building the local church in Delta.

During the 1950s and 1960s uranium was in demand due to the United States building a nuclear arsenal to protect us from potential Russian attack. A person could make a lot of money selling the material to Uncle Sam, there were uranium veins running through Colorado.

In plotting uranium claims, we had to make sure each was a thousand yards square. Glen would plant a post topped with a metal disk bearing a claim number then plot outward using a hundred-foot measuring tape. At each corner we'd also plant a post with a metal disk bearing the same claim number. We'd go out for days at a time, often climbing up and down hills and up vertical cliffs staking these claims, using Glen's Jeep pickup as our base of operations.

We staked a lot of claims in the southwest corner of Colorado near a little town called Dove Creek. We also went into Utah, around Moab. By day the temperature would reach 110 degrees. At night it would still be so hot we couldn't get to sleep until after midnight.

There were a few small uranium mines around Dove Creek. The miners would pick and shovel the dirt and rocks into steel carts on wheels, then push these loaded carts to the mine entrance, and dump the cart's contents into a chute. When the chute was full, a truck would haul it away.

A man near Moab, Utah, hit a big vein of uranium, a mine so big that he used front-end loaders to haul out the ore.

Glen wasn't so lucky, but he must have produced enough uranium to make the staking worthwhile or we wouldn't have spent so much effort climbing around in desert heat.

***

Fifty dollars was the amount needed to buy my first car, a 1947 four-door Plymouth. I was sixteen years old that year, 1958. The family of my friend Sky Fairlamb hired me to drive along canals and ditches on their property to make sure everything was clear. They bought the car for me and took five dollars a week out of my pay; I don't remember how much extra they paid me.

Though somewhat experienced driving farm trucks and tractors, I studied a driver's handbook prior to taking my driver's test, and successfully earned my driver's license.

A while later, driving home with Mom and my sister from seeing Uncle Fred in Norwood, about sixty miles from Delta, the Plymouth's motor blew up. Our landlord Mr. Shelby towed my car back to Delta to a junkyard. In those days before cell phones, we had to wait for another car to stop to take us to a phone at someone's house or store.

***

My next car was a 1949 Pontiac convertible, but just before my senior year of school I traded it for an almost new 1959 Pontiac from a man whose farm I'd worked on, Robert Reed.

. One afternoon I told Kenny that if he paid our way, I would drive us to his mom's place in the southeast corner of Colorado, about 200 miles away. We left Delta about dark that day. We had to go over Monarch Pass, elevation 11,100 feet, before we got to her house in Alamosa after midnight. She made us late dinner and some sandwiches to take with us. We stayed about two hours and left, heading back over the Continental Divide and Wolf Creek Pass, from the top of which you can look down and see every curve in the road for miles.

Along the way we picked up a road reflector next to a broke-down truck and were chased by an angry driver. We headed to Norwood where Uncle Fred lived. We had been up one night and two days when, about ten miles out of Norwood, we chewed some fifty milligram caffeine tablets to stay awake. Those pills should always be swallowed, never chewed because they leave a very bad taste in the mouth. We raced to the Dairy Queen in Norwood for two large milkshakes to get the nasty taste out of our mouths, and then killed a couple hours at Uncle Fred's pool hall. Heading back home, about midnight, we arrived in Montrose a town twenty one miles south of Delta, where we stopped at a service station to gas up.

As I turned back on the highway, Kenny said, "Hit it!" I stomped the gas pedal, and we were doing a hundred miles an hour going out the north end of town. A police officer in his own car, a 1960s Chrysler, gave chase. At Olathe, half-way between Montrose and Delta, we turned off and circled back toward Montrose before returning to the highway to Delta. The policeman had turned around and was going back to Montrose when he saw us and made a U- turn and the race was on again. In Olathe, the high school had a barbed wire fence at the end of the baseball field. I turned on a road near there, went about half a mile and parked on a hill under a tree.

A few minutes later the policeman came by us, driving along a canal shining his spotlight, He was really mad at us because he'd run his new car through the barbed wire fence.

With headlights off, I turned around for the highway, navigating the back roads, which were broken into one-mile squares. We crossed the highway, but I didn't know which direction to go. But Kenny did, so we swapped seats while going fifty miles per hour. We ended up about four miles west of Delta. Five miles further west, at the local dead man's curve, we saw the blue lights of the police. We maneuvered to the north end of town, parked at a friend of Kenny's, and changed license plates.

We left for Dove Creek, and messed around most the day then returned to Delta around 6 p. m. A Delta cop who didn't like me said that if he hadn't had his wife and kids in the car he would have chased us the night we left. We'd left Delta on Tuesday evening and this was Thursday evening: we had been rambling around two days and two nights. I don't know why he was mad; on Tuesday night we were only doing sixty miles per hour on the two-lane highway when the posted speed was seventy.

***

A couple days after my little trip with Kenny, a man I barely knew asked if I would take him to Vernal, Utah, about 180 miles away. I told him I would for thirty dollars plus food and gas. He gassed up my car and put a twenty-gallon drum of gas in the trunk. We started driving in the middle of the night and got to Vernal after sun up. On the road home, an oncoming pickup truck pulling a two-wheel trailer lost a wheel and axle off the trailer. The tire hit the front of my car then slid along the side with its axle poking a hole in the fender above my back tire. I was lucky it didn't puncture my tire because I didn't have a spare.

Back home, Uncle Howard's wife Lucille called me to take her and her daughter Wanda to Utah. It turned out my encounter with the flying tire and axle had broken my car's universal joint. With my Pontiac left at a local garage for repairs, I had a good excuse to tell her no.

It turned out that if I had taken Aunt Lucille and Cousin Wanda to Utah, I would have been put in jail.

Aunt Lucille had stolen all of Uncle Howard's savings bonds. When I declined to drive her, she got some random guy to take her and Wanda all the way to California, with Lucille cashing bonds and spending money so fast that the California police called Delta to ask if a bank had been robbed. I could have been arrested as an accessory and for transporting a minor, Wanda, across state lines.

Those car repairs saved me some trouble that time. As it was, in the two months I had it before the bank repossessed it, I put about 20,000 miles on that 1959 Pontiac and all but one original tire and rim had been replaced.

***

The fall of my senior year I started going steady with a girl named Jean Castoe and Kenny was going with a girl named Jackie,

Back then we could go to Davis Clothing and buy brand-name Stetson cowboy hats. Kenny and I bought low-crown black Stetsons with six inch brims. We put the girls' names on our hats in beads.

The night before Christmas break, Kenny and I got someone to buy us a quart of Jim Beam whisky. Like fools, we chugged it down without Coke chasers. The next morning, I was sicker than a dog. I made it to school, went to my bookkeeping class and told Mr. Hughes I was sick and that I was going to the gym to lie down. That afternoon I rode the bus out to Jean's house, eight miles out of town. We tried everything to settle my stomach: I drank baking soda and water, salt and water, and other things. Just before supper, I was feeling better until Jean's dad came in with a pint of Jim Beam. The sight of it made me sick again. For about ten years after that, I couldn't drink any hard liquor.

***

That spring, I went out for track again, still wearing the track shoes Uncle Howard had given me back in ninth grade. They had five spikes on the toe and two spikes on the heel because you are supposed to run on your toes - but I ran on my heels. I'd find that wasn't good for long runs.

Full of excitement for my final year of track, I thought I would train like a triathlon runner and run about twenty miles to build up my wind and endurance. I rode to Hotchkiss one evening and the next morning started to run back to Delta. I figured I could make the run in hours, so I traveled light, wearing my track shoes and carrying no water.

I jogged on the gravel beside the road. The farther I went, the more my feet hurt. Blisters formed on my feet. It took over five hours to get home, by which time I was limping something awful. It took a couple of days rest before I could get back into warm-up exercises, wind sprints, and mile runs. I did letter again that year, as I did in my previous years in track.

***

Graduation came at the end of spring. That last week, we turned in our books and received our report cards. The ceremony was held the night before the last day of school. The atmosphere was sufficiently formal as we wore caps and green gowns to receive our diplomas.

The next day, the last day of school, I filled five or six balloons with water, ink and ammonia and carried them in a shoe box to the school activities that morning. I kept them safe for their ultimate purpose.

After school, I rode the bus out to Jean's house. I knew that as I left the bus at Jean's, the Nickel kids, who lived on the next farm on the route, would still be on the bus. They were my targets. And so as I passed the Nickel kids to exit the bus, I threw the balloons at them.

My plan did not account for being caught. Floyd the bus driver made me stay on the bus back to the high school for discipline. Vice Principal Wigham said it would be a nice gesture if I cleaned Floyd's bus. But, I had graduated and there was nothing to force me to do it. Over fifty years have now passed, and I've never cleaned that bus.

***

In June I worked for Robert Talbert bucking hay. He would bail the hay in fifty-pound bales. An escalator on the front of his Ford tractor would pick the bale off the ground and carry over the tractor to the front of the trailer being pulled. I grabbed the bale as it came off the escalator and moved it to back of the trailer and stacked five rolls high. When the trailer was full, we went to the haystack - twenty bales wide by sixty bales long. By cross-stacking and lashing them together, we piled the stack fourteen or fifteen bales high.

At noon we'd break for lunch. Mrs. Talbert and her daughters Shannon and Louie would cook fried chicken, mashed potatoes, corn, bread and desert cake or fresh cherry pie and ice cream.

After sweating all day and getting hay dust all over me, I would itch so fiercely that most evenings I would go swimming in a canal.

Working for farmers during the summer and fall was great, but I didn't know what I would do during the winter months. It was the first time I wouldn't have school to keep me busy.

President Kennedy had taken office earlier in the year, and there was talk of building up the military to fight communism, so I decided to join the Army.

So on July 11, 1960, I met with the Army recruiter. He gave me a short test:

"Did you hear that car backfire?"

"Yes," I said.

"Put your left hand over your eye. What's the sign on the door say?"

"Recruiter."

"Can you write your name?"

"Yes."

"Good. Go home and pack a small suitcase: two shirts, two pair of pants, two t-shirts, two pair of shorts and two pair of socks. Meet me here at 6 o'clock tonight."

I did, and that recruiter put me on the bus to Denver for a trip that changed the course of my life.

Chapter Two

Fort Riley Shuffle – 1961-64

At the induction center, they prodded and poked us, gave us eye exams, listened to our hearts, watched us do knee bends. After we passed all of this, they gave us an aptitude test to see what jobs we were best suited for.

I tested pretty high in mechanic abilities. The recruiter had also noted what fields were best suited for. I was going into air defense missiles, to be stationed at San Antonio, Texas.

They swore us into the Army.

About 6 o'clock that evening they put some of us on the train The Spirit of St. Louis headed to Fort Riley, Kansas. We arrived at Junction City, a small town at the edge of Fort Riley, after the sun was up. A van was waiting to take us to the replacement company barracks in the old wooden hospital complex. The Department of Defense had activated the First Infantry Division, known as the Big Red One, so most of the soldiers were deployed – and we would be replacements. This was just after the Russians built the Berlin Wall.

They fed us breakfast then assigned us our bunk beds. There weren't any lockers. They gave us each ten dollars and a list of things to buy at the Post Exchange, or PX: two tooth brushes, two combs, two towels, and two cans of shoe polish.

The sergeants marched us to the barber shop. The barber asked me how I wanted my hair cut. I said just a little off the sides. He shouldn't have bothered asking. He set his clippers to leave a quarter-inch stubble. We had to pay for the haircut ourselves: thirty-five cents.

The sergeants took us to get our shots - inoculations for malaria, tuberculosis, etc. - and our uniforms. The sergeants showed us how to make our bunks with the sheets folded in hospital corners and the blanket so tight a quarter could bounce off it.

We were at the replacement barracks just long enough to fill a training battalion. Since we were making up the Division the sergeant asked me if I would sign a waiver foregoing my assignment to San Antonio to stay put. I did.

The cadre didn't teach us any military customs. We went from the replacement company area to Camp Funston, on the east side of Fort Riley, and were broken into companies. We lived in old wooden barracks from World War II, maybe even World War I, with twenty men per floor, two rows of double-high beds on each side of a center lane. On the center poles we put one-gallon cans for cigarette butts. Finally, we were issued footlockers. The top shelf was covered with a white towel, on one side of which we displayed comb, toothbrush, razor, and shaving cream. On the other side of the tray, a five-by-seven-inch card with brass and name tag, shoe polish and shoe brush. Along the edge were individually rolled socks. On the bottom shelf were individually rolled T-shirts, shorts, towels, a shaving kit and shoe polish kit. Our uniforms hung on a wood bar under a shelf.

Designated with a military occupational specialty, or MOS, category of lllB, I was assigned to be a combat infantryman in A Company 2nd Battalion 28th Infantry, the Black Lions; the unit won its name and crest in Europe during WWI. We launched into three weeks of basic training. We did PT (physical training) wearing t-shirts, pants and combat boots. The PT test included pull-ups, pushups, dodge-run-jump, horizontal bars and a one-mile run in boots. For the obstacle course, the sergeants placed a machine gun on a platform six feet high and fired live rounds over our heads as we crawled under barbwire. The idea was to simulate battleground conditions, but anyone standing up would actually be shot.

We learned to fire the M1 rifle, reliable and used by the military for decades, and the bazooka, which was more exciting. The sergeants loaded us into two-and-a-half-ton trucks, fifty soldiers in each, to go to the range. They instructed us on how to assemble the bazooka, load it and hold it on the shoulder. Most importantly, they advised not standing right behind it because of back blast. Then, we were allowed to fire the bazooka – definitely a highlight of training.

Excitement at the firing range was offset by the necessary but boring kitchen duty. We had to pull KP (kitchen police) one weekday twice a month and one weekend every three months. When the soldiers were done eating they'd drop their food trays in a window by the back door where the KP would scrape off the uneaten food in to the trash, rinse the tray, put it in a rack, and run the full racks through the big dish washer where boiling water sanitized the trays. Another KP would take the trays out, dry them, and return them to the door coming into the mess hall. KPs also swept and mopped the dining room floor, washed the tables, set the chairs, and washed the big cooking pots and pans.

Eventually, we were also assigned guard duty. The first sergeant chose a staff sergeant from his duty roster, three buck sergeants as relief commanders, and thirty privates to man the post.

One of our sergeants was Staff Sergeant Leonardi. He was a good-natured guy who was tough as needed. He guided us through our training. Another sergeant was Staff Sergeant White. He was six-foot-eight-inches tall and weighed about 300 pounds. He had played semi-pro football, so you didn't get in his way anywhere within a hundred yards – but at 105 yards, you could get out of the way.

My pay amounted to $67 once a month. There was a process to being paid. An officer and a guard from the battalion would go to Division Finance to pick up the money for the whole battalion. Then the pay officer from each company would pick up and count the money for every man in their company, according to each man's pink pay slip. First he would pay the officers and NCOS (non-commissioned officers), then the lower ranks would report for pay. You would salute and say, "Sir, Private Russell Babcock RA-176XXXXX reporting for pay, sir." The pay officer would count your money and hand it to you, and then you counted it, saluted and left.

After you got your money, you had to run a gauntlet of sorts – a line of people wanting to be paid. First in line was the first sergeant wanting donations for pet projects like the Red Cross or USO, then the supply sergeant wanting $20 dollars a month for doing laundry, and then just out the door were the loan sharks wanting payment of debts. You had to rely on loan sharks if payday fell on a holiday or a weekend, otherwise you sat in the barracks instead of going to town; the sharks would loan $5 if you paid back $10. Sometimes a man would borrow from several sharks, and by the time he worked through the line he had to go back to the first loan shark to borrow enough to pay everybody.

Everybody ranked below sergeant was subjected to bed check every night. You had to be back from town and in bed when the CQ (charge of quarters) came in about 11 o'clock. It was a regular routine for the MPs (military police) to go down with trucks haul soldiers out of the bars.

We would wake at 5:30 a.m., dress, make bunks, and be outside for PT at 6: chin-ups, pushups, and running. After PT, we would hit the mess hall to eat. The cooks and KPs gave you two strips of bacon, a large spoon of powdered eggs, two pieces of toast, a bowl of cornflakes, some fruit. We had ten minutes to eat before the sergeants started yelling and pulling us out of our chairs.

As we progressed in training, we took classes in the use of radios in the field. The PRC 25 radio weighed twenty pounds, and had a short antenna and a long antenna with a range of thirty miles to allow contact with artillery that could provide support from a distance. The PRC 10 weighed five pounds and had range of one mile for use by squads coordinating in their immediate area.

Classes also covered First Aid, map reading, bayonet training, battlefield formations, how to dig and build foxholes, and fields of fire (the area that can be covered with the firearms at hand).

We would take to the field on Fort Riley's Custer Hill, most of the time marching up in battlefield formation along the tank trail. There we set up a company defense perimeter. Staff Sergeant Leonardi would tell us where our foxhole would be, and assign two-man positions. Most of the time we made overhead covers for the foxholes. When night came, one man slept and one stayed on alert. Sometimes the coyotes that lived in the brush would come up to us. At 4:30 a.m., Staff Sergeant Leonardi would wake us to send us down to the mess for breakfast.

After five weeks of advanced individual training (AIT), we started testing in groups. First, squads tested, and if they failed they were retested. Then platoons, companies and, finally, the whole battalion tested.

It was November when the battalion tested. We loaded trucks with our equipment and traveled in convoy on Interstate 70 from Fort Riley to Goodland, Kansas, where we stayed overnight at the fairgrounds. We proceeded the next morning to Limon, Colorado, and then took Highway 24 to Fort Carson we stayed on post for three days doing PT: marching and getting used to high altitude and thin air. On the third day, the trucks delivered us somewhere in Pike Peak National Park.

We unloaded equipment and set up a company perimeter, everything we did at Fort Riley – except that now we were doing it in snow up to our knees. The mess sergeant picked a fine time to serve us ice cream for desert.

Staff Sergeant Leonardi assigned our positions. We broke pine limbs to bunk down on the ground, and stoked fires to stay warm. After a week of this, we returned to Fort Carson then Goodland and Fort Riley, where the next few days were spent cleaning equipment.

Back in time for Thanksgiving, the mess sergeant cooked turkeys, mashed potatoes, dressing and pumpkin pies. However, the rest of the holiday weekend and the weeks up to mid-December were spent on classes and work details. When Staff Sergeant Leonardi found I could draw, he assigned me to paint our unit's Black Lions crest on some parking signs.

Mid-December marked the first time we were granted leave. Half the men would be given 10 days of leave while the other half remained on post to keep things operating. I was among those left behind, but fortunately we only had to work half days.

One day after completing my duties, I went into the town nearest the base, Manhattan, Kansas. You could ride the bus for fifty cents or you could walk the two miles. I went to a movie, which at that time also cost about fifty cents. As I walked outside, I saw three or four guys from the company had gotten off the bus. We talked a bit then a couple of them went in the theater. PFC Orth invited me to go with him to the café where his sister worked. He was a skinny guy, a little slow; I remember once while we were cleaning weapons, someone handed him a Coke bottle with some cleaning fluid in it and he drank a little before he realized it wasn't Coke. At the café, I ordered a Coke, a hamburger and fries. We were sitting there talking, and Orth told his sister I wanted to take her to a movie. I hadn't said anything to that effect, but the three of us ended up going to a movie. It was better than sitting in the barracks.

Finally, a couple days after Christmas, the Army granted me leave. The bus trip to Delta, Colorado, took two days and when it arrived I still had to walk two miles out to Mom's house at the Shelby farm. We had a nice reunion for the evening, and the next morning I walked eight miles to my high school girlfriend Jean's house, where I stayed a few days before going back with Mom for a day. Then, I caught the return bus to Fort Riley.

The end of holiday leave meant getting back to the business of learning war. We dug into target practice.

I carried a Browning Automatic Rifle (BAR), weighing twenty-three pounds and firing a twenty-round magazine. It had short bipod front legs for stability when firing from a single position and a strap for us to carry it into assault while firing from the hip. All the BAR gunners in the company went to the 1,000-meter range to qualify on it. At the far end of the range were the targets, beneath which ran a trench where men lowered the targets to mark our shots and raised them back up for us to shoot again.

We started 100 yards away from the targets to zero our guns, or calibrate our gun sights, firing three rounds at the bull's eye. The man in the trench pulled the target down and marked the hits with black or white tape then ran the target back up to show the results. Ideally, you zeroed your weapon within twelve rounds, at which point you moved from the 100-yard line back to the 900-yard line, where everybody fired twenty rounds at the targets. Then, we moved up to the 800-yard line and fired twenty rounds. The hits were counted and they'd figure up if we qualified or bolo'd (failed). The qualification levels are marksman (lowest), sharpshooter (middle) and expert (highest). Experts can wear all three marksman badges on their Class A dress green uniforms if they want.

In February or March the battalion went to Camp Irwin, California, for two weeks of desert training. The sergeants told us to take our long johns, but we were going to the desert so some of us didn't believe them. We flew from Fort Riley to Edwards Air Force Base, arriving at night. The wife of our football-playing Staff

Sergeant White had fixed him a large box of fried chicken for the trip; he ate the whole the thing on our plane ride.

At Edwards, they loaded us on open semi-tractor trailers, basically cattle cars. We bounced along 75 miles across the desert to Camp Irwin. Unloaded from the trucks with our sleeping bags and field packs, we went to sleep almost immediately under some tin shelters.

After breakfast, we bounced on the trucks some more until we were in the middle of the desert. We dismounted the trucks and set up a company perimeter. The sergeants were right: It was cold in the desert. I was wearing a t-shirt, a wool shirt and a field jacket, and field pants. After dark I even put on another set of fatigues to try and stay warm.

The next weekend they trucked us to a shower. We rinsed off the dust and grit and changed clothes, then we went right back to the desert for another week. The next Friday we went back to Camp Irwin, but not before the desert claimed my Timex Electrica wrist watch. It felt good to shower again. We relaxed on Saturday, and it was warm enough to strip down to t-shirts – a nice break before the cattle-car ride to Edwards for the flight back to Fort Riley

***

That spring Kansas State University in nearby Manhattan sent its ROTC cadets to Fort Riley for a week's training to give them an idea how to lead troops as lieutenants. I instructed one squad of cadets, designating the squad leader and helping them simulate an ambush scenario. They were given five minutes to write a patrol order for the squad in reaction to an ambush. In the meantime, another ROTC squad instructed by one of my fellow soldiers was farther down the trail setting up the ambush. The two ROTC squads would follow their courses of action and engage in a mock fire fight. Afterward, we instructors would tell each group what they did right and wrong.

For the Fourth of July, the Air Force put on an air show by the Tuttle Creek Lake Dam outside Manhattan. One of the planes accidentally released a bomb. It didn't explode, fortunately, but no one was sure where it had landed. The next day our battalion went to Tuttle Lake to search the woods for it. We hunted all day and didn't see it. Finally, somebody in a helicopter spotted it by the dam. Had it exploded and destroyed the dam, the area would have been flooded.

In August our battalion flew to Norfolk, North Carolina, for two weeks of amphibious training with the Navy. The Company Commander made Staff Sergeant White stay at Fort Riley; he didn't want to take a chance that Staff Sergeant White would get stuck between decks on boat.

The first week was PT: raft training, climbing up and down rope nets to get in out of landing boats. The Navy food was great; if you left the mess hall hungry, it was your own fault. In the evenings and weekends, we were allowed to go into the city of Norfolk, but only within the main six blocks. Navy SPs (Shore Patrol) were positioned in pairs on each side of the street corners and each side of the streets to keep Army, Navy and Marines from fighting.

On a Sunday afternoon we boarded a troop ship, going below to where they would stay. For three days we floated up and down the coast. We slept in hammocks, the same as you see in war movies with ships. Thursday we practiced hitting the beach. As usual, it was raining. We went over the side of the boat, climbed down nets to the landing craft.

The crafts ran in circles before getting in line to charge the beach. Our craft hit the beach on an angle. You are supposed to walk to the end of the ramp and step off with your outside foot. I ran and jumped as far as I could, and as my feet hit the ground, a wave hit me, knocking me over. I was on hands and knees looking my BAR in the surf. Finding it, I ran up the beach. The landing was like that for everyone. It was such a disaster that our platoon leader, who'd never sworn at us before, started cursing a blue streak. We loaded back on the Navy's front-loading troop crafts for return to the troop ship.

I had to completely disassemble my BAR to remove the salt water: gas piston out, gas port, take the bolt apart, trigger group, rifle butt, oil recoil buffer, then reassemble. It felt good to shower and put on dry clothes. Maybe it was the exposure to the salt water, but I found my leather watch band wore the skin off my wrist. I wouldn't wear it the next day.

Weather for the next day was calm. We went over the side of the ship, climbed down the nets into landing craft. We charged the beach, leaping from the ramps into ankle-deep water.

This time, we looked like pros.

***

Back at Fort Riley, the platoon sergeant took me out of Staff Sergeant Leonardi's squad and put me in the weapons squad. I'd been promoted to SPC E-4 (Specialist 4), and placed as first machine gunner with two people under me on the gun crew, an assistant gunner and an ammo bearer. I and the assistant gunner each carried .45 cal. 1911 pistols and two seven-round magazines. The ammo-bearer carried the M1 .30 cal. rifle with an eight-round clip, along with a seven-clip bandolier across his chest.

The ammo bearer had to be strong. The .30 cal. machine gun weighed thirty pounds. Then there was the spare-parts bag with traversing and elevation, spare barrel, an asbestos glove, a headspace and timing gage, and tripods.

You took the back-plate off, pulled the bolt out, then separated it and put in the firing pin, reassembled the bolt, replaced it in the receiver, and replaced the back plate. Next, you screwed the barrel into the receiver then cocked the gun, pulled the cocking handle back, put the thick part of headspace, released the cocking, pulled the trigger. Firing adjustments can be made according to the headspace and timing gauge positions.

***

In fall 1962, my girlfriend Jean back in Delta, wrote me saying someone was harassing her about me and she would not be writing me anymore. I called her to get more information, and she agreed to keep writing me.

I wrote the person who harassed her. I used profane words that are today in common use, but were considered so offensive in the 1960s that people like the comedian Lenny Bruce were taken to court for using them in public.

That person reported my letter to the Postal Service, and it caused me problems for years.

***

The platoon sergeant switched me out of my weapons squad and into a rifle squad. Another SP4 E4 named Perry was assigned with me to be team co-leaders, usually a sergeant's position, so a war broke out between the two of us. On days we had work details, we'd argue about which person would go on what detail.

On Thanksgiving, we were in the field and just knew our dinner would be run-of-the-mill rations, but the mess sergeant at the base didn't let us down. He made a full Thanksgiving meal of turkey, mashed potatoes, sweet potatoes, dressing and pumpkin pie. The mess hall sent the food in insulated containers nested inside bigger insulated containers, allowing us to have a nice, hot Thanksgiving meal.

Around December 20 I was getting ready to go home for Christmas. I was on the main post when two MPs came up to me and asked if I was SPC4 Russell Babcock. When I verified it, they put handcuffs on me and took me to company headquarters outside the main post and had me sign out of the company. Then they drove me back to the military police station on the main post, where two U.S. marshals were waiting for me. An MP took his handcuffs off of me, and one of the marshals put a chain around my waist running through his own cuffs and then slapped the cuffs on me. The marshals signed for my custody and drove me to a lawyer's office. By this time it was about 6 p.m. and dark outside.

The lawyer read off the charges to me: three counts of using the mail for profane and obscene purposes.

The person I cursed out by letter for harassing my girlfriend in Delta turned me in. I sat in jail for about three weeks before posting bail. There would be no Christmas homecoming for this soldier.

***

In February 1963, due to pending legal action on the postal obscenity case that would send me to federal court in Topeka, Kansas, I transferred to a different unit that was remaining at Fort Riley, 2nd Platoon C Company 2nd Battalion 12th Infantry. This unit was based on Custer Hill.

The barracks were newer, multi-story brick buildings, nicer than the old WWII barracks. On first floor were the orderly room, mail room, and training room. On second floor were the 1st Platoon and day room. On third floor were 2nd and 3rd Platoons. Each floor had a small hall with two-man rooms for single NCOs (non-commissioned officers).

When I mentioned to my platoon leader that I could draw, he put me in training to do all the art work for the unit. I also became the mail clerk, repair man, and a team leader in the field.

The field platoon sergeant sent me to the company headquarters tent to be a runner taking messages to the platoon sergeant. The company took me to Battalion to be runner to the company. Battalion took all the different company runners back to the barracks. But my company was out in the field, so the sergeant yelled at me for going back to the barracks.

***

My lawyer sent me word to be at court on a date in March. I signed out on pass to catch the bus to Topeka. When I got there, my lawyer told me the prosecutor couldn't be in court so the trail was postponed. I returned to base.

***

A few days later, as the company was going to the field, the same thing happens as the first time they went to the field and I went to the barracks. The company returned, and my squad leader and platoon sergeant screamed at me. They took me out of the training room and gave me KP and guard duty.

When the mess sergeant wanted to partition dining room with an area for officers and NCOs separate from the peons, the job was mine. I built the wall with two-by-fours and plywood. I used a blowtorch to burn the grain in the wood for extra endurance, then varnished it.

***

When the time came to go to Topeka again, I caught the Sunday afternoon bus. By the bus station was a small restaurant. On entering, I noticed a cute blonde waitress name Nancy, so I took my time eating to visit with her. Since I had nothing to do except get a hotel room for the night, I decided to do something nice for Nancy. After eating, I visited a five-and-dime store to buy a scarf, model car paint and small paint brush. I went back to the restaurant, sat at the counter and painted her name and a rose on that scarf.

The next morning, I arrived at court only to find out it had been postponed again. Back at Fort Riley, the platoon leader decided that I wouldn't be going to the field until the court case was finished. If somebody needed something drawn or other chores done, I was ready and waiting in the training room.

But when the platoon sergeant wanted me to paint the unit's crest on the side of the ninety-foot water tower, I said, "No way, Jose." I'm afraid of heights.

The company commander requested some art work in our recreation rooms. Along a long wall I painted a four-by-ten-foot mountain scene, with a man standing on a cliff looking into the valley at a deer standing by a lake. In the next room, where we played cards and wrote letters, I painted the six codes of conduct with a picture and what each code said. The next room had a pool table and a closet, and in the closet I painted the Last Supper, Crucifixion and Resurrection. I did all these pictures in enamel paint that was like model car paint; it dries so fast it's hard to blend but everything turned out swell.

***

My trial was finally to be held the next month. My accuser was put on the bus at Delta, Colorado, headed to court in Topeka, Kansas. As the bus got to Gunnison, Colorado, the highway patrol received word the trial had again been postponed, and they took my accuser off the bus drove them back to Delta.

Frustrated as all-get-out, I told my lawyer I would plead guilty and bypass a trial if it got the process over with. The judge gave me two years' probation. I thought, "Now, maybe I can get back to doing something in the Army."

***

In March 1964, I was still hanging out in the training room, so I was drafted to learn how to operate the film projector, which played 16mm reels of film. It was used to show instructional films during training and Hollywood movies on some evenings. In the military, it seemed as if you have to have a license to operate anything, and this projector was no different. It was a piece of equipment that thousands of school teachers around the country operated in their classrooms after reading an instruction book, but I had to be sent to a weeklong training session to be certified to operate the projector.

After this training session, I went on a week's leave to go home to Delta, Colorado, to my girlfriend Jean Castoe's high school prom. I'd sent her $150 for her dress and other expenses, and I spent $125 on my own clothes for it: a black Sammy Davis Jr.-style hat, white shirt, a white dinner jacket, black dress pants and black shoes.

After finishing my last projector class, I prepared to leave the base, finally getting on the road about 9 p.m. Driving my recently purchased 1958 Chevrolet, I headed west on Interstate 70, doing ninety mph. About midnight I was twelve miles from Oakley, Kansas, when I saw a black calf standing in the middle of the highway. I couldn't swerve at the speed I was going so I slowed down as quickly as possible, which wasn't much, and I hit it square and threw it over the car.

A while later, a farmer came by and towed me to a garage in Oakley. The next morning the mechanic pulled a used radiator out of a junk yard and installed it. I complained about how rusty it was, but the mechanic tells me it would take another hour and half to put in another radiator. With another 300 miles to go on a time crunch, I declined.

Leaving Canyon City, Colorado, doing about fifty miles, I was stopped by a cop who said to slow down. It was a warning I should've heeded. Further along the way, I was driving along a valley when I come to a town with a speed sign that slowed from forty-five to thirty-five. Calling it a town is more than polite; it had only four buildings – a house on each of three corners and a general store/post office on the fourth. A highway patrolman in an unmarked car stopped me and wrote a ticket for speeding. He was going to take me to court immediately – back to Canyon City, an hour in the opposite direction.

He asked if I wanted to drive my car or ride with him. With only $5 and a half-tank of gas in the car, I opted to ride with him instead of wasting my resources. I told the judge I was on leave. He said that when I get back to Fort Riley, I needed to mail the court $25 for the fine, and he released me.

After the hour ride back to my car, I start driving toward the Continental Divide. I'm almost to the top of Monarch Pass, elevation 11,000 feet, and snow starts falling. Soon I can only drive about twenty miles an hour. I arrive in Gunnison about 9 p.m., twenty-four hours after I set out on what was usually for me a ten-hour drive. Gassing up in Gunnison, with seventy-five miles to go to Delta, I called Jean to say it'd be another two hours before I hit town.

We had a heated talk and broke up over the phone.

After all that bull I went through, I just turned around to go back to Fort Riley. I took my hat, jacket and pants to Jack and Dick's Pawn Shop, and pawned the whole lot for $10.

***

In June 1964 the first sergeant said the company was going to take the EIB test (Expert Infantryman Badge), that my weapons qualifications didn't count since I hadn't trained with the unit. The good duty, mail clerks and repair people thought I would be a dud, but they didn't know me.

The first thing we did was a twelve-mile road march with full field pack and rifle, with a limit of three hours to complete it. I did it in two-and-a-half hours. Some other tests were map reading, calling for artillery, disassembling and assembling an M60 machine gun. We went to the land navigation range for daytime land navigation, and we had to find our way to a designated place on our map.

I started true but realized I was off course, so I started over. Everybody finished ahead of me and was bused back to the company area for supper. When I got done, I started walking along Highway 77, making it to the company and finally eating. We did night land navigation too, and I didn't get lost on that one.

Fifty-nine people in the Battalion passed all their tests and received the EIB. I was the only one to receive the EIB who was not an officer or NCO.

***

My four-year enlistment was up August 11, 1964. I had to make up twenty days lost time due to being in jail on the obscenity charge. I got to thinking, "The Army's not so bad. I'll reenlist." The battalion recruiter wouldn't talk to me. He told me to talk to the recruiter downtown. The recruiter downtown said he didn't know what was going on, so I talked to the battalion man again.

He said bluntly that since I spent three years at Fort Riley due to legal problems instead of getting shipped out, I was a bad prospect. If I really wanted to reenlist, I had to stay out 90 days and lose a stripe.

***

One night in July I loaned my car to one of the guys. That was a mistake. He was drag racing or something and tore out first gear and reverse. I went to the loan company to borrow $300 to buy and install a new transmission.

During the last week of July and first week of August, I was turning in equipment, and clearing medical requirements and finances to be ready to be discharged from the Army. A week before I started the process, the post Ford dealer told me to bring my car in to be fixed from hitting the calf. I took my car to the shop and they said it would be fixed in three days.

Those three days turned into weeks. I had to ride the bus for my last few busy weeks, and then when I was discharged from the Army, the mechanic still had my car. I saw the car sitting in the alley behind the shop, so I went to the Ford dealer and told the manager his repair shop on Third Street was bull hockey. His men were supposed to fix my car in three days but it had been sitting in the alley for weeks. The next day he called me to pick up my car; they put on a new hood and hood latch and painted it.

***

When my last day on the post arrived in early 1964, I moved in with a woman I met in Manhattan. Mary Jane Schultz and I had started dating the summer before, when I drove past her on Sixth Street as she was pushing her daughter Nora's stroller on the sidewalk. I'd been on my way to an auto salvage yard for a part for my 1958 Chevrolet, and she was walking to her mother's house. I stopped and chatted her up, and she gave me her name and address. We grew close quick.

Mary was born June 10, 1944, so she was two years younger than me. She grew up in Junction City and was married to a soldier named Little, who was stationed elsewhere. I never met him. Their daughter Nora had been born in January 1963.

While staying with Mary, I was trying to find work around town. Mary and I went to the post to talk to someone with my former unit. While leaving, we were stopped by MPs who gave me a ticket for not having a post sticker on my car. When I told them I wasn't in the Army anymore, they called a wrecker and had my car towed to an impound yard in Manhattan. The next day I went to the yard, where they charged me $25 to get my car. I wasn't cheerful about being there.

Two policemen approached me at the yard, saying the police chief wanted to see me and they took me to the police station. The chief asked if I was working. I said no but that I had been looking. He told me to get out of town or he would arrest me for not having a job or a place to live.

I continued to live with Mary and Nora until November, when my ninety-day reenlistment limit ended.

***

Since my "obscene literature" offense was a federal felony charge, the Army would have to waive it before allowing me to reenter the military. They did waive it, and the Army recruiter put me on the bus for Denver and the induction center.

This time I knew what was happening. I arrived at Denver, was taken with the group to a hotel, served a good breakfast the next morning, and driven to the induction center. The doctors prodded and poked us and we passed the physical. Then they swore us in.

The sergeants asked what MOS we wanted. I requested infantry, wanting to go airborne, and was accepted. That evening they put on the train the Spirit of St. Louis bound for Kansas City. Off the train, the recruiter put us on a military bus for Fort Leonard Wood, Missouri. A couple hours' drive through scenic wilderness brought us to the post, outside the very small town of Waynesville, where walking five blocks in any direction would put you out of town.

We signed in as the replacement company. `The NCOS took us recruits to the barbershop. The four or five of us prior service men hung in a group and followed to the barbershop. We laughed as the barbers asked the recruits how they wanted their cuts. The recruits may have said, "A little off the sides," but the barber set the clippers for quarter-inch stubble. When we prior service guys said, "A little off the sides," that's what we got.

The NCOs next took the recruits to the dispensary, where everybody received their shots. I didn't get any because I was up to date. At the quartermaster store, we received our issue of uniforms. When I pinned my EIB badge on my uniform, a PFC told me I couldn't. I begged to differ. The discussion ended when an NCO told the PFC to shut up.

We could get passes to go into town. I put on my khakis with my collar brass, one U.S., one cross-rifles with blue background disk, blue infantry rope, and black tie folded between second and third button, my EIB badge and national defense ribbon, black belt, pressed line down my khaki pants, shirt buttons lined up with the edge of my buckle and pants fly, and boots shined.

I looked sharp.

We walked to the post bus station to catch a military bus to town. At the main gate, the bus stopped for an MP to check all our passes. We arrived in the big city of Waynesville. Small as it was, it had several pawn shops where you could buy Army rank brass and stuff. The recruits would buy general stars, sergeant stripes, ropes and put all this stuff on their uniforms and wear it around. Then as the bus back to post stopped at the gate, the MP checking the passes would make the recruits take off their junk decorations. It's technically a crime to misrepresent your rank.

***

In December, I took my girlfriend Mary to Colorado, to get married. I'd paid for the divorce from her husband. In Delta, my friend Ross Smith rented the local recreation hall and found a preacher. With Mom, Donna, Kenny and a few other people present, Mary and I were married.

While in Colorado, I received orders to go to Fort Benning, Georgia, for jump school in January 1965.

Toward the end of my leave, we took a bus to Grand Junction to catch the train the Spirit of St. Louis for Chicago, where we transferred to a train southbound for Fort Benning Georgia. I rented a trailer home just off post for Mary and Nora. At this time, Mary was about six months pregnant.

I went to Finance to file for an allotment for Mary. The clerk looked at our marriage papers and her divorce papers. He said he couldn't file the allotment yet because our marriage wasn't valid – we hadn't waited ninety days after the divorce was finalized to tie the knot. We had to get married again by a local justice of the peace.

***

At Fort Benning, I started airborne training to prepare for jumping out of planes. The three-week training included: ground week, tower week and jump week.

In ground week you practiced three-point landings in a jump harness that goes over your shoulders and two straps that go between your legs and snap in front of chest. You run up the stairs of a thirty-foot tower, and an NCO would hook you to a cable. You then yell and jump off the tower, and bounce down the cable to a landing berm.

For tower week, you simulated with a parachute. At the top of a 60-foot tower, your harness would be hooked to a big metal ring to hold the chute open. You'd then be released to float to the ground.

Finally, the third week was jump week. A C-130 plane would take us up and we'd jump out the back. After making your second jump, you'd be awarded with your wings pin at the landing zone (LZ).

Unfortunately, I failed ground week. That Monday I was supposed to have KP, but went on sick call. I told the doctor I'd fallen and hurt my back. He ordered me three days of bed rest with pain pills.

Eventually, I did pass jump school.

***

Early in the morning of April 30, Mary went into labor. I woke a neighbor to take us to the hospital, and called the base to inform them. In the hospital waiting room, I played solitaire, fell asleep for a while, then played some more. I was awake when the nurse brought the good news that Mary had a baby girl. We named her Loretta Lynn Babcock.

I went to company headquarters for the first sergeant to sign me out on a ten-day leave, but he presented me orders that our unit was going to Korea, so I was granted thirty-days leave that would give me family time and a chance to put our affairs in order.

We caught the train back to Junction City, Kansas, where Mary's mother, brothers and uncles lived. We decided Mary would have the easiest time living with so much family around.

Her sister Helen was living there, too, while her husband Rick was in the Air Force on the island of Guam. For Helen's birthday, Mary went bought a two-by-six-inch tube of bologna, which she then wrapped in blue and pink ribbon and tied on little baby boots. She put it in a shoe box wrapped in paper gave it to Helen. Helen got mad but their mom thought it was funny. To this day Helen still gets mad at the mention of that bologna.

Chapter Three

Camp Casey, South Korea – 1965-66

With my leave up and my family settled, I caught the train for San Francisco. It was a two-day trip, but I rode in a sleeper car so it was relaxing. In San Francisco my company hung around for a week waiting on enough people to fill a troop ship with Army and Navy families going to Hawaii, Japan and Korea.

San Francisco was still a couple years away from becoming the Mecca of the Hippie era, but it was still a happening place. I went to a go-go bar where they had three kinds of dancers: skinny, nice, and fat. A glass of beer was $3, which was overpriced but they knew servicemen would pay it. I rode a trolley to the top of Knob Hill and walked Lombard Street, the one with all the switchback-style curves. It's not worth driving on.

When the troop ship had enough passengers, we sailed out under the Golden Gate Bridge. The bunks on the ship were four beds high; and you wanted to sleep as high you could to lower your chances of getting puked on. At night, movies would be shown on deck. The ship made big circles across the ocean for several weeks, stopping in Hawaii and Japan before landing in Korea.

Although most combat was happening in and around Vietnam, the United States maintained bases in South Korea and elsewhere due to threat from communist forces. U.S. policy was based on a "domino theory" that if one nation in Southeast Asia fell to communism, others would follow. As years have passed, the theory has come to be seen as lacking basis – but that can't change the past. So, there I was in Korea.

At Camp Casey, South Korea, forty miles north of Seoul and ten miles south of the DMZ, the main post had a few brick buildings, like Division headquarters, but most were Quonset huts. There was a theater, a recreation center run by USO volunteers, a baseball field, and a golf course with a creek running by it. The post gate was flanked by a chest-high brick wall.

The main road ran all the way through the post to a Korean village called Tongducheon. It has actually become a big city, but in 1965, it was a village that was only as shady as a big city. The only lights off post were from the shops and bars along the main street. Boys would steal wallets and transistor radios from soldiers' pockets. Young and pretty girls worked the clubs. When they got too old for the bars, they walked the streets. When they were too old for the street, they went to the fields.

Houses were made out of paper, tin, wood and plastic. The ancient forests outside the village had been burned during the Korean War, so the trees were few and only about 6 feet tall. The older men, the papa-sans we called them, planted rice in marshy fields using water buffaloes.

The DMZ (Demilitarized Zone separating South and North Korea) was a short distance away, and had only been established barely a decade before my posting at Camp Casey. There was a ten-foot-tall barbed wire fence with wire strands six inches apart, with high wooden guard towers every 500 yards. The North Koreans would broadcast over loudspeakers, "Hey, GI, come over!"

***

One day the USO gave us tickets to see the Hollywood actress Martha Ray perform in a stage show of "Hello Dolly." She had been performing for troops in the field since WWII, and if you sat far enough away, you couldn't count the lines on her face.

We rode the train from Camp Casey to Seoul, and returned the same way after the show. Unless you had an overnight pass, you had to be on post by 2400 hours, or midnight. Naturally, we'd like to have remained in Seoul longer.

***

In December, the leadership school gave us a two-week course on counter-guerilla warfare. The Vietnamese were fighting using guerilla tactics, that is without declared battlegrounds, uniforms, or rules; the attacks were often done hit-and-run style by small, mobile groups or individuals who may or may not be dressed as civilians. Outside of the Korean War, America hadn't fought an enemy like that.

The first week covered radio calls, map reading, land navigation, and how to distinguish civilians from combatants.

During that week three Red Cross volunteers came out the day we were rappelling on a cliff. One woman wanted to try, so the NCO took her to the top of the cliff, put a Swiss seat harness on her, and hooked her on the rope. She rappelled down just fine. Watching her gave us a good break.

The second week of training was spent in field. Unfortunately, it had snowed about eight inches. We loaded into trucks at 1900 hours (7 p.m.) on a Sunday to be taken to the training area. My platoon sergeant pointed to a ridge line with a gap, and told me to get us there.

In talking, I had stood my rifle against a truck fender and told a guy that if the trucks started to leave, grab my rifle; the trucks left and the guy didn't get my rifle. It turned out that when the driver left for base, he took my rifle with him and put it in the arms room.

I was the only man out there without a rifle. Luckily, I didn't get an Article 15 citation.

When we settled for the night, I had two shelter halves to make my tent. I raked snow away and spread pine needles on the ground for cushion. Instead of my regular sleeping bag, I had the shelter halves sewn together along with a poncho and wool blanket. During the time in the field, if I wasn't taking a patrol, I was telling one of the other acting jacks to go on patrol. Our company made the highest score to that time, 950 points. Individually, Sergeant Miles and I tied for first place.

In January 1966, I was promoted to buck sergeant E-5.

***

.In April the Division commander's wife visited Camp Casey. I and a couple other NCOs took her to the rifle range to show how they fire a twelve-gauge shotgun, an M60 machine gun, and an M79 blooper (grenade launcher). She fired all the weapons, but she wasn't ready for the first one. That shotgun pushed her down on her butt. She steeled herself after that.

***

In May my year was up with the unit. I turned in my field gear, cleared Finance and took a bus to Seoul and then a plane back to the States. Thinking ahead, I had shipped my uniforms and other baggage ahead, so I would only have to carry one suitcase with one set of fatigues and one class-A uniform.

Some of the officers had Korean girlfriends, called yobos. These yobos met our bus at the airport, these girls were all crying alligator tears, "Don't go, I love you!"

It was funny watching them. As soon as the new officers got off the plane and came through the door, a new love began.

***

Being in Korea was an experience that exposed me to another culture and helped me adapt to interacting with people from that culture. Although much less dangerous, it was excellent training for what lay in store for me in Vietnam.

Above: The division commander's wife wanted to fire some weapons. After this photo was taken, an M79 grenade launcher knocked her on her butt.
Below: Training in Korea prepared me for Vietnam.

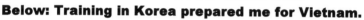

Camp Casey, South Korea, 1965. Above: Soldiers pack for exercises.
Below: Korean farmer with ox and cart.

Camp Casey, South Korea, 1965. Above: Trucks take soldiers out on exercises.
Below: Quonset huts used as barracks.

Above: Counter-guerilla training. I'm second from right
Below: Platoon leader, sergeant and NCOs; I'm at right.

Training in Korea.

Chapter Four

5th Infantry Division
C Company, 2nd Battalion, 10th Infantry
Fort Carson, Colorado – 1966-67

We flew into Travis Air Force Base in California. From there I went to the local airport to fly to Manhattan, Kansas, where I then caught a cab to Junction City, where my wife Mary was living. I spent most of my thirty-day leave around Junction City. My orders posted me next with the 5th Infantry Division at Fort Carson, Colorado.

Since Mary was pregnant again, we decided to swing through Delta to pick up Mom to help care for her and Nora and Loretta.

Mary, Nora, Loretta and I headed west on Interstate 70. While I'd been away, interstate highway speeds were decreased from seventy miles an hour to fifty-five to conserve gas supplies. The trip took much longer than normal.

At Fort Carson I rented my family a room at the guesthouse on post. Just before I arrived at Fort Carson Colorado, the Department of Defense activated the Fifth Infantry the Fifth Mechanized infantry Division,

The next morning, I reported to the company and learned the 5th Infantry Division had been activated already, so I would be joining the replacement company.

At Personnel, I turned in my 201 file, finance records, and medical records. Then I reported to the post quartermaster and was issued TA-50 field gear: Helmet and liner; two ammo pouches; first aid pouch; pistol belt; field pack with straps; shelter half with three section poles, rope and ten stakes; canteen and cover; entrenching tool and cover; poncho; sleeping bag with mattress; duffle bag and two waterproof bags; two wool shirts and wool pants; two pairs of field pants; over boots; and mess kit with knife, fork and spoon.

I signed for it all, and packed it up.

***

The replacement company assigned me to the 2nd Battalion 10th Infantry Regiment.

For reasons unknown, the Department of the Army gave Division hundreds of extra staff sergeant stripes and sergeant first class stripes. Usually in the Army at this time, about twelve months were required to make a higher rank, though that could be waived. Division was going to distribute these stripes sooner than later, which meant I was at the right place at the right time.

Although a buck sergeant with just six months' time in my grade and just thirty days in the division, I was promoted to staff sergeant. Usually such a promotion would require being in the company over six months.

***

The battalion was at Camp Red Devil for training. When I joined them, my platoon sergeant, Sergeant First Class Runyon, thought I would have to go to a promotion board, and sent me back to garrison to get the proper uniform. We didn't have a promotion board, but I straightened out the uniform problem and Mary drove me back to Camp Red Devil.

The first day I went to the field with the company, Sergeant First Class Runyon told me to march our company from station to station. The NCOs from another company were teaching the classes. The first class was battle field formations, and the buck sergeant teaching it didn't know his subject. He demonstrated the wrong hand signals for various formations, and I stopped him and took over his class. Though I was wrong for taking over because I hadn't studied or made a lesson plan, I knew what he was supposed to teach. After finishing, I marched the troops to the next class. I looked up to see the buck sergeant was marching his next group to me, and he quit giving classes that day.

The word got back to the company commander and first sergeant, and my status was boosted.

One morning about sixty trainees went on sick call to miss training with that sergeant. Boy, was he mad. The next morning at reveille formation, he screamed at the troops, "I can't stop you from going on sick call, but I can get a medical book and make every one of you show me in the book where you hurt!"

On one side of the barracks door, the men wrote "Runyon's Raiders" and on the other side "Babcock's Clowns."

***

For Fourth of July weekend, the battalion commander decided that instead of taking the troops back to garrison to clean the trucks and equipment, he would have the soldiers' wives and kids bused to the field to eat and play games.

But, on Monday we returned to post to start cleaning equipment. That morning, Mary went to the hospital in labor, and gave birth to our boy Alvin Ray.

***

I was the weapons squad leader for 2nd Platoon, where the rifle squad has a staff sergeant, squad leader, two sergeant E-5s as team leaders, two M79 men, and five riflemen. Each platoon has three rifle squads and one weapon squad, with ten people per squad.

For the record, as you go up the ladder, three rifle platoons and one weapons platoon make a company. One headquarters company and three rifle companies make a battalion. Four battalions make a division, five divisions make one corps, and five corps make an army.

***

One time there was a demonstration for the division commander and other VIPs. The company commander thought it would be impressive for my weapons platoon to hit a target part-way to the objective: A hill at which all eleven of the company's armored personnel trucks would be charging and firing live rounds.

When the trucks reached the top of the hill, the back ramps would drop and troops would run out in front of the trucks, get in line and charge over the hill firing in a blaze of glory.

Once a week was a company maintenance day. I would tell my men to clean all weapons and equipment, but as I was not always able to get to the company to check on them, they didn't. It came back to bite me.

As my truck reached our first objective, the driver slowed to five miles an hour and lowered the back ramp almost to the ground and we ran out to the front of the truck with two machine gunners firing at the main objective. When the company was close to the objective, my crew ceased fire and remounted the truck on the move. We practiced all afternoon, waiting for the tank battalion to arrive.

We practiced one more time with the tanks. Here was where the lack of my men's maintenance caught up to me. Everybody started charging across the ground, stopped and mounted up. My men were in the truck, and I ducked down to hop in when the ramp cable broke. The ramp hit the ground and bounced up to catch me between the 500-pound ramp and the top of the truck, breaking my watch and squashing my chest and back. I fell into the truck on my knees. By the time the driver stopped, I was curled up on the floor trying to breathe. Meanwhile, the company and tanks hit the objective.

The driver alerted the company commander, who sent an ambulance. It seemed like a long fifteen miles to the post hospital. They X-rayed and checked me over. Luckily, I had no cracked ribs or broken bones. The doctor released me to go home with Mary.

I decided to take a hot bath, thinking the hot water would ease the bruised muscles, but it relaxed the wrong muscles and I really started hurting.

Mary took me back to the emergency room. I was hospitalized overnight, and released at noon the next day to three days' bed rest. It was a week before I returned to the company.

Fortunately, the company spent the rest of the year on work details and training, no big projects.

Before Thanksgiving, we took Mom home to Delta.

At Christmas, we took my recently purchased 1961 Ford Falcon to Mary's mom's home in Junction City for a couple of weeks.

Also for Christmas, I went to Sears and bought a color TV, washer and dryer, and I also bought the old lady an electric sewing machine. They gave her a few lessons on how to use it, but Mary couldn't sew and kept tangling the thread. I finally pawned the sewing machine.

***

In March, Division sent a CMMI team (Command Maintenance Management Inspection Team) to the battalion, checking maintenance and cleanliness of equipment and trucks in the motor pool. We had to lay out the pike, shovel, pry bar, screw drivers, pliers, grease gun, five-gallon water and gas cans. They also inspected the TA-50 supplies and weapons in the arms room. The team inspected my M60 machine gun, spare-parts bag, one of the spare barrels, and took the ends off the gas chamber. The gas piston was rusted to the cylinder wall and they had to take a hammer and chisel to knock the piston loose.

***

That spring a battalion of British soldiers came to Fort Carson to train with us.

We went to the field near camp Red Devil to practice attacks, defense and live-fire exercises. Once in the morning and once in the afternoon we'd stop to drink a spot of tea, as is the British tradition.

At the end of the month-long training, our two battalions did a parade. First, our battalions marched around the parade field at regular cadence, 120 beats per minute.

We were standing in formation at attenuation when a British trooper moved and one of the British NCOs reach up and bopped him on the head. Then, the British battalion went around the parade field in a tribute to the Bataan Death

March, one of the tragedies of WWII where Japanese force-marched prisoners to camp in the Philippines.

It was a real tear jerker to watch. They marched so slowly it seemed like it took a minute for each foot to hit the ground. At this pace it took them a half hour to go around the parade field.

***

The next month about thirty West Point cadets came to train. One night just before dark, we were moving a column for an attack maneuver. I walked up and popped a gas grenade so the cadets would put their gas masks on. I put on my mask, but I heard one cadet coughing in the smoke. He was choking badly enough that I put him in a fireman carry to take him out to fresh air. I weighed 135 pounds and he weighed about 180 pounds; jerking his fat ass around cracked three of my ribs.

***

A couple days later, my platoon leader and I went to Panama for two weeks of expert jungle training.

The lieutenant and I flew to Charlotte, North Carolina, and at the hotel bar happened to meet other people going to Panama. The first class in Panama involved getting in water and flipping over our rubber raft, turning it right side up and then getting back in it. We went up the Chagres River to where the NCOs had a training area. We climbed a rope ladder up a tree, where a zip line ran a thousand feet to a tree across the river. An NCO hooked me to the line, and said to drop to the water when I hit a knot in the line about ten feet from the river's bank. When I hit that knot and dropped, boy, my ribs hurt. My lieutenant built a raft out of our ponchos and some brush, put our equipment on, and we dog paddled it back across the river.

On a Sunday afternoon, the NCOs instructed us to make shelters in the jungle. The lieutenant and I built the floor of ours two feet off the ground so snakes couldn't reach us. For supper, the NCOs gave us a cup of rice and a live chicken, which we killed, plucked and cleaned before cooking; it was no trouble for me since I grew up on a farm. They showed us heart of palm (the inner core of a palm tree) and other things in the jungle we could eat.

We went on day and night patrols. Our black work gloves came in handy if we slipped on a hill and needed to grab a tree branch with two-inch thorns or a nest of red fire ants.

At the end of the two weeks of training, we received expert jungle patches that we sewed on our fatigue jackets. We hoped the training wouldn't fail us in real situations.

***

Back at Fort Carson, my orders came down to go to Vietnam. It had taken long enough for it to happen.

Chapter Five

Vietnam – 1967-69

I sent my uniforms to Vietnam by whole baggage, and our household things to Junction City, where I rented an apartment for Mary and the kids.

At the end of my thirty-day leave, I caught the train to San Francisco and then a plane to Travis Air Force Base and another plane. With one stop for fueling in Alaska, we were Vietnam bound. Altogether, the plane ride lasted about 18 hours, but we crossed the International Date Line going backward so we technically landed the day before we departed.

***

We flew into and remained a couple days at Tan Son Nhut Air Base in South Vietnam before a group of us were sent by C-130 transport plane a short distance to the 25th Infantry Division at Cu Chi, in the northwest part of Saigon.

In addition to filing our 201 files and finance records, we turned in our U.S. green-back dollars for military pay scripts, or MPCs. This was a measure to prevent U.S. currency from influencing local economies, such as fueling the black markets that developed in Europe during WWII. MPCs were distributed from the end of WWII to the end of Vietnam, when it was decided they didn't work.

We spent a week being trained about our enemy, the Viet Cong: the people, booby traps, tunnels, hangouts, habits.

The trainers told us there were three types of people that we were fighting: Viet Cong (aka VC or Charles or Charlie), snipers, and North Vietnamese Army soldiers.

The Viet Cong comprised a roughly connected group of guerilla fighters, often villagers, who supported Communism and the North Vietnamese, and were the least trained and least equipped of the three groups, however if you gave him a shovel, he'd dig a tunnel to China.

They were skilled at setting booby traps in the jungle. You'd want to stay off the main trails because of the traps, some as simple as tree limbs with spikes. They had tunnels where they may place unexploded artillery rounds in the openings. Or they might place a thin wire loop around the hole, and it would close around your neck as you start walking in. Or they would catch a poisonous snake and tie him by the tail near the hole and not feed him so he'd be one pissed off snake guarding that spot. Or Charlie would sit in the hole just out of sight, waiting for Americans. One of Charlie's favorite tricks was to take a flag or pistol or something that would make a nice souvenir and tie it to a grenade that would explode if touched by a GI. Unless Charles outnumbered you, he'd more than likely just fire a couple rounds and run.

The second group was snipers, expert shooters who hid in the jungle or buildings and picked off his enemy one at a time. His rifle usually was a bolt action rifle with a three-round or five-round magazine with a scope, capable of firing a round 1,000 yards. Some of the deadliest snipers were women. They were good enough to put two bullets between the eyes or in the heart before the target fell dead. Very few snipers were cowardly, but if they were then their commander had them chained to a tree so they couldn't escape,

The last group was the North Vietnam Army (NVA). NVA soldiers started out in North Vietnam carrying all of their equipment. If a soldier was going to be a mortar man, he and two other men would carry the mortar tube base plate and tripod legs. As they moved down the Ho Chi Minh Trail, they practiced setting up and firing the mortar. They often had to hunt or scavenge their own food and endure American bombing. The trip to the Saigon area took around six months, and by the time they reached the Hobo Woods they were angry at us for making them suffer all that way, and they would stand toe-to-toe with us and fight.

***

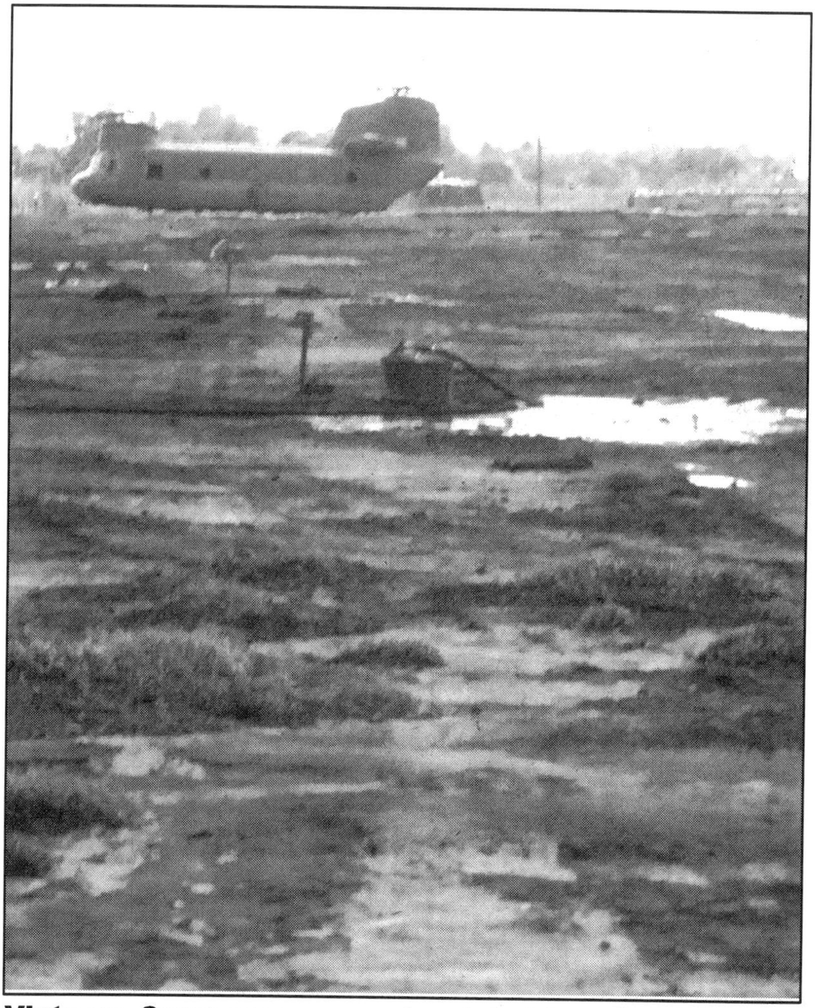

Vietnam. Some areas were desolated from battle.

Above: Vietnamese countryside from the air.
Below: Preparing to touch down.

Above: I and several other soldiers were decorated in the field. I believe this was for my Bronze Star for valor. Below: Troops came out to see Bob Hope and his girls.

It was September 1967, and I was twenty-five years old. I was assigned to D company 4th Battalion 9th Infantry Regiment, known as the "Manchus" due to being sent to China for the Boxer Rebellion of 1899. They also saw combat during WWI, WWII and Korea.

My first week in D Company was spent assembling my TA-50 field supplies. I had my equipment all set up in a duffle-bag with extra clothes, steel pot helmet with liner, entrenching tool, shirt, pants, underwear, socks.

They sent me to the field camp one morning on the "chow chopper," the helicopter with the morning chow, ammo, water, and cases of C-rations, the food we ate at noon. Each case had twenty-four boxes. In the individual ration, the main meal was a can of stew, spaghetti and meatballs, or ham and lima beans (which I hated for being too salty). There would also be a can of fruit, a pack containing sugar, salt and pepper, coffee, crackers and jam, a pack of four cigarettes, and, most importantly, toilet paper. Sometimes you'd get a can of date pudding, which was a bad-tasting cake, but the rats in the bunkers really liked it.

The chopper took me to our unit's forward base camp in the Ho Bo woods and rubber plantations across the river from Saigon. Around us were Communist strongholds. It was an area later portrayed in the movie *Platoon.*

The platoon sergeant was waiting by the chopper pad when we landed, and some troops unloaded the chow and ammo. In the company area, the platoon sergeant took me to the officer and NCOs tent and introduced the three buck sergeants to me, then he got on the chopper and I never saw him again. I took over as first platoon sergeant/acting platoon leader.

The buck sergeants were Sergeant William Byrd, Sergeant John Collins, and Sergeant Robert Cochran. We talked for a few minutes and I told them a little about myself. Then they took me to one of the enlisted member (EM) tents, where I introduced myself to the troops.

I told them what they could expect from me as a platoon sergeant: 1) that I would not tell them to do something that I would not do myself; and 2) that if I sent them somewhere and they were fired on, that I and the rest of the platoon would be standing next to him before the sound of the shot was done echoing.

A few days later we were assigned a new second lieutenant, whose name was Thomas. He was black, and this was at a time when there weren't many black officers, so he had overcome a lot of prejudice to get achieve his rank. Lieutenant Thomas, Sergeant Bob Cochran and I were all within six months of the same age and within six months of the same time in service, so we bonded pretty well.

We went out on an all-day sweep and returned to camp that evening. The unit had a policy that at night every man would get one Coke and one beer. I traded my beer for one of Sergeant Cochran's Cokes because I didn't drink. It had been years since my senior year Christmas break when I got drunk on Jim Beam, but I still couldn't stand the smell of alcohol. However, I did smoke Hav-a-Tampa cigars, which were smaller than regular cigars and had a wooden tip.

***

The next month, October, was a good month or a bad month depending on how you look at it. For awards, it was a good month. For my health and safety, not so much.

I already had two unit citations that I had been wearing – the blue Presidential Unit Citation and the red Meritorious Unit Citation – however, if I was in a unit that hadn't received these awards, I couldn't them. My new unit in Vietnam was fighting to earn those awards, and once they did I could wear them again. On an individual basis, I had earned and could wear the National Defense Ribbon and the Good Conduct Ribbon.

Over the course of October 1967, I would earn the Bronze Star for valor (October 9); my first Purple Heart (October 10); the Silver Star, the third highest medal the Army awards (October 15); and my second Purple Heart (October 25).

On October 9, Army engineers and our company found a complex of 15 Communist bunkers. We used all of our C-4 explosives to blow most of the bunkers, but there were three left. The company wanted somebody to stay there to wait for Charlie (the Viet Cong) to return home. I placed one machine gun five feet in front of each bunker. My men – my radio man, three machine gunners, three assistant gunners and three ammo bearers – and I all sat quietly until we heard Charles coming in the back door. We waited a few minutes until the Viet

Cong combatants were inside the bunkers, and then we opened fire, killing them. We verified the casualties, and returned to camp in file formation.

***

On October 10, we were strolling through the jungle looking for the VC. After our noon meal, I took Sergeant Collins and another sergeant to explore around the bend of the trail. There we saw three VC; we shot and killed two, but one got away. As we assessed the situation, I felt something in my right forearm. It was a piece of metal shrapnel that had hit me during the skirmish. The platoon medic bandaged my arm, and we continued strolling through the jungle and returned to camp. At the battalion aid station, I had my arm cleaned and checked.

On October 15, we had been at Cu Chi and were returning to the forward base camp. We got into such thick jungle, the only way we could move was down the trail. The 2nd Platoon of twenty-five men were leading the way for headquarters platoon with the company commander, his radio man, company medic, and Air Force forward observers. Then my platoon came next. I was the last man in the company line.

I had a claymore mine bag on my pistol belt in which I carried blasting-cap crimpers and a block of C-4 blasting caps so if I saw an unexploded round on the trail I could blow it up. This came in handy on this day.

As the 2nd Platoon was leading, they walked right up the middle of a VC battalion base camp, and Charles was home.

I placed one of my machine guns pointing back down the trail we were on. I lay there watching bullets cut the grass while waiting for the company commander to say something. After a few minutes, I called Lieutenant Thomas to tell him I'd take two machine guns forward. I left my steel-pot pack and M16 on the ground, but took my nine-shot .22 pistol, and crawled forward. I put a gunner on the trail, telling him that when I gave the word, he should aim high in the trees and keep firing to make noise.

We opened fire. A 2nd Platoon man yelled, “Stop firing, you’re hitting us!” but Charles was the one hitting them. Both sides stopped. The platoon starts moving back. I crawl forward and find a body with a damaged light anti-tank weapon (LAW) on it, which I cut off, and drag the body back to one of my men.

I then crawled up to the foxholes. Lieutenant Thomas and another man were a-ways behind me. The VC started firing at me. I jumped in the foxhole and yelled at Lieutenant Thomas to fire high because I was coming back.

I get back to the damaged LAW and put piece of C-4 next to it. I waited to see what the commanding officer was going to do, but after five minutes he still did nothing. I yelled out, "Fire in the hole!" and set off the C-4 and we got out of there.

We moved back down the trail, with my men helping 2nd Platoon with their wounded. The company commander called an airstrike on the VC base camp. We called in medivac for the wounded. I think there were four dead and eight wounded after the strike. We waited for C Company; there were about 60 men who joined us and we then went back to the VC camp and captured a doctor and a nurse, and recovered a radio and machine gun.

Our battalion thought we would be attacked by the VC so the company supply sent water, apples and a case of ammo per man. Fortunately, the VC didn't attack. When 3rd Platoon joined us, we found more of the VC camp before sweeping back to our camp the next day. What was supposed to be a four-hour jungle stroll had turned into a three-night, four-day adventure.

My last fun for the month happened October 25. The company commander wanted 1st Platoon to send out an ambush patrol. I took out a fifteen-man patrol. We set up along a trail. We formed an L-shape ambush.

The M16s we had were some of the first ones, with the three-prong flash hider and the weak extractor spring. If the rifle was a little dirty, it would jam. So we carried the cleaning rods assembled under the rifle, and if it jammed we played Daniel Boone. The three-prong flash hider, though, was great for cutting the wires of C-ration cases.

I was relaxing, leaning against a berm, with my steel-pot helmet lying on the ground with my M16 and nine-shot .22 pistol. For some reason, I didn't have any grenades on me.

Another company was manning an ambush setup a down the trail from us. Once in a while they'd fire close to us. I called the CO to ask if we could come in, but, no, he said that other group was coming in.

So, I was sitting by my berm reading a comic book. Don't ask why I had a comic book, where I got it or what it was about, but I was sitting there reading it when I thought I heard noise from a bamboo hedge about ten feet to my right.

No one else heard it.

The third time I heard it, I asked Specialist Bayer, who'd been in my platoon at Fort Carson, to throw me a grenade. He did and I set it by my equipment. About thirty minutes later a VC poked his head through the hedge, and I saw him. I picked up the grenade, pulled the pin and pitched it. The grenade hit him in the head and exploded.

I had my flak jacket on, with my compass in the left pocket. A piece of shrapnel went through the bottom of my compass but not into me thanks to the flak jacket. But, another piece of shrapnel went into my right elbow. Shrapnel also hit Specialist Bayer and the M79 gunner. I broke up our ambush setup and marched to camp. The three of us were then taken to the military hospital in Cu Chi.

While awaiting treatment, I probed my right elbow for the shrapnel. For my wound earlier in the month, they used a scalpel to cut into the wound. For this wound, the doctor showed off his upbringing as a Kansas farm boy. He jabbed pinchers in the wound and pulled the handles open like a set of fencepost-hole diggers to expose the shrapnel, which he then pulled out.

The three of us spent a week in the hospital raising hell with the nurses. Twice a day they gave us shots: one early morning and one late evening. When the nurse came to one of us to give us a shot, the others would yell, "Watch it, she's going to stab you!" We wore t-shirts, pajama bottoms and cloth flip-flops. There were a couple days when pretty Red Cross volunteers would sweep through in short skirts and play cards or dominoes with us.

I enjoyed cooling my heels because a couple weeks later, November 12, would be the day I reenlisted in the Army, a staff sergeant first class with six years' service.

Chapter Six
Tet Offensive

On November 12, 1967 I was sworn into the Army again, and given the bonus of $1,500 tax free plus a thirty-day leave.

From Tan Son Nhut, I caught a plane to Travis Air Force Base in California and another plane from Travis civilian airport to Denver. For my first order of business, I rented a car to drive to the finance company office and paid off my two cars. Then I went to the Pontiac dealer and bought a 1967 Firebird convertible, green with a white top. The salesman helped take the rental car to the airport.

It was about 6 p.m. when I drove out of Colorado Springs and got on Interstate 70 headed to Junction City, Kansas. About a week earlier, in early November, my wife Mary gave birth to our fourth kid, a girl we named Nancy Lee.

We packed up the house and I rented a U-Haul to move Mary and the kids to Delta, Colorado, to again be closer to my mom. We made the most of the trip.

A few months previously, during the summer, John Wayne and Glen Campbell made the movie True Grit, and filmed parts of it in Ridgeway, Colorado. During my leave, my buddy Kenny and his wife Lola joined my family on a visit to Ridgeway. We saw the buildings made by the movie people, such as the hotel and saloon, and other parts of town that were authentic from the old mining days. Whenever I watch "True Grit," I think of that trip. From there we went to another mining town, Silverton, which had a train called the Galloping Goose that was the only narrow-gauge train still running in the United States.

***

About December 4, I returned to Cu Chi. We Americans celebrated Christmas and our New Year, but Vietnamese New Year (or Tet) was not until January 30. North and South Vietnam usually agreed to a cease fire for the holiday. The Tet Truce of 1968 was agreed to run January 27 to February 3.

However, the leaders of the North Vietnamese Army had other plans.

They came down in force the night of January 30 to capture Hue and other big cities, and almost overran the American embassy in Saigon. More than 100 towns and cities were attacked.

During the Vietnam War most Americans couldn't find Vietnam on a map, and probably still can't. Though the Vietnam War was the first war to be broadcast on TV, and a daily presence in American homes, many people thought Vietnam was a young country, younger than ours. In fact, Vietnam's first king unified the region almost 5,000 years ago, and it has been frequently engaged in conflict ever since.

I feel that one of the best portrayals of our experience in Vietnam was in the movie *Full Metal Jacket*, which follows a group of young men from training to combat. At one point the men emerged from the jungle to fight in the city of Hue, in the thick of the action of the Tet Offensive. Hue had been the capital of Vietnam from about 1800 to the end of World War II. Its jewel then and now is the emperor's palace in the Imperial City, behind a brick-walled citadel.

American troops faced a tough battle because commanders wouldn't bomb the city from the air due to the historical importance of the Imperial City and the royal tombs along the Perfume River (Huong River). Unlike European castles made of stone, the emperor's palace and surrounding buildings were made mostly from wood, as was the emperor's throne. When I visited the palace later, I also noticed a room behind the throne that held about twenty Buddha statues. One aerial strike could have sent the Imperial City and its treasures up in smoke.

The troops fought block by block through Hue, and as the troops got closer to the citadel, they were ordered to not even use artillery fire.

But, U.S. commanders changed their minds as their wounded and dead increased. When the battle was over, only a small portion of the Imperial City remained. Fifty years later, it is still being restored.

While Hue was about to be attacked that night of January 30, 1968, my unit was to the south, in the Ho Bo Woods outside Cu Chi.

The time was about 0430 hours. The sun hadn't risen, and the roosters hadn't even woken up, when on the Armed Forces Radio Service an official from the Air Force starts yelling at the top of his voice with maximum volume that the Viet Cong was launching its Tet Offensive in cities across the nation.

The Vietnam War wasn't like any war America had fought, with front lines of combat and the enemy on the other side. In Vietnam, there were no lines. The Viet Cong were everywhere: regular-looking Vietnamese people shopping in a market, walking down the street, waiting tables in restaurants, doing civilian jobs on American bases like cutting grass. Even children planted bombs and fired weapons.

***

Most nights it was just after dark when I set out my night forward security post, which served as our listening post (LP), to get ready for the night in our defensive position.

I always waited till after dark to send out the listening post so the enemy wouldn't see them, and it was my policy to place the LP man myself that way I knew where he was. At night the platoon leader, our two radio men, the platoon medic and I would each pull two-hour radio watch listening for warnings from our listening post. I always pulled last shift.

The LP called in a radio report every thirty minutes to let us know everything was quiet. If the LP missed two radio checks, whoever was on radio watch at the time would wake me, and I would call the LP. If he didn't answer, I'd grab my helmet grab and weapon and go out to the LP position. If everybody was asleep I would pop a CS gas grenade on them. They would wake up and I wouldn't have to worry about them falling asleep for a while. In fact, I found a CS gas grenade to be the best wake-up call for anyone I caught asleep at their position while I was checking our platoon perimeter.

***

Not long after the Second Platoon's new sergeant, Sergeant Bill Byrd, was assigned to us, the enemy caught us in a firefight.

We'd returned to the forward base camp and were making a sweep around the base. An hour into the sweep, we came under fire for about five minutes then it stopped.

Somebody started yelling for a medic. I was leading my medic in the direction of the shouting but ran into a thirty-foot patch of knee-high wait-a-minute vines – so called because their thorny vines grabbed you and tried to trip you. You'd have to watch out not to fall against a tree with a nest of red fire ants that would swarm over you or you'd have to take your clothes off to swat off the ants then get dressed again.

The calls for a medic continued as we fought our way through the vines. I called back, "We'll be there!"

We arrived, and there on the ground was Sergeant Byrd. He had sunglasses on, something he knew not to do in the jungle. He'd been walking down a clear trail, which was another no-no because the likelihood of booby traps increased on trails. Indeed, he had tripped a booby trap. Shrapnel entered the side of his neck.

My medic bandaged the wound, but Bill had lost too much blood. He died in my arms. He had a little over sixty days before going home. If he hadn't been wearing sunglasses, if he hadn't walked a trail, maybe he'd have lived to make the trip home.

I told the machine-gun crew to take his body back to base.

The medic and I returned to the platoon. Some firing started again then stopped a few minutes later. I made my way to the company commander's area. Lieutenant Thomas and Sergeant First Class White were there. I asked them if Byrd's body had made it back. They said no. I told them that he was dead. Both Lieutenant Thomas and Sergeant First Class "Pappy" White were men of color, and our backgrounds probably couldn't have been more different, but the three of us stood there crying over our fallen friend.

We decided to retrieve Sergeant Byrd's body ourselves. They followed me into the jungle. We found Byrd's body and made it back to base as firing started again.

The CO called in gun helicopters. Two of them arrived and we directed their fire. One was a Cobra gun ship, the other was a Huey chopper.

Somehow one of our men, Sergeant Robert Cochran, had gotten ahead of the platoon, and was pinned down and wounded. The Huey flew out, picked him up, then came back for Byrd's body and took them to Cu Chi. Sergeant Cochran spent a week in the hospital then returned to the company, and was promoted to staff sergeant of 2nd Platoon. Sergeant First Class "Pappy" White rotated back to the world.

***

On another patrol, we came to a stream too wide and deep to wade across, so we cut a tree over the creek.

In walking over it, I used a machete to cut off extra branches as I went, to make the crossing easier for the men following. Unfortunately, I cut my middle finger. That afternoon when I returned to base camp, I went to the aid station to have a medic clean and dress it. The medic didn't give anything for pain. He poured mercuraform, an antiseptic, on a gauze pad and in the cut, and then started scrubbing like he was washing dirty socks. I pulled my hand back in pain but the other medic pushed it back.

The cut was bad enough I was sent back to Cu Chi for a bit.

Sergeant Bob Thomas extended his tour of duty for another six months. It was his second extension. When he took a five-day in-country R&R, he bought eight bottles of liquor. When he returned to the company, we were at Cu Chi and the platoon was having a party.

While we were waiting for noon meal, the battalion chaplain came by carrying a mongoose on his shoulder. It was a furry gray thing with a bushy tail, just larger than a rat. We asked him, "Does your mongoose drink?" Then we let the mongoose take a sip from a glass of rum and Coke.

A few minutes later, one of the men in the mess hall asked me if he could have a drink. I gave him the glass that the mongoose drank out of.

I was going to drink the rum and Coke, but I found that even though ten years had passed since I got sick on it in high school, the smell of liquor still made me sick

***

We stood down for a week in Cu Chi. We performed equipment maintenance. We haunted the PX (Post Exchange), enjoying things we missed out in the field, like soda and candy. We also caught up on gossip.

I heard about one of my former lieutenants, one who became platoon leader but turned out to be a dud. Someone in his platoon fired at a tree near him and wounded him. After a hospital stay, he returned to different assignments: S-3 intelligence, S-4 supply in head-quarters then A Company, B Company, C Company. I don't know where he landed, but it was apparent that everyone figured out he was a dud.

There was an NCO club that was open from 1300 hours to 2300 hours, and it had slot machines. If you won a jackpot the manager would verify it before handing over your winnings. The drinks of choice were Pabst Blue Ribbon, Budweiser and liquor.

About this time a scandal rocked the base's clubs – the officer, NCO, and enlisted men's clubs. Some high-ranking NCOs, first sergeants and sergeant majors were stealing money from the clubs and falsifying their records. For instance, they claimed to have bought twenty pallets of beer for $5,000 when they only bought two pallets and pocketed the rest of the money. Most of them got caught and were court-martialed, busted to private or sent to Fort Leavenworth. After that, Finance made five copies of all paperwork.

After our week of relaxation, we went back to the Ho Bo Woods.

Chapter Seven

Rumbling in the Jungle

Sweeping across an open field, heading back toward camp, we started receiving fire. We took to the ground.

I couldn't see the enemy because of a bamboo hedgerow. I lay there watching glowing rounds of ammo cut and chip the bamboo. I know the enemy's about 200 yards ahead, between us and camp.

In front of us, on the other side of the enemy, the CO ordered the company's weapons platoon FO (forward observer) to give the 81mm mortars a fire mission. With a bursting radius of fifty yards, the 81mm mortars can be walked about 50 yards closer to the enemy; we hoped they wouldn't fire a long round.

Meanwhile, behind us, the battalion FO called a 105mm howitzer battery to fire over us. A 105mm howitzer can be heard when fired ten miles away and will whistle until it lands. It had a bursting radius of 100 yards. We hoped they wouldn't fire a short round.

Fortunately, all calculations were accurate, and we weren't hit by friendly fire.

***

On another afternoon patrol, we found a bunker complex. The engineers and I ran out of C-4 explosives with a few bunkers left to blow, so we set up a perimeter and called the CO for a resupply of C-4 and an evening meal.

I was lazy digging my foxhole. I should have dug two feet wide by four feet long by five feet deep, but I only scraped three inches deep. Around midnight the enemy launched mortar fire. I came out from under my poncho shelter, grabbed my rifle, put on my helmet, and ran to my foxhole – but it was so shallow I just sat on the edge, put my feet in and put my arms over my head.

It would have been safer just to lie down. I learned my lesson.

***

Eventually, the company moved part of the mess hall to the forward camp, in the Ho Bo Woods. Some cooks set up a functioning mess tent. It was nice not to have to eat food while sitting in mud.

In the mornings, Bob Cochran and I would wake the troops and send half to chow. He and I would stand outside the mess tent drinking coffee, counting the troops through the chow line then we'd eat.

About 0630 hours the squad leaders would pick up the day's supplies. Each squad leader picked up ten meals for his men, and took ammo as needed – twenty-round boxes for M16s, 100-round boxes for M60s. While the troops were at mess, they would fill their water canteens.

Around 0700 hours the company commander would say move out. If my platoon was leading, I'd tell the lead squad to move out. I always felt a sense of patriotism when marching out a front gate because it reminded me of so many westerns in which John Wayne did the same thing. The compound gates in Vietnam were a bit more threatening, made with concertina wire, razor wire in three-foot loops.

Once outside the wire, the squad broke into columns: one file on the left and another fifty yards to the right. Lieutenant Cochran and his RTO (radio telephone operator) walked in about the middle of the left file, and on the right side, my RTO and I took the end. I was the last man.

As we strolled through the jungle, I would look for unexploded artillery rounds on the ground. If found, I cut a two-inch piece of C-4 and take a blasting cap from my claymore bag, use my crimpers to poke a hole in the C-4, place five-minute timed fuse in the C-4, light the fuse and stroll on.

On one patrol we came upon a big house. Nobody was home. We checked around then moved on. About a half-mile farther, the company stopped for noon meal. We set our perimeter, and took our C-rations.

There was spaghetti and meatballs or ham with lima beans (too salty). Included was a blue heating tablet to cook the food, one can of fruit, a can of crackers with jam, a packet of salt and pepper, spoon, toilet paper. There was also a pack of four cigarettes until 1968 when the surgeon general said that smoking could be hazard to people's health.

The squad leaders also included bullets – because we could never have too many.

After eating, I took my RTO and my platoon medic back to better check around the big house. As we were returning, I heard on the radio that Bob's OP (observation post) had been fired on. Bob said he'd be on the way to the OP. He carried a twelve-gauge shotgun on patrol, and he grabbed it as he left with his RTO.

Within minutes, Bob and his RTO were shot and killed by one or more snipers. Most snipers were so good they could hit their target twice, either in the head or heart, before the target fell. Some of the most deadliest and ruthless were women.

The CO called in artillery fire. It sounded like 105mm, with a bang-to-boom time of about five minutes, whistling all the way.

We tried to get to reach the bodies of Bob and his RTO but couldn't due to artillery fire lasting through the afternoon and into the night.

About midnight we got to them. I helped carry his body back to base camp. Three days later we went back to Cu Chi. On the fourth day, we had memorial services. Then it hit me that Bob and I wouldn't ever again be standing at the mess hall drinking coffee while the troops go through the chow line.

***

Caught in a game of musical chairs because of his incompetence, Lieutenant Bob Thomas was transferred to C Company then back to D Company and placed as my platoon lieutenant. Thomas wants the same man and same squad on point every day.

I tell him no. It would cause stress that would follow us everywhere, and eventually lead into ambushes. He overruled me.

At 0700 hours the CO said head out. I tell the squad that has point to move out. We get to the gate, go through and form a couple columns of ducks, one file on left and one file on right. After an hour or so I get a call from the CO.

"Plat sergeant, this is the CO," he said. "Go get your plat leader."

The trouble was my lieutenant had seen something and took his radio-man wandering around out of formation.

On a sweep we stopped and waited for Charlie Company. The field was wide open for over 1,000 yards. Then, I saw men running all around not in any formation. I called back to the CO to ask if he could find out who they were. I knew that Charlie Company was around that area.

The battalion commander was flying around overhead, so I set to battalion radio frequency to ask him when the Lieutenant Thomas comes running up screaming, "Get off the radio! They pop purple smoke! They are VC! They pop purple smoke!"

I lay down behind an M60 machine gun, put down the bipod legs, check the pre-loaded 100-round ammo belt, and adjust the rear sight for 1,000 yards. I see a man running along a berm, so I open fire. I see the rounds hitting right behind his heels as he dives behind the mound.

A couple days later I saw Lieutenant Thomas on the forward base. He yelled at me, "You son of a b-, you were putting rounds two inches above my head!" In the meantime, this dizzy lieutenant had all the troops in the platoon ready to revolt. The CO sent him to Cu Chi, supposedly to ship out to a mechanized infantry unit.

***

We were preparing to go on patrol when the company commander walked up with a platoon of ARVNs and their advisors – South Vietnamese soldiers, their lieutenant and NCO advisors. As we moved outside the wire, there was a stream in the middle of my plat and ARVNS.

I tell Private Luck to get in the creek, and I wade in after him. We're wading along and getting hung up by wait-a-minute vines. Then a VC gets behind us; I look back and see the top of his head above water – he's tangled up in wait-a-minute vine! I reach down and cut his throat. We wade along farther and another VC gets behind us. We see him easily enough and shoot and kill him.

That evening, with perimeter set up and C-rations passed out, the CO has a meeting with the plat leaders. We settle down for the night, but wake hours later to hear the battalion camp behind us being hit with mortars. The battalion commander calls to tell the CO to sweep in, but I tell the CO, "You can go, but I'm not taking my plat. We let two VC get behind us. I'm losing my men in deep holes in the creek."

The CO tells the battalion no.

After sun up we swept into camp. The ARVNs left.

***

We stayed away from villages that are no-fire zones because we'd have to call Saigon and they won't give permission to return fire.

One person who only wants to be left alone is the farmer during the day. When we came upon a farmer's house, we'd search all through it: under the eaves, in the closet, under the bed, in the rice paddies. If we found weapons, we'd take the family into custody and burn the house. At night, the VC would come through to take pigs, rice and chickens. If there were young men and women, they'd take them and force them to be VC.

***

In May our company was attached to a mechanized infantry company. We set up at the outskirts of a large village with the purpose to hold elections and keep out the VC.

It was like a real carnival came to town. We took a 600 gallon water trailer that we called a water buffalo, added fifty pounds of sugar, and mixed up packs of Kool-Aid: grape, orange, cherry, lime. We gave the kids gum and candy, but we'd watch that they didn't approach in big groups. The VC would tie grenades under the kids' arms, and send them at soldiers in a group.

We were there a week. The last day my platoon gathered at a farm house where I pulled water out of the well so we could take baths.

After release from the mechanized infantry, we moved back to base camp with 2nd Platoon leading, 3rd platoon in the middle and 1st Platoon last, and I was the last man in the company.

The 2nd Platoon came under fire. Somehow my platoon had a 60mm mortar tube and some rounds but no sight and no bipod legs or base plate. I put the mortar tube in my steel pot. Holding the tube in my right hand I eyeballed my aim to the front of the company. It looked good.

I dropped the round. The 2nd Platoon said I was too close. I went to the front of my plat, dropped another round, but they said I was still too close. I dropped my steel pot, M16 rifle, and pack to go to the back of 2nd Plat. I grabbed an M60 machine gun and moved forward. Another gunner joined me. I told him to move down to a nearby berm because when we started firing, they would fire on us.

I commenced firing straight ahead. A VC to my left shot me in the right chest. It felt like somebody came up and gave me a kidney punch. I rolled off the gun, cussing and calling the VC everything but a human.

A couple people asked if I was hurt, and dragged me behind a bamboo hedge. They put patches on the front and back of my wounds. I told somebody to find the company medic because he was carrying a stretcher. About twenty minutes later, the soldier came back and said he couldn't find the medic.

I made my back to the main company myself to find the medic, and was then put on a chopper.

***

That third time I was wounded was May 28, 1968.

After surgery, I was placed in intensive care. Breathing was a problem. I couldn't catch my breath. When I started flopping around in bed, two nurses ran up to tell me to lay still.

I told them I couldn't catch my breath. They had me raise my head then lower it, then raise a foot and lower it, and so on. Finally, I got comfortable and went back to sleep. The next morning when I woke up, I wasn't in pajamas. All I had was a towel wrapped around my bony butt.

I had to pee what felt like a gallon. Walking outside to the latrine, I found I couldn't do it. A couple hours later, my teeth were starting to float, but I still couldn't pee. It felt serious, so I told the nurse. She stuck a catheter in me. Oh, what a relief!

The nurses gave me pajama bottoms the third day in the hospital, so I looked presentable for when my medic and a couple guys came by. They said Lieutenant Thomas had won the respect of the platoon, but the price was too high. One or two of the point men were shot. Thomas tried to get them and was killed.

Early on my fourth morning in the hospital, the nurse put me out before I woke up. I don't know if they put any stitches on the inside of my wounds but they put eleven wire stitches in front and thirteen in back. When the doctor was cleaning my gunshot wound, he spread my ribs. I couldn't take a deep breath for three months.

The fifth morning they put me on a plane to Cameroon Bay. The nurses gave me so many pills I lost my appetite. I'd get up in the morning starving to death, so at the mess hall I'd load my tray to overflowing. I'd sit down and eat ten or fifteen bites, but couldn't eat any more and throw the food away. We'd sit on a beach or I'd wade around the rest of the morning. Before noon I'd be starving again, and go to the mess hall and fill my tray, eat a bit and throw the rest away. This went on two weeks. While at Cameroon Bay, I lost twenty pounds, hitting 135 pounds.

I returned to Cu Chi around June 7.

The 25th Division had a policy that a soldier wounded or hospitalized three times didn't have to go back in the field, so for about three months I ran the enlisted men's club.

The club was like all the "buildings" on base a GP (General Purpose) medium tent stretched over a wood frame and wood floor. A twenty-year-old Vietnamese woman served the tables; we called her Baby-san. The drinking age was sixteen, so younger soldiers could come in. Five fifty-gallon drums held beer, including Pabst Blue Ribbon, Budweiser, Ballantine, Pabst's Red, White and Blue, and others. We chipped ice off a thirty-pound block to put over the beer. The tables were repurposed big wooden reels left over from electric or phone wire. Soldiers could also work our nickel, dime and quarter slot machines.

Due to the recent embezzling scandal involving the clubs on base, in operating the enlisted men's club, I made sure to have multiple receipts for everything: paying Baby-san, buying beer, etc. Fifty years later, I remember the Red, White and Blue and Ballantine cost $3 a case while Bud and PBR were $6 a case; there were forty cases per pallet.

The accounting measures put in place after the embezzling proved to take too much effort, so the battalion decided to close the club.

I went to 25th Division Personnel to request assignment to Saigon security. The clerk said the Division leadership school was looking for instructors. I submitted a lesson plan for a one-hour class, and was accepted to be an instructor.

Chapter Eight
Division School

In September I extended for six months. With the thirty-day free leave, I went home to Colorado.

Returning to Division school, I threw myself into the new routine.

The school's commandant was a captain. Other personnel included one first sergeant, a supply sergeant, a mess sergeant, a training sergeant, five clerks and twelve instructors. The course was two weeks long for SPC-4 and E-4s to give them an idea of their duties and responsibilities.

***

All students had to go on two ambush patrols outside the wire around Camp Cu Chi.

To attend the school, the SPC-4s need orders from their units promoting them to sergeant E-5. The soldiers who made honor student would be promoted to staff sergeant E-6. With guys bumping up two ranks in two weeks, our ovens were kept hot shaking and baking people out of classes. To give everyone a break, the middle weekend of the two-week school usually offered some kind of floor show like singers, comedians or dancing.

Some instructors taught a map-reading radio course. I taught the M60 machine gun and the .50 cal. machine gun, one hour per weapon per course. Each instructor led a one-night ambush patrol per two-week course.

If we instructors didn't have class or patrol, we could go to the PX, club, or swimming pool. With so much time on base, I bought a small TV for my room.

One day while going into the club, I met a sergeant named Babcock. We had a good laugh about sharing our last name. We entered the club and had fun with some girls, telling them we were brothers with different mothers but the same father!

Just before Christmas, Bob Hope came to Cu Chi with his troupe of gold diggers and Miss Universe. Bob Hope carried the show; the others didn't do a lot.

For the class on the .50 cal. machine gun, I set it up on its tripod on a table. It weighed 125 pounds and had an effective range of 2,000 yards. I disassembled the gun for my students.

The .50 cal. round itself is four inches long and one inch around. If you are hit by one, you lose a whole lot of area.

Each instructor would take out a ten-man patrol once during the course, and each student would go on two patrols. Before I started at the school, one patrol made contact with the VC and half the students ran, and the same thing happened again shortly after I got there.

From that time on, when I took out a patrol I'd give the patrol orders as we moved, telling the people where we were going and what we were going to do, and specifically what each person would do.

First, as I started giving the patrol orders, I told the students the enemy was Viet Cong, and that unless VC outnumbered us three to one, he'd probably fire a few rounds but then he'd run.

Second, I told them that if we made contact and any students ran, they had better run back through the wire to the school, pack their bags and go back to their unit before the patrol and I got back – because if they only came back to the school I'd kill them there. Lucky for them, my patrols never made contact.

On some of our patrols we would have a dog team. There were two types of dogs we used: a scout dog trained to sniff and find the VC and a security dog for keeping away intruders.

The scout dog was friendly like your dog back home, and anybody could pet it. The security dog you didn't pet. If a security dog team was with you, you didn't even try to touch the handler. If you were stupid enough to try, you wound up with your hand in the dog's mouth. The dog wouldn't bite it off, but he'd let you know, "Don't touch my master."

If we were outside the wire and made it to our ambush site, set up and laying there quiet waiting for Charles to come by, and if three hours later we noticed the dog handler was asleep with his security dog, we didn't reach over and smack him. We threw small pebbles at him.

***

I found out the 25th Division was going to hold a promotion board either in November or December. I told the first sergeant to turn my paper work in to the board. He told me that if I made sergeant first class E-7 I would have to go back to the field. I said I didn't care because if I didn't make sergeant first class, I'd be on the Department of the Army's promotion list and make AFC in a few months. They turned in mine and another sergeant's paperwork to the Division.

Around December 1, the two of us went to the board.

The promotion board was made up of first sergeants and sergeant majors, and when you went before a promotion board, you walked up to the president of the board, sitting in the middle, you salute and introduce yourself.

"Sir, staff sergeant Russell Babcock reporting, sir," I said. The president of the board can then ask you questions or tell you to go stand in front five or six other people on the board who ask questions.

"I see where you have the Silver Star," one sergeant major said to me. "How did you get it?"

I told him.

Another sergeant major said, "I see you extended. What did your wife say?"

"She told me if I don't extend don't come home because you won't have a home to come to."

Well the two of us passed the board. In January, we received our orders. I was promoted to sergeant first class. I don't know if the other sergeant had to go to back to the field or not.

We instructors threw a party for ourselves. I tried a rum and Coke, and I still almost got sick from the smell of alcohol, years after my last encounter with it.

In February 1969, I returned to the world.

Chapter Nine

Fort Gordon, Georgia – 1969-70

My orders assigned me to Fort Gordon, Georgia.

I started clearing out of Cu Chi. I turned in my TA-50, went to the aid station for my medical records, went to finance for my monthly pay and to draw travel pay for airplane tickets, and *I* requested a two-month advance.

Finance wanted to charge me for one of my free leaves. I said no and showed them where the leaves said free, not accountable. With the thirty-day leave I took first going to Vietnam, then two free leaves, and leave going back to the world, I counted 120 days of leave time. Normally, you'd get thirty days once a year. I guess I used four years leave time in eighteen months, but was granted it fair and square.

I went to the transportation department to set up an appointment to pack and pickup my baggage, clothes and things I didn't want to carry on the plane.

The day arrived that I left Cu Chi and went to Tan San Nhut. I processed through and got on the Freedom Bird back to the world. Crossing the International Date Line caused us to jump ahead a day. The flying time to Travis Air Force Base was about eighteen hours. We finally land, go through their supply depot and are issued the new Army dress uniform, Army Greens; the Army was doing away with the old tan uniform.

I went to the civilian airport and bought a plane ticket to Colorado. After landing, I called my buddy Kenny Sanders to pick me up at the airport. My old lady had moved and I didn't know where.

I knew the route and box number, so we went to the post office and found out where that route started. We drove to the route and followed it till we found the box number and house.

We stayed there a few days. I noticed all the tape recorders and speakers were missing. I asked my wife where they were at. She said she pawned them and lost them.

I found out from my friend Ross Smith that Mary would pawn the system every month, and he would redeem it and return it to her.

There was work to do in moving my family to Georgia. I rented a U-Haul trailer for the furniture and loaded Mary and the three kids in the back of the Firebird bound for a first stop in Junction City, Kansas. We took the highway south out of Delta. It had snowed about eight inches before we left Delta, and when we neared Gunnison, we saw around 200 head of deer and elk out in the fields

Mary wanted to drive, so I let her. Snow plows had cleared the roads, but there were a few snow clots left behind. I tell the old lady not to hit any because I was afraid they might be big snow-covered rocks. Well, she hit some and one of them really was a big rock that put a small hole in the oil pan. When we got to Junction City, I took the car to a garage, and they welded the oil pan for about $50.

We stayed in a motel for a few days while visiting Mary's mom and brothers.

When I left Fort Carson going to Vietnam years earlier, I sent an allotment of $200 a month for Mary to live on, but also had Finance take $25 from each paycheck for $50 savings bonds that could be cashed later. She had these savings bonds with her while we were in Junction City and went to one of the banks to cash them. She had the four kids with her, and it got hectic.

***

After a week and a half in Kansas, we drove on to Fort Gordon, Georgia. We arrived there right at the time when the Masters Golf Tournament was being held and we couldn't find anywhere to stay during that week. Everybody and their dog were there. A lot of local people rented out their houses and left on vacation;

some houses rented for $1,000 a week. I managed to rent us a room at the guest house on post.

I sign in at Fort Gordon a start in-processing. There is a battalion infantry training school and the Southeastern signal school. They assigned me to the signal school. I tried to tell them that my MOS is infantry and that I'm a certified infantry instructor, but no dice; they send me to the signal school.

After I processed in and the Masters was over, I looked for an off-base house for my family. A realtor offered us a three-bedroom house with living room and dining room, a big kitchen, a garage, a great big screened-in front porch, and a smaller screened-in back porch. The floors were hardwood, the kitchen stove was electric, the heating stove was diesel fuel, and on a standard size lot of land for $11,900. Mortgage payments were $100 per month.

At the signal school all the students attended night classes. I didn't check to see what MOS the students were, that is the jobs they'll work in the military. Some took radio repair classes, which started at 1800 hours and went to 2400.

If a student was sick and wanted to go on sick call, he had to wake up to go to the orderly room company office, have the CQ night duty NCO fill out a sick slip and then go on to the aid station.

My work day started at 0800 and went to 1700. It was my job to make sure students attended appointments and any mandatory training such as weapons qualification. We woke up the students at 1100, made them take showers, get dressed, make their bunks, eat, then clean the barracks, cut grass, study, eat again at 1700, make formation at 1745. The commandant counted the men, passed out any information of upcoming events, then sent the students marching to class. My title was Field First. At 1630 I'd go to battalion for news of things happening the next day, and then I went home for the day.

***

Back home, Mary said she hadn't received a couple of her allotment checks and savings bonds. I told her I'd have the post office check it out. One inspector came to the house and had Mary and I write our names over and over, then about three weeks he came again and had us write our names again. A month after that, he came to the house and told me the allotment checks and bonds were cashed at one of the banks by a woman with four kids.

He said he had a copy of the bank's security video, and could find her. He said he could charge the woman for theft of a government check from a government office, and that the woman can go to jail for one to five years, or fined $1,000 to $5,000. He asked me what I want to do.

His description fit my wife. Mary then admitted she cashed the checks, and none were missing.

***

There's a woman who lived across the street and Mary had a personality conflict with her over the six months since we moved in. I hadn't said a dozen words to her, but if I stayed up late to watch a movie on TV, the next morning my old lady would start nagging. “Did Shirley call? Did Shirley come over?”

Our bedroom was right off the living room, and if anyone called or came by, Mary would hear them. I finally tell her, “You can go over to her house and talk, stand in the yard, but Shirley doesn't come in my house.”

That fall our daughter Nora started school. We lived four blocks from the school, and Mary and the other three kids walked her to school for a week to make sure Nora can do it.

One day either Nora or Loretta slammed Nancy's hand in the door, cutting the tip of the pinky finger off except a little piece of skin. They said Alvin did it.

Mary had to suck up her dislike of our neighbor Shirley because Shirley and her sister were the only neighbors who could watch the kids while we took Nancy to the hospital.

After we returned from the hospital I found out it was Nora and Loretta that had shut the door on Nancy, so I administered that one spanking that they'd remember for years to come.

Mary was pregnant again and the evening of October 19 she went into labor. The pains were three or four minutes apart before she decided to go to the hospital. I sent Nora across the street to see if Shirley could watch the kids while I took Mary to the hospital.

After the pregnancy, Mary kept walking Nora to school and dragging the other kids along. I wanted her to stop because I knew that if it rained, she would drag all four kids out in it too.

So, in the mornings I got up, shaved, showered, ate and drank my coffee, woke Mary and together we bundled up the kids and threw them in the car. Mary dropped me at the base, kept the car for the day and would come to get me at 1700.

***

After eleven months in Georgia, I went to Personnel to send a request to the DA (Department of Army) to be posted to Fort Steward in Panama. They wrote back that you can't specify a particular post, so I had Personnel send a request for the Caribbean.

***

One Saturday about twenty students had to go to the firing range for weapons qualification. I arrived at the company at 0700, and the CQ said he had trouble getting one student up. I went to his room, he's asleep so I grab his arm and pull him out of the bed and he hits the floor. I told him to get up. Ten minutes later I check on him, and he's back in bed asleep.

I marched to the latrine and filled a gallon can of water, went back, pulled off the covers and dumped the water on him. Then he was up!

I took the students to the range to qualify. Some hit marksman, the lowest level, most hit sharpshooter, and a few hit expert.

On Monday, the first sergeant told me I shouldn't have gotten that lazy student's sheets and mattress wet. "Oh, well," I said.

A few days later the company commander, first sergeant and I had a big argument about it. They removed me from Field First duty and sent me to the motor pool, the vehicles available for use by authorized personnel, usually higher ranking guys.

I don't have to be in the motor pool all day due because the vehicles were mostly used in morning and evening, but I usually went in to pass the time instead of being home.

My job in the motor pool included being there from 0600 to 0800 and 1600 to 1800, for before-and-after maintenance like checking water and oil, tire pressure, change flat tires.

The motor-pool sergeant, Sergeant First Class Rodrigues, gave me a driver's test, and I got my license to drive all the vehicles in the pool.

I decided to work at the motor pool during the day, so I have Mary take me to work in the morning and pick me up in the evening. It was more productive than staying home all day watching TV, arguing with the old lady and playing tiddlywinks with my toes all day. Things were tense at home. Mary would harp at me, "Who'd you see? Who'd you call?" I'd say nobody and she would go on and on. I would have to walk out of the house and around the block to cool down to keep from smacking her in the head.

It was better for me to work in the back of the motor pool doing something or drive the supply sergeant or quartermasters to the store to pick up supplies.

***

Around the end of June, I received a packet from Fort Bragg, North Carolina, saying it would be a pleasure to welcome me to a six-week training course.

I had Personnel call the Department of the Army to see if I was on orders to go. At first DOA said no, but I decided to ask again a few weeks later. This time I had Personnel call Fort Bragg for an order number relating to my letter, then Personnel cross-checked the number with DOA and asked if I was on orders. "Yes," DOA said, "he has to be at Fort Bragg by August 1."

Knowing I'd be leaving Georgia for a while, I decided to send Mary and the kids to her family in Junction City and prepare our house to rent out. I decided it'd be safer for them due to riots around the country and locally over the military, Vietnam, Civil Rights, etc.

There were even riots in downtown Augusta, Georgia, and the governor requested the National Guard come in to control it. I recall the reason for those riots was the federal government stopping segregation in schools. In the state next door, Gov. George Wallace protested this ruling at the University of Alabama in Montgomery, and the 101st Airborne Division was sent there for control.

For my house, I got the supply sergeant to buy me paint, varnish, and brushes, and I painted the inside of the house and varnished the floors.

One night I took the survival knife I brought back from Vietnam and spent two hours filing it sharp so I could later shave with it in the field. After we'd painted the house's front porch, Mary decided to use my knife to scrape paint spots from the cement floor. I got so mad I could've cut her throat with it.

Once the house was ready, I went to the realtor, told her I was going overseas and asked her to manage renting out my house and then send the checks to the Office of Veterans Affairs to make my mortgage payment. She said she'd rent the house but not send the checks to the VA, so I told her to send the checks to Mary at Junction City.

I drew two months advance pay and travel pay, and had the transportation office ship our household things to Junction City.

***

I loaded Mary and the five kids in the '67 Firebird Convertible and we drove back to Junction City, Kansas. At the time Mary was pregnant with our last kid.

On arriving, I started looking for place for Mary and the kids to live while I went to training at Fort Bragg and then back to Vietnam.

I found a three-story stone house out in the country on Lyons Creek Road, with a fence all around the yard. It was owned by a doctor, who told me the history of it. It was called the Locust House because one year in the late 1890s locust swarmed into the area, destroying all the crops, hay, wheat, corn. Supposedly, the farmer went to England where some of his rich friends gave him money to help the poor Kansas farmers. He spent his share building the three-story Locust House. The living room had a sliding door that could open to make the room twice as big. The second floor held the kitchen and two bedrooms and a bathroom, and the third floor was all bedrooms. Altogether, the house had thirteen bedrooms, but by the time we moved in, the third floor was unusable because the walls had holes.

A week before my leave was up I got on the train to Fort Bragg. Mary found $300 in travelers checks in my stuff, and asked why I had them. I said I was going to a six-week school and had no idea where I would stay.

***

At Fort Bragg I went to the school area to sign in. We had a choice of staying in the barracks or renting rooms in a motel. We were drawing COLA pay, cost-of-living allowance, which would have covered the motel, but I chose to stay in the barracks along with most of the students.

I don't how the Army picked this class. There were seventy-seven of us senior NCOS: three or four first sergeants, six or seven staff sergeants, and the rest of us were sergeants first class. And, most of us were headed to Vietnam for a second time.

We all had signed to the school setting in the auditorium waiting for the commandant to say what we would be doing during the next six weeks. First he told us classes would run 0800 until 1100 and 1300 to 1700. In class we'd have PT, study Vietnam history, learn our duties as military advisors, and read, write and speak basic Vietnamese. Our Vietnamese instructors were women and we were to call them "Ba," which means Mrs.

The commandant said we wouldn't need NCO club cards to enter the post club. In his words, all women fat, slim and ugly went to the NCO club; all the men needed was an ear of corn to get into the club. A couple NCOs went to the grocery, and bought two dozen ears of corn. They sat by the dance floor at the club and started throwing the ears on the dance floor. The club manager came up and asked what they were doing, and they told him they heard only pigs came in there.

There were two other classes in progress at Fort Bragg, but their courses were eight to ten months long had mixed military services – Army, Navy, Air Force – in them.

There was a young marine staff sergeant instructor who taught us the new policy of pacification. The strategy involved us driving out the Viet Cong from villages and then teaching the villagers combat and policing techniques to fight Charles so the villagers would no longer be afraid of threats from guerilla forces.

Someone who spoke to our class was an ex-VC named Chou Hoa who gave up and came over to our side.

I didn't blame the VC for giving up. He was poorly trained and equipped with his coolie-hat, a rifle and a few bullets against us with our B-52 bombers. When you hear the plane engine, you turned around and headed home; they could drop over a hundred 1,000-pound bombs, each one able to make a 30-foot swimming pool. Then, we had Puff the Magic Dragon, a C-130 cargo plane with four 20mm cannons, mini eight-barrel guns on each side of the plane firing 1,000 rounds a minute, with the rounds hitting the ground about one inch apart. We also had the Cobra gun helicopter, with 40mm high explosive guns, two twelve-rocket pods, plus mini guns. If any one of those weapons was used on me and I lived through it, I would be like a VC and turn in my rice card and join the other side. So, the VC really were underdogs.

The military called these turncoats coyotes. They were useful as guides.

***

After a week, everybody on base knew about our class. They partied hearty. The ones that drank mixed drinks would have handkerchiefs filled with ice and wear sunglasses to keep from bleeding to death from bloodshot eyes. The partying wasn't limited to Friday and Saturday, but continued Monday, Tuesday, Wednesday, and Thursday. Sundays were for resting.

A few people drove their cars to Fort Bragg. Sergeant First Class Creed had a blue '60s model VW Bug. Usually Sergeant First Class Creed, Sergeant First Class Sanchez and I would go to the NCO club or go downtown to a Vietnamese restaurant or bars. Creed drank rum and Coke, Sanchez drank tequila, and I straight Coke. It didn't matter what nationality a woman was, we practiced the military's pacification policy on her.

We did stupid things that we knew better about, but did them anyway. Still, when Memorial Day weekend arrived, we graduated. Leaving Fort Bragg, we were given a week to get to Fort Bliss, Texas, for more training.

***

I bought plane tickets to Manhattan, Kansas; Grand Junction, Colorado; and El Paso, Texas. I stayed a couple of days with Mary and the kids. While I was home, Mary's doctor wanted to know if, because Mary and the kids were alone, would I want his family's German shepherd. It was a good women-and-children dog, and the doctor's two kids were at collage. I accepted. He brought the dog over and within thirty minutes, I was leading it around and petting it.

The next morning I flew out of Manhattan to Delta, Colorado. I said hello to Mom and stayed three days with Ross Smith and his family: wife Nancy, and kids Linda, Dale, Terry and Diane. The last night Ross took me to the airport

The flight to El Paso had turbulence all the way. When I got off the plane, I went into the restroom, got out of my uniform into civilian clothes, put my bags in a locker, and caught a cab into town. I walked across the toll bridge into Juarez, Mexico. Back then the cost was one penny.

I went into a bar called Caesar's Palace. The inside you wouldn't believe. The floor was carpeted red. The bar and the walls were black with large squares of red velvet hanging up. There were a bunch of sofas and stuffed chairs, and the tables were littered with cans of cigarette butts. Men lounged around with girls on their laps. Prostitution was technically illegal, but so as long as the women stayed inside the bar, they were OK.

I sat and drank a couple of Cokes. That was enough sightseeing for me. I left and walked back across the penny-toll bridge to the USA. I get a hotel room for night.

The, next morning, Sunday, I went to the airport to collect my bags and get dressed in my uniform then headed to Fort Bliss. When I signed in, the CQ told me that my wife had called. In the phone booth, I called collect since I paid the phone bill anyway.

“Where have you been?” Mary asked, with an edge to her voice.

I told her I went and saw Mom.

“Why didn't you tell me?”

“I don’t want to hear your mouth,” I said. “Why can't I see mom?”

We got into an argument screaming over the phone, and some of NCOs came out to see what was going on. I told her I was tired of her jealousy bull hockey and to stop or I'd divorce her.

***

We’d be at Fort Bliss for two months. The commandant told us the language course would teach us to say things like, “Me Tarzan. You Jane. Us go party.” He told us if we had a hard time writing, don't stay in the barracks, just go get drunk but make sure to sit in class next to someone smart and look over his shoulder and copy what he writes.

There were three or four more language courses going on there, some Vietnamese and some Russian. Classes ran 0800 to 1600.

Just as at Fort Bragg, after a couple days all the other students knew my class as partiers. After class, we’d eat supper then go to the club or bars until two or three in the morning. The first Friday night, I went along with a Mexican named Sanchez and a Puerto Rican named Raul in a cab to downtown El Paso then walked across the bridge to Juarez.

They talked to a Mexican cab driver who then took us to a bar. Inside, the walls and ceiling are covered in mirrors and a three-piece band was playing. The band came over to our table, and Sanchez and Raul join in singing then I start singing too. I have no idea what the hell I'm saying.

I'm drinking Coke, Sanchez was drinking tequila, and Raul drank a beer then rum and Coke then tequila. He says, “I know an alcoholic drink that you can drink. You'll like a screwdriver." It was vodka and orange juice. I did like it and I couldn't smell alcohol in it so it didn't make me sick.

After a couple of hours Raul was drunk and passed out. Sanchez and I grabbed Raul and left him with the cab driver that brought us. Sanchez and I then made a deal with the driver to take us from bar to bar all night. He took us to Caesar's Palace because I've told Sanchez what it looks like. Sanchez and I dragged Raul inside and sat him in a stuffed chair. We ordered drinks. Sanchez was talking to one of the women when Raul reached for and missed the butt can and threw up all over the red carpet. The bartender came over and politely spoke to Sanchez and me "Please take your drunken friend and get the hell out of his bar."

Sanchez had the driver take us to a sidewalk cafe where we ordered some food for the driver and us to eat. The driver then took us back to the first bar of the night. Sanchez and I took our time with our drinks, and finally about 0530 the driver returned us to the toll bridge. By this time, Raul was awake, and we took our shoes and socks off and paid the tolls and weaved and staggered back across the bridge.

At an all-night café, we put our shoes and socks back on and staggered in for breakfast. We caught a cab to the barracks for class.

Then at 1630 we hit the mess hall then grabbed a cab back to Juarez. This time the cab was licensed to go over the border to Juarez so we rode through customs and across the bridge and the partying lasted again until early morning.

***

One day I received a letter from the VA telling me I'm three months behind on my mortgage payments. I go to Finance and draw a month advance and send a $400 money order to get caught up.

On a Saturday evening, I was sitting in the day room watching TV when three black NCOs came in saying they were going to Juarez. They were all high, and I told them, "Wait a minute, I'll go with you. I don't want you all getting arrested in Juarez being high."

We caught a cab and stopped at a Holiday Inn to pick up some more classmates, who were also black. We then went across the street to a colored bar. I was the only light skinned guy in the club. Not too far in the club, I was caught by four black women at a table and we started dancing and continued until closing.

We partied like this through September and October until graduation at the beginning of November. Most everybody was put on a plane and sent to Vietnam.

A couple like me received ten-day leave because Mary was due to deliver our baby. I arrived in Junction City a week later and there was a young couple over at the house. I didn't know them but Mary did. Then Mary went into labor. I asked the couple to watch the kids while I took her to the hospital. They claimed they couldn't stay long. I called Mary's mom and told her to send Johnny and David out to watch the kids.

Mary was famous for waiting till labor pains were three or four minutes apart, and that's what she did this time. I threw her suitcase in the car we hot-footed the ten miles to town. We passed Johnny and David on the way.

I was racing up Washington Street, the main street of Junction City, at 60 miles an hour looking for cops. I didn't see any. I got to Grant Street and made a two-wheel right turn onto Grant. We were less than a mile from post and a little over two miles from the hospital when I saw a cop. He didn't follow but called the military police.

I raced across the bridge onto post and an MP jeep met me there. I didn't stop or slow down, and he turned on his lights and siren and called ahead and another MP jeep got behind me with his lights and siren. So, I had two MPs escort me that last half-mile to the hospital.

At the emergency room doors, I got out, yelling, "Woman in labor!" They started to bring a wheelchair, but I made them get a gurney.

I opened Mary's door, and one of the medics threw her on the gurney, but then the baby fell on the ground. Mary had given birth in the car while the MPs were chasing us!

This was our daughter Ella May. The medic picked her up and put her with Mary on the gurney and wheeled them into the hospital. I returned to the parking lot for the suitcase and spoke with the MPs. They understood what was happening. The lieutenant asked if I was OK.

At the door a buck sergeant whose wife just gave birth to a boy gave me a cigar. The nurse asked me what we had. I said, “Another raggedy-ass girl.”

I signed in Mary and took the suitcase to her. The baby spent two days in the incubator. Back home, I told Johnny and David she had a girl and they left.

The next morning, I fed the kids. Tammy, our next to last daughter, was in diapers, but I don't change diapers so I got her aunt Ruth to watch her until Mary got out of the hospital. I fed cleaned and took care of the others: Nora, Loretta, Nancy, and Alvin.

A few days later I flew to Travis Air Force Base and then back to Vietnam.

Chapter Ten

MACV – Hue, Vietnam – 1970-71

On arriving at Tan Son Nhut Air Base, we were loaded on a bus by an officer from MACV, the US Military Assistance Command - Vietnam, the commanding entity for American military activities there.

The bus drove us across the airport to the MACV compound, a facility just a few years old that also headquartered the command for Army of the Republic of Vietnam. It was so big, some referred to it as Pentagon East.

The NCO showed us our barracks, and issued bunks and linens. After we put our bags in the wall lockers and made our bunks, the sergeant took us to the mess hall for supper and then continued the tour to the PX, the theater and the NCO club.

At 0600 the CQ woke us up. We dressed and ate before being marched to the auditorium for briefing. We thought we'd be told we'd be advising Vietnamese officers about combat, but most of the officers had been fighting. Our orders were to aid them in getting air strikes, artillery fire, and supplies.

Unit assignments were made. I was assigned to MACV Team 3 - Hue.

The military divided South Vietnam down to four areas. I Corp comprised the area from the DMZ line between North and South Vietnam down to Da-Nang. II Corp runs from Da-Nang to Pleiku, III Corp from Pleiku to Saigon, and IV Corp from Saigon on south.

"Saigon is off limits," the instructor told us. "You can't go into Saigon."

That was the wrong thing to tell a bunch of GIs.

As soon as the day's briefings were over, we were off for the day. So, we ran back to the barracks, changed from our uniforms into civilian clothes, then galloped to the main gate and signed out. A few cabs provided quick transport to Saigon's bars. When we ordered drinks in Vietnamese, the waitresses asked us how long we'd been in Saigon.

"Two days," we told them.

"No way!" they said. We finally told them we'd gone to language school.

In a couple hours we proved we could go to Saigon and get back to the compound before the instructors missed us.

***

After three or four days of briefings, the sergeants took us across to the airfield to catch a C-130 transport plane to Hue. There the command sergeant major took us by bus to MACV's Team 3 complex, a two-block barbed-wired area in which the main building was a four-story French hotel where the I Corp commander and other high-ranking officers stayed. On the second floor was the officer-NCO club; on the first floor was the orderly room where the unit commander and first sergeant ran the unit mess hall. Altogether, there were about three dozen buildings in the compound.

The next morning I needed to take my financial and medical records to the 101st Airborne Division's base camp, Camp PHU-B1, which was twenty miles to the south. The first sergeant told me his driver would drop me off there and then I could call when ready for pick up.

After completing my processing at Division base camp, I tried to call the first sergeant but couldn't get through. I walked to the main gate and off post. It was not recommended to leave base without helmet, flak jacket and weapon, but I hadn't brought any. I walked about a mile down the road to a village along Highway 1, the main road north to south. A Vietnamese man with a three-wheel Lambretta, a cross between a scooter and a truck, took me back to Hue for $10.

***

MACV Team 3 comprised about 500 people and worked with the ARVN 1st Division in their area of operation from the DMZ to Da Nang. The first team of U.S. advisors I was assigned to supported the 3rd Battalion.

Our compound was five miles north of Hue off Highway 1. There was a marine major in charge of our group. In the rainy season, we wore rain suits with pants that had suspenders on them, and the Major looked like Farmer Brown from Kansas – but he wasn't as smart.

He wouldn't pay the working girl at the compound $2. Instead he went to a village by the highway and paid the working girl there $30, messing up the low prices that had been charged to the truck drivers hauling supplies and ammo.

He also thought we ought to carry the 1911 Colt 45 cal. pistol with a live round in the chamber. He wrote and sent a message to all team members of Team 3 about it. Before the message got around to everybody, he'd shot himself in the leg and foot twice.

The compound had about a half-dozen GP medium tents stretched over wood frames with wood floors. They held twenty men, a mess hall, aid station, and latrine. On top of the latrine were two fifty-gallon drums that we'd fill with water; the sun would heat the water and when flushed down it would amplify the smell of the waste. During the rainy season when it rained on and off every day, the water wouldn't get so hot, and the smell wasn't as bad (but it still wasn't good).

Some Vietnamese women worked in the camp. A few cleaned trays in the mess hall, but most worked as house girls making our bunks, shining our boots, etc. They would hand-wash, starch and iron our uniforms. They earned money that helped them and their families, and made our lives easier. Most men didn't know how to starch and iron shirts because their wives or mothers did it back home.

A week before Christmas the battalion went to the field for thirty days. A captain and I were attached to the battalion commander in Headquarters Company. The other three companies each had an American lieutenant and a NCO. The unit had about a dozen coyotes, former Viet Cong. ARVN provided RTOs (radio telephone operators). Our guy would carry the radio when we moved from place to place and help dig the foxhole when we set up defense positions.

We'd move from place to place every two or three days.

We'd hang a hammock between two trees and stretch our poncho over that for shade and to keep the rain off. I brought a bunch of books to read, including some of *Mack Bolan: The Executioner* books by Don Pendleton. C-rations were passed out for noon meal, but breakfast and supper meals were cooked by the battalion commander's cooks. The captain and I would eat with the commander and his officers.

On Christmas morning 1969 a resupply of food stuffs arrived. That evening the cooks fixed potato and octopus soup. It was pretty good, but definitely different for a Christmas meal.

After dinner, the battalion commander brought out a quart of Crown Royal, and the officers and I had a couple of Christmas cheers.

***

When we returned to our compound I spent a couple days at MACV compound.

For New Year's 1970, I received three letters.

The first letter was from the VA saying I was three months behind on mortgage payments. The second letter was from the Red Cross saying my wife Mary had a car wreck and the damage to the other man's car was $100. The third letter was from Mary herself saying that unless I sent her $50 she'd no longer write me.

I sent the VA a $300 money order for the mortgage, borrowed $100 to send for vehicle damages, and then wrote a letter to Mary.

It was a long and not a nice letter of the sort that had gotten me in trouble with the post office years before. Briefly, it went:

Dear Mary:

1. The VA wrote and said we were three months behind on mortgage payments, which means you signed and cashed the checks yourself.

2. The Red Cross told me about your wreck and $100 damage.

3. I'm not sending $50. So write or not, I don't give a damn.

***

Some good news was that I was told I'd be enlisted advisor for the ARVN 1st Recon Company, replacing a jarhead (marine) gunny sergeant E-7.

I moved all my things from my former camp north of Hue back to the main MACV compound, where I was assigned a room on the second floor of one of the enlisted quarters.

The lieutenant advisor for the recon company told me it was his policy that we would alternate going out in the field with one of the recon squads for a week at a time.

The lieutenant told me that since I just joined the company and hadn't met any of the people, he would go to the field first and I would go the next week.

During that week, the team he was with engaged the enemy in a fire fight. The lieutenant was wounded and medivacked to some hospital; I never saw him again.

G-3 assigned us another lieutenant, William Altman. His basic MOS was PIO (public information officer), but we made a real infantry grunt out of him. The major from G-3 told Altman and me to go where the company commander or the assistant commander (XO) went, and not to go in the field with any of the recon teams.

We spent most of the day driving near the Citadel, Hue's inner walled city near the old imperial palace, because the ARVN company commander's house was in the neighborhood. When we finally found the captain, I introduced him to the Lieutenant Altman. The captain said was staying in Hue that evening. According to our orders, we needed to remain near the captain. It was coincidental that our payday was that day.

The stars were aligning to allow Altman and me a night out in Hue. Just to make sure, Lieutenant Altman talked to the G-3 major, who said that since the company commander was staying, we could too.

Unknown to us, later that evening the commander decided to go to the firebase at Xa Hoa, where the recon unit had part of the defense, along with the 101st Airborne Division. The firebase was a two-part hill on the shore of Tonkin Bay. About halfway up, the ground was graded flat to land helicopters. At the top was an artillery battery run by a company from the 101st Airborne.

Sometime late that night the Viet Cong attacked from the sea. A couple sappers made it to the top battery and destroyed two cannons. As the VC came up the hill, they fired an RPG, a 40mm self-propelled grenade, which went into the bunker where Altman and I would have been.

The next day, when I found out the recon commander was at the firebase and that the firebase had been hit, I rushed back to our compound, grabbed the lieutenant, and we raced to firebase Xa Hoa. We arrived at the base, went to the helipad, and reported to the I Corp commander, a three-star general. I had been on the job a week and it was just the second day for Altman. The general proceeded to chew our asses for not being there the night before. The general was ready to chew out the recon commander when I told the general he couldn't because the recon commander was at the firebase. The lieutenant and I got another ass chewing.

When the general was done with us, we went to check out the bunker that'd been hit by the RPG, where Altman and I would have otherwise been sleeping during the attack. It went through two one-inch steel interlocking planks and a foot of dirt, right over my bunk.

I had laundry bag under my bunk, holding two sets of fatigues, towel, T-shirts, shorts, socks, three or four cans of pork & beans, a one-pound tin cracker box, twenty five-packs of Hav-a-Tampa plastic-tipped cigars. The RPG round tore holes in some of the clothes, didn't hit the cans of pork & beans, and tore the hell out of the cracker can and my cigars. I was left with no more than two packs of cigars.

The lieutenant was upset about being chewed out by a three-star general after two days on the job.

"Bill," I told him, "look at it this way: If we'd been here, we would have been wounded or killed and they would be replacing us. I can take an ass chewing any day, but I can't take a B-40 enema."

***

In February 1971, the nearby 3rd Brigade from the 101st Airborne was getting ready to return to Fort Campbell, Kentucky. I drove a two-and-a-half-ton truck to Camp Eagle at Phu Bai to see if they were leaving any equipment that I might take for my troops. The supply sergeant gave me a deal: one scrunch up, 110 aluminum cots, 105 steel pots and sets of TA-50 packs, straps belts, shelter hafts, thirty machetes, forty pin-flare guns, forty strobe lights, four PRC-25 radios, two 291-foot-tall radio antennas, two starlight scopes for weapons, .45 cal. pistol, .38 cal. pistol, automatic twelve-gauge shotgun, M90 recoilless rifle, ten M72 Law rockets, forty twenty-round and forty thirty-round magazines for M16 rifles, six cases of combat boots.

I gave the supply sergeant an AKA rifle for all the goodies. The AKA was a semi-automatic rifle so he could register it with the unit and take it home to the states.

The boots were too big for the ARVN men, so when I returned to Hue the next day I took the boots down to a flea market and sold them.

My supply expedition earned me a reputation as a deal maker. The ARVN recon commander wanted to build a patio on his house and asked if I could get him some cement. I took the big truck and drove about eight miles down Highway 1 to Da Nang Air Force Base and traded an AKA rifle to a supply sergeant for a twelve-gauge shotgun and another AKA rifle to another supply sergeant for four pallets of cement.

I told the recon commander the cement would cost him two medals for Lieutenant Altman and two medals for me. He awarded RVN Gallantry Crosses to us both, plus a RVN Staff Service First Class for Bill, and a RVN Staff Service Second Class for me.

A couple nights later the recon commander ordered an ambush. Bill and I took our shotguns and pistols; I gave Bill the .38 and I kept the .45. A couple hours after we set up, the VC walked in. After springing the ambush, we called for illumination, rounds fired over the area to light it up to check for kills. We didn't find any bodies but there were a lot of blood trails leading out of the ambush site. We returned to base.

***

We American advisors were not allowed in downtown Hue without our ARVN counterpart. One afternoon the recon commander, his wife, his jeep driver, Altman and I were at a sidewalk cafe eating when American MPs approached and harassed Bill and me. The ARVN captain told them he was our counterpart and to leave us alone. The MPs left.

***

An exercise was coming up to prepare for the possibility of sending the ARVNs into Laos, a nation on Vietnam's western border. Although the U.S. was secretly bombing Laos from the air to disrupt North Vietnamese supply chains, American troops couldn't fight on the ground.

I talked to the 75th Infantry Rangers at Phu Bai about training our ARVN recon company to repel from helicopters. The Rangers' commander agreed to a two-week training session. Our men learned to repel first from a thirty-foot tower and then from 100 feet off a real helicopter. The troops learned how to hook up to the different types of choppers. After the course, the ARVN recon commander, Bill and I all took the Rangers' commander and first

***

The motor in our jeep started making noises and overheating. I drove to one of the American motor pools in Phu Bai. The motor pool sergeant had his mechanics replace the motor's head and head gasket. I told the motor-pool sergeant that I'd take him and the mechanics out to dinner off post.

One day a VC came out of a tunnel near battalion headquarters. Personnel sealed the tunnel, but Charles seemed to infiltrate the base anyway. A little while later someone cut the security chain off our jeep's steering wheel and stole the vehicle. After that, Lieutenant Altman and I carpooled with the ARVN captain.

Bill and I alternated trips into the field with the recon group. The captain, his wife and his driver would pick up one of us in their jeep. When Bill got into the jeep with them, they made him sit in the backseat, but when I got in, they made me do the driving.

We trained the recon company to the point where they could call for their own air strikes, supplies and medivac. We worked ourselves out of our jobs.

The recon commander, his officers and first sergeant threw us a goodbye party, and we got drunk. Unwisely, I drove us back to the compound. We were lucky we weren't stopped.

Back at the MACV compound, I was given busy work until a new assignment was given. The first sergeant had me check all our bunkers every week to make sure the equipment was ready. With that done, I'd go talk to the waitresses at the NCO club.

***

The next assignment came soon enough. Lieutenant Altman and I were put in charge of security for a visit from a two-star general. Years before, he had been advisor to the governor of Hue, and they were to reunite on an excursion down Hue's Perfume River and visit several emperors' tombs. Bob and I recruited two squads of rangers for security.

On a Saturday before the event, I took two men and a PRC 25 radio on a rented sampan down the river. Every half hour I used the radio to call two people on a gunship helicopter to make sure there weren't any communication dead spaces. At the halfway point, we put the sampan to shore and walked around a tomb. Pop-a-san, the older man who piloted the flatboat, said he'd go back now. I pointed to one of my men and told Pop-a-san if the San-pan started to leave my man would shoot and sink the sampan and we'd all walk home about fifteen miles. Pop-a-san decided to tour the tomb with me, and we returned to Hue all together. I told the G-3 major that we had radio contact all the way down the river.

The afternoon before this shindig, I drove to Phu Bai to pick up the two squads of Rangers. I told them not to think too badly about our barracks because all our support comes from the ARVNS. The Rangers settled into one of the barracks then Bill and I took them to the NCO club for BBQ chicken, potato salad, beer or liquor. We partied down for a few hours to make the trip worthwhile for them.

Early the next morning, Bill divided the Rangers into two squads. The chopper took one squad to the first tomb then returned for the second. In the meantime the general and governor and VIPs arrived at the chopper pad, loaded up and flew to the first tomb. They walked around for about ten minutes, got on the chopper to fly to the second tomb. Bill's chopper then picked up the first squad and flew to the third tomb.

While that was happening, I was speeding up and down the river on a WWII PT boat. I stop at the turnaround point where the VIPs are supposed to land in an open field, walk twenty-five yards to the river's edge, cross the river to the tombs, walk around and eat lunch. The artillery major in charge of the sampans had them sitting a half-mile away; I asked him to move them closer, but he declines. I asked his counterpart, the village chief, but he tells me the county chief would be there in a few minutes.

The county chief arrived and I explained that I wanted the sampans moved to the edge of the field so the VIPs wouldn't have to walk so far. He told the major to move them. After getting this straightened out, I returned to patrolling.

Bill dropped half the Ranger squad in the open field, and held up the other half until after the VIPs had crossed to the sampans. The Rangers were then supposed to load on a truck to go a half-mile to another tomb. The squad leader asked the troublesome artillery major if the squad could load, and the major told them to march there double-time instead. The squad does.

After this tomb the VIPs flew back to Hue. Bill ferried back the squads on the helicopter. While everybody had gotten back to Hue the quick way, I was still racing up the river. I made it back to join everybody to load on buses to drive to the Citadel and the castle for a special tour arranged by the governor.

I've mentioned this castle before. Unlike European castles, Hue's was more wood than stone, and so was the throne. The governor also showed the party the room of Buddha statues behind the throne. The structure had been damaged during the Battle of Hue in 1968, but was still impressive.

Bill and I thanked the Rangers, and we drove them back to Phu Bai. One squad leader told me about the trouble with the jerk major making them march.

***

Soon thereafter, Lieutenant Altman was cleared to return to the world, and I followed a bit later.

There was a captain I knew who arrived in country a month before me and our running joke was he kept telling me, "I go home before you," and I'd say, "Yeah, you got here first."

Well, I received orders giving me a three month drop, and when I showed him, saying I was going to the world in September, ahead of him, he was pissed!

I returned to the world unassigned. I didn't know where I was going – in more ways than one.

Chapter Eleven

Fort Leonard Wood, Missouri – 1971-73

A plane took me from Hue to Tan Son Nhut, and another, a freedom bird to the world, took me to Travis Air Force Base in California. There we were issued a set of new green uniforms.

I went to the civilian airport to fly to Manhattan, Kansas. The Manhattan airport is about halfway between Junction City and Manhattan, so I caught a cab to Junction City, where my wife Mary was living with our kids.

They were living in a house in the middle of town, somewhere between Third Street and Walnut. Her mishandling of money had lost us the old stone house in the country, the Locust House. She had cashed the checks I'd sent to pay the mortgage. Needless to say, when the cab dropped me off, I was not in a good mood.

My 1967 Firebird convertible was sitting there in the driveway. I looked at both the front and back bumpers, and neither was bent to indicate it had been in an accident that would have done $100 damage to another car.

I took my bags in the house. I noticed that the German shepherd I bought the kids was missing and my old lady had thrown out all the pictures I'd left or sent home, like the ones of the imperial castle at Hue. Mary claimed the dog wouldn't let our son Alvin play, and my stuff was lost while moving.

It was a Monday when I walked in, and the week didn't get any better. The atmosphere simmered until the weekend.

"Mind if I take the kids to a movie Saturday?" Mary asked.

"There's the car," I said.

Around dark on Saturday, Mary loaded the kids in the car and left.

Around 11 p.m. Mary's sister Helen stopped by wanting to know where Mary and the kids were. I said they were at the movies. Around 1:30 a.m. Mary and the kids finally got back.

"Helen stopped by and wanted know where you and the kids were, then she left," I told Mary.

Mary started yelling, "Are you trying to put the make on my sister?"

"She was here five minutes and left!" I said.

Then Mary asked me what I'd say if she wanted to go to California for a few days. I told her it would take three days to drive to California, three or four days resting, then three days to drive back – that'd take over a week of my leave. "Not no," I said, "but hell no!"

Then the real knock-down fighting started.

It turned out Mary had been going out with a Fort Riley cook named George. Evidently, she got rid of the German shepherd because it wouldn't let Georgy -Porgy in the yard. And she hadn't taken the kids to the movies; she dropped them off somewhere and met George.

I weighed 135 pounds and Mary weighed 170 pounds, and we started throwing punches and wrestling. We kicked out the front door, and fought into the yard then to the middle of the street. After around fifteen minutes of this, we broke up. I threw my bags in the car and told her I'd drop it at her mom's house, because it was near the bus station.

I thought I'd take a bus to Delta, Colorado, but the clerk at the station said no more were leaving that night. I decided I'd hitchhike instead, so I left my bags there to be taken on the next bus.

My intention to leave the car at Mary's mother's house was met with a surprise. Two police cars were there. They woke her mom up and checked through the house looking for me. I drove to a little park on Grant Street and slept. Early in the morning I returned to Mary's mom's and told her brother Johnny to take me to

Abilene where I could start hitchhiking on Interstate 70, and he could take the Firebird back.

***

There I was on I-70 hitchhiking home to Delta, Colorado, wearing my uniform. I'd get a ride down the road a-ways, get dropped off, walk a-ways, and then get picked up again. By midnight, I'd made it to the east side of Denver. It took
me two hours to walk across Denver, and by then I was awfully tired so I climbed up under an overpass bridge and curled up to sleep.

At a service station a few hours later, I cleaned up and bought some snacks and water. I caught a ride over Loveland Pass. I wouldn't have wanted to walk it. The elevation was 11,100 feet, and the roads go up for eight miles at a stretch and go down about the same. That driver dropped me at the edge of Aspen. I got another ride to Glenwood Springs.

Along the road west of town in the Glenwood Springs Canyon, a Colorado highway patrolman stopped me and asked where I was walking. I told him Delta, and he said OK, and drove off. About two feet off the right of the road was the Colorado River and on the left side mountain cliffs. Most of the way through the canyon the speed limit was sixty miles per hour. There weren't many cars coming by, but when one did, it was close. I finally reached Grand Junction and caught the bus to Delta, fifty miles south on Highway 50.

I stayed with my mom a couple days. I called Mary to tell her that when my assignment orders arrived, she could to send them to me there.

I also reconnected with my former high school girlfriend Jean Castoe, now White. She had a house on the north side of town where she was raising her four kids. I stayed with her for the rest of my leave.

When Mary forwarded my assignment orders, I found myself assigned to Fort Leonard Wood, Missouri.

A week before my leave was up I caught a bus to Fort Carson to draw my pay. While there, I went to the PX and bought a hard-case Samsonite briefcase to carry my paperwork.

With my marriage on the rocks, and Mary already throwing out my stuff, I decided I needed dependable storage container for my documents and photos. Anytime I watched TV there would be an ad with a gorilla throwing luggage around a cage showing how tough it was. I thought the ad was for Samsonite, so I bought a Samsonite. Almost fifty years later, that case still holds my important papers, but finding the commercial on the internet shows it was actually for the American Tourister company, Samsonite's competitor.

The time left on my leave was winding down. There was no express bus to Leonard Wood. The regular bus took three days there, and I swear it stopped at every cow pasture along the way. Fort Leonard Wood was a basic training post that covered about 100 square miles deep in the middle of nowhere in the Ozarks. There was one small town just off post, Waynesville, in a canyon; you walk five blocks in any direction and you are out of town.

At Fort Leonard Wood, I processed in: I turned in my 201 file to Personnel, turned in my finance file and got paid for leave and travel, turned in medical records to the hospital, then reported to the quartermaster to receive a TA-50 helmet, field pack, shelter half, and sleeping bag.

I was assigned to Headquarters Company 3rd Training Battalion. The first sergeant assigned me a room in the barracks. I put my clothes and gear up in the footlocker and wall locker, with my TA-50 on top.

Once settled in, I headed out to buy a red Dodge pickup. If you wanted to get anywhere off base, you needed wheels.

***

Mary hired some shyster lawyer and filed for divorce. She wanted $300 child support per month. I told the shyster, "No, I will do $200 for four kids." Nora was from a former marriage and Alvin was not mine. After some haggling we agreed I wouldn't pay for Nora and Loretta, but I'd pay for Alvin because he was a boy and had my last name. Altogether, I'd pay child support on Alvin, Nancy, Tammy and Ella.

One weekend, I hopped in my truck and drove the back highways: Highway 13 to the Lake of the Ozarks then west on Highway 54 to El Dorado, Kansas, up Highway 77 to Junction City. It was about a seven-hour drive.

I visited the kids a couple hours then I got a hotel room. The next morning Mary wouldn't let me see the kids, so I left to return to the post.

***

One day I got a letter from a Mrs. Jimmy Turner. I didn't know any woman named Jimmy Turner. It turned out to be from my sister Donna. I hadn't seen or heard from her for about eight years. I guess she got my address from Mom, whom I was still writing and calling.

Donna was married and living in Chattanooga, Tennessee, with her husband and two kids, aged about three and four. I took a three-day pass and went there, driving the winding two-lane Highway 54 to Paducah, Kentucky, then the twisting two-lane Highway 41A through Nashville, and the last six miles into Chattanooga on a fancy four lane. I called Donna from a payphone and her family met me and took me to their house, on the side of Chickamauga National Military Park, where the Civil War battle took place.

We had a good reunion. One night we went bowling with Donna's next-door neighbors, the Blackwells. I hadn't been bowling since high school, so we had some laughs at my expense.

I left early that Monday morning to drive back to Leonard Wood. With all the hills, the distance was about a thousand miles and took about sixteen hours to drive.

***

At Fort Leonard Wood, I was made NCO of a firing range. At first, I did the 25-meter zero range, where the trainees would calibrate their sights.

The next range I was in charge of was the qualifying range. The trainees would qualify as marksman with twenty to twenty-five hits on a pop-up target, sharpshooter with twenty-five to thirty-five hits, or expert with thirty-five to forty hits.

At the firing ranges, a lookout sergeant in a tower would give the all-clear signal once everyone was out of the line of fire. My tower operator was Staff Sergeant Dobbs, and he gave all commands on the firing line. I'd take him a cup of hot coffee, and he'd take a few sips then let the coffee get cold.

The DIS (drill instructors or drill sergeants) marched the trainees from the barracks area out to the ranges. One morning a drill sergeant marched a company of trainees on the range, and I knew he looked familiar. I knew Sergeant Jerry Peeler from C Company 2nd Battalion 10th Infantry Regiment at Fort Carson years ago. He left Fort Carson for Vietnam after I did, where he served in the 1st Cavalry. At Fort Leonard Wood, he was a staff sergeant, but a couple months later he made sergeant first class.

***

I took a ten-day leave for Christmas in 1971 and drove to Colorado, I'd had battalion CQ the night before I left, so I didn't get started till noon the next day. Around midnight I drove into Salida, a little town at the bottom of Monarch Pass. I felt the right front tire shimmying so I stopped to check it and there were only two lug nuts holding the wheel and one was loose. I tightened the lug nut and kept going.

A highway patrolman stopped and asked me where I was going.

"I'm trying to get over the pass before it's closed," I said.

He looked at his watch, then at me. The time was 12:30 a.m.

"Where did you come from?" he asked.

"Fort Leonard Wood," I said.

"What time did you leave?" he asked.

"About noon," I said.

"How far is that?"

"About 800 miles."

"I'm writing you a speeding ticket."

I almost punched his ticket for writing me a ticket.

Leaving Salida and driving over Monarch Pass at 3 a.m. I'd slowed from 90 miles an hour. When I arrived at Jean's parents' house around 5 a.m. there was one lug nut holding the tire on. Being Christmas and no parts stores open, I borrowed a car to visit Mom a couple hours then went to Jean's.

The next morning I got five lug bolts and lug nuts and fixed the wheel, but going back to Leonard Wood, the heater in my pickup stopped working. I put on a couple pairs of pants and shirts and wrapped up in a heavy blanket. From Canyon City, Colorado, across the state of Kansas and half of Missouri, I was freezing.

When I got back and took it to the mechanic, it turned out the wire to the heat adjuster had just come off.

Just before the weekend of my birthday, January 14, 1972, Mary wrote me wanting me to come up to Junction City. I got there and we left the kids with somebody and went to a movie. After the movie, we went back to the trailer house she'd moved to. She told me her man George had left and she wanted to know if I wanted to get back together.

Just then, I was saved by the bell. Georgy Porgy himself walked in.

It was only going to be a few hours until I had to leave, so I just slept on their living room floor. A while later, a drunken girl came in, waking me up. I don't know who she was, but it made me question the living situation there.

The next day I drove back to Fort Lost in the Woods.

***

In about six months' time I put 20,000 miles on my pickup. Many of those trips I'd drive seven or eight hours to see the kids and spend 30 minutes or an hour then get in an argument with Mary and leave. I started visiting my sister in Chattanooga, 1,000 miles, and I would drive home to Delta, Colorado, 1,100 miles.

About twice a month I drove to Chattanooga to see Donna. They always wanted to go bowling, so I bought a fifteen-pound bowling ball, a blue-and-white bag, and bowling shoes.

To give an idea of how far beyond regulations I was pushing my traveling, here's a list of the pass restrictions at the time:

1. Normal pass from end of work day 1700 hours or 5pm to 2400 hours or midnight - 50 miles

2. Overnight or 24-hour pass - 75 miles.

3. Three-day or 72-hour pass or - 150 miles.

You were allowed to go farther than these distances if you had a plane ticket.

I'd get a seventy-two-hour pass and drive a round trip of 2,000 miles to Chattanooga, Tennessee, or Delta, Colorado. The cost for gas would be about $50.

I'd get a forty-eight-hour pass and drive a round trip of 300 miles to Junction City, Kansas.

Had I ever been late getting back to post, I'd have been in trouble.

I came close to it. My pickup motor blew up, so I sold it to a junkyard and bought a 1960s Ford convertible. During a run to Junction City to see the kids, something went wrong with the car. I had my foot on the gas pedal all the way to the floor but was barely doing twenty miles an hour. It took an hour to drive past a service station.

The man there checked out the motor and found one of the head gaskets had blown. I left the car there to be fixed. I phoned Mary, but didn't get an answer. So I started the twenty-mile walk to White City where Mary lived. The sky was clear and the temperature was around 100 degrees. The walk took four hours.

The old lady and kids weren't home, so I went to a cafe for a bite to eat and a drink. I went through three bottles of water, and took a fourth one with me to Mary's. About 7 p.m. the streets rolled up for the night. It wasn't until 10:30 p.m.

that Mary, Georgy Porgy and the kids got home from fishing all day at the lake. I told George to leave; I was going to stay the night and have the old lady take me to get the car the next day.

The mechanic said he had the heads milled and put in new lifters, pushrods, and head gaskets it cost me around $150. I paid up and started back to base.

A new officer was assigned to the range, Captain Peatree. We started arguing over the running of the range. It was serious enough I arranged with the captain at the survival, escape and evasion range to go to work there.

In the summer at the survival, escape and evasion range, the range cadre arrived at work around 1700 and started preparing for the night's training. We started a fire in the pit and let it burn down to red hot coals. We took big ammo cans without the rubber seals (so they wouldn't pressurize) and fill them with ears of corn and chunks of potato, then add water and place near the coals to cook.

We took a dozen store-bought trout, buttered them and wrapped them in foil, some with lemon juice and some with BBQ sauce, and set them on the coals to cook. Next we put game hens on long poles to roast over the coals. When everything was done, we spread it on big trays.

The trainees marched on the range around 1930. We'd break them into three groups: shelters, traps, and food. For shelter we showed them how take vines, branches and leaves to make shelter. For traps, we showed them how to weave small branches into box traps to catch small birds and fish. For food, we showed them how to get a fire going and prepare the food then we had them sample the food we'd been cooking.

The next part of the training put the men in a POW (prisoner of war) situation and an escape scenario.

Their drill sergeant formed them up and marched them into our classroom. The range officer told them that they would see POW camp personnel dressed in red helmets, green shirts and black pants. One of us would walk in so they could see. Then Sergeant First Class Crow, a short, stocky guy would come running through the door yelling. He'd run up to a trainee, and pull him to his feet by the shirt. Crow would hip-throw the trainee to the ground, without letting go of the trainee so he wouldn't get hurt. Five or six more of us would rush in and start taking the trainees out of the classroom, forming them up in four groups to march to the prison.

The prison was set up in two sections. The small section had a 10-foot-tall cyclone fence with two rolls of concertina wire lining it. On the ground were six wall lockers lying flat on each side of the compound, a chin-up bar, and two small sheds where we simulated interrogations.

The other section of the compound was open ground.

The trainee cadre issued the group in the small compound their boxes of C-rations. The trainees would eat while in the big compound. The groups formed large circles. For about thirty minutes we'd make them double-march in place or do sit-ups while eating.

Some members of the cadre were not dressed as guards, but rather civilian who were partisans, or underground civilians friendly to U.S. troops.

The partisans would throw noise grenades and fire blanks in a mock attack on the prison, then run up and open the gates and tell the trainees to follow them out.

The partisans would lead them back to the classroom, where the range commanded showed the trainees a map of the range for their "escape."

The "escape" area was one mile square, each side bordered by a road. The commander told trainees that diesel fuel smudge would cloud the area for cover.

"If you are near one of these roads, stay put and keep an eye out for the rescue truck," he said. "But beware enemy troops along the road who will capture you."

While the trainees were still in the POW compound, the smudge pots would be lit and start smoking. For the enemy forces for the roads, we used the trainees who'd gone through training the night before.

Thirty minutes after the trainees were released from the POW camp the truck would start picking up men. The trainees who'd been "captured" would be put in the small compound. They'd be made to lay a wall locker while we'd pound, or do chin-ups or sit-ups for fifteen minutes.

We'd also take them into the two small interrogation sheds. There was a two-by-four nailed to the floor on which the subject would put his toes, and then he'd bend forward to place three fingers of each hand on a desk. Their legs would have to be bent. We'd ask them questions to which they were supposed to only give their name, rank and service number. If they let their knees fall, we'd kick them to straighten up.

After about forty minutes they were released to their drill sergeants, who took them to a smoke-break area. They'd hang out while we picked up the rest of the "escapees" and smudge pots. Usually we'd have the range closed by midnight, but once in a while some trainees would lie down and fall asleep while awaiting "rescue." We'd take the jeep around the range with the siren and flashing lights until they were found.

***

Mom sent me a letter telling me one of my cousins was in basic at Leonard Wood. I think he was Aunt Nelly's son from Gnome, Colorado. I didn't get the letter in time. I remembered a couple of "interrogators" questioning a kid who said he was from Nom. I didn't know which training group he was in, and I never saw him after.

On the weekends when I wasn't going to Delta or Junction City or Chattanooga, I'd drive to Rolla, a college town twenty-five miles north of Leonard Wood. There was a USO club run by an older lady volunteer, where service men could play pool, watch TV, read, and get Coke, tea and snacks.

This lady knew me and what range I worked on. Some of the trainees would tell each other how rough the survival, escape and evasion course was, with the throwing them on the ground and breaking arms and legs. Some of the trainees recognized me and visited.

Sometimes the course did get rough.

One night the truck that set out the smudge pots had its bed covered with diesel fuel a d one of the light pots fell over catching the floor on fire. Instead of stopping and putting out the fire, the sergeant driving it raced around the range. The truck burned up. The sergeant had to pay for the truck.

There was a Friday night when we were done with the survival class and I started to open one of the ammo cans on the hot coals that had corn and potatoes. It still had some of its rubber seal and the can got pressurized like a pressure cooker. When we tried taking off the lid, it exploded, nearly making me instant mashed potatoes.

My eyes were protected by sunglasses, but my chest, arms, neck and face suffered burns and one of the trainees was burned a little too. We were taken by jeep to the hospital. The emergency room nurses iced my chest. They also soaked towels in ice water, wrung them out and put them on my arms and neck.

I asked one of the nurses if she'd put some iced orange juice and vodka in a glass for me. After two hours of this treatment, they put salve on and put me in a room where I didn't get much sleep. The next morning they gave me some lotion and a slip recommending light duty for ten days.

After the trainee and I got burnt, the range cadre stopped cooking on coals and the trainees went to the mess hall, where corn and potatoes were cooked in a five-gallon pot with a non-sealing lid.

***

When fall 1973 finally rolled around, I decided to leave the Army after twelve years active service.

The last week of October I received my discharge orders and clearing papers. They would take two weeks to clear, so I began tying up loose ends. I started by washing and cleaning my TA-50 and turning that in. I went to the company's arms room, drew my M16 rifle clean and oiled it, then turned it back to the armory. Supply signed off on my cleaning and that I had paid for my quartermaster laundry. I went to the battalion aid station to get my medical records and then to the hospital take a physical.

I went to Finance to sell my forty-five days of leave back to Uncle Sam, and they also figured up how much money they owed me from Nov. 1 to 12.

At Personnel, we read over my 201 file:

January 1966 – Korea – promoted to Sgt. E-5

October 1967 – Vietnam - received Silver Star, Bronze Star & two Purple Hearts

1969 – Vietnam – promoted to SFC E-7

November 1970 to 1971 – Vietnam – posted to MACV HQ at Hue

Summary: two-and-a-half tours in Vietnam and five combat hash marks.

***

We made sure everything was right so they could issue my DD-214. By November 10 I had the standard-issue five copies of my DD-214, my honorable discharge certificate, and a letter of appreciation saying "thank you for a fine job," signed by President Richard M. Nixon.

I signed out at 0001 hours on November 11, 1973.

The world would hold opportunities and frustration in alternating doses, but I was used to that.

CERTIFICATE OF APPRECIATION

FOR SERVICE IN THE ARMED FORCES OF THE UNITED STATES

RUSSELL ALVIN BABCOCK SFC US ARMY 13NOV67-12NOV73

I extend to you my personal thanks and the sincere appreciation of a grateful nation for your contribution of honorable service to our country. You have helped maintain the security of the nation during a critical time in its history with a devotion to duty and a spirit of sacrifice in keeping with the proud tradition of the military service.

I trust that in the coming years you will maintain an active interest in the Armed Forces and the purpose for which you served.

My best wishes to you for happiness and success in the future.

Richard Nixon

COMMANDER IN CHIEF

SEAL OF THE PRESIDENT OF THE UNITED STATES

DD FORM 1725

On leaving the Army in 1973, I was given a certificate of appreciation signed by President Nixon.

Chapter Twelve

Civilian Life

During spring 1973, when I was still at Fort Leonard Wood, the fuel pump on my car failed while driving on base. I left the car on the side of the road and went to get a fuel pump. When I got back, the fire department was putting out a fire that was eating my car. Insurance totaled it out, and with that money I bought a 1972 Ford Ranchero.

The Ford Ranchero was a low-riding pickup truck, more like a car with a truck bed on it. But mine had the 400 cubic-inch small-block V8 engine that was also being used in that year's Ford Torino. The motor was so powerful I could sit on a dry cement slab, hold down the brake, floor the gas, let go of the brake and have smoke roll off the tires. That truck is a classic now.

I outfitted the truck with a SSB-22 sideband two-way radio with a 100-watt booster. The SSB radio had a longer range than a regular CB radio without the booster. CB radios were popular at this time. In those days before cell phones, truck drivers used CB radios to communicate with each other about gas station locations and police speed traps. By 1970 the radios were small enough that regular drivers started using them too.

My radio was strong enough that when I was once at Monarch Pass in Colorado, I talked with a guy in Bakersfield, California, 900 miles away.

One day I was driving near the Lake of the Ozarks and was tired so I pulled onto a dirt road for a nap. I turned off the car and I thought I'd turn the switch to accessory mode to listen to the radio while I slept. When I woke up ready to go, I realized I hadn't put the switch on accessory and the battery was too low to start the car.

But, there was enough power that I could talk on the radio. I started calling for help, and a guy answered, but he was in Little Rock, Arkansas, too far away.

A woman driving to the Lake of the Ozarks thought I was a patrolman and stopped. She jump-started my car and I showed her the turn-off she needed for the lake.

***

That winter after leaving the military I hung out in Colorado.

I stayed for a bit in Delta with Jean Castoe White's brother John, his wife Judy and their four kids. Winter was setting in, and John and I got an idea to sell firewood.

The forestry department permit cost $100 to cut a hundred cedar posts. We figured we could make $25 per truckload, and there would be a lot of truckloads.

I put studded snow tires on the Ranchero, and bought a gas power saw. We went up the side of Grand Mesa at sunrise to start cutting. We filled the truck a little above the bed and the tailpipes were lowered to three inches off the ground. We sold four-to-six-inch around by eight-foot long poles for a half-dollar and ten-to-twelve-inch around by ten-foot long poles for a dollar. We made some good money.

Jean and a couple friends of hers were working at Russell Stover candy in Montrose, twenty miles south of Delta, for $90 a week before taxes. I told her they were crazy to work for so little. I was getting $90 a week in unemployment checks for eleven months.

One night John and Judy wanted to go dancing or to the movies, so I told them I would watch the kids while they went. They had two girls and two boys. The youngest boy Bobby started screaming at them using profane words and ran in the bathroom and locked the door. The next day I left before I killed the little monsters. If Bobby had been one of my kids and he cussed me and then ran in the bathroom, I'd have kicked down the door and used my belt to make his butt rosy red.

I slept in my car for a few days.

Judy's dad Frank Nicholas heard about it, and invited me to stay with his family. He had some grown married kids and four or five still at home. It was nice of him to take me in.

For extra money, I started baking eight to ten pies a week. Then sugar prices increased $1.50 per pound, so a five-pound bag of sugar cost more than $8. It turned out the town's sugar-beet factory was eating up the sugar supply. I gave up on the pies.

Mr. Nicholas had a bunch of car bodies he wanted cut up, so he put me to work on that. Using an acetylene cutting torch, I'd cut the frame up into three-foot pieces (which get a better price than bigger sizes), load them on the Ranchero and creep down the quarter-mile driveway. That stuff was heavy. My tailpipes would be one or two inches from dragging the ground.

I'd drive eighty miles to the junkyard at Grand Junction, and sell the scrap iron. I'd get around $100 and subtract the cost of acetylene, oxygen tanks and gas, then split the money with Frank. Around this time the price of gas started rising from under a dollar a gallon to around $1.50 a gallon, so that was an expense we watched out for.

After hauling the car frame, I'd return for the car body, winching it onto a flatbed truck to haul to the junkyard. It didn't bring as much money as the frame.

Frank had a ten-foot by twenty-foot trailer house that he wanted moved from Cedaredge Mesa to town.

There was a mile-long winding road off the mesa. I used a tough Willys Jeep pickup to move the trailer. When I lowered the trailer stand, the pickup really squatted at the top of the mesa. I put the truck in four-wheel drive, in low gear, and started creeping down the hill. Every so often I stuck my foot out the door and dragged it so my speed wouldn't build up. I finally reached the foot of the hill. The rest of the drive was easy.

After finishing the work for Mr. Nicholas, I struck out on my own again.

I found a one-bedroom apartment for $90 a month. In January 1974, I joined the Colorado National Guard, the 157th FA (field artillery) unit, with 155 mm self-propelled guns. We drilled one weekend a month, for which I drove thirty miles to

Montrose. Because the people came from all over the state, the battery commander would leave the drill hall open at night for us to sleep in after going out partying.

We'd get a full day's pay for every four hours of drill. For eight hours on a Saturday and eight hours on a Sunday, we'd get four days' pay.

The battery had a sergeant first class battery fire chief who would use a surveyor's scope to line up the cannons. When we went to the field the sergeant would also set the perimeter defense. Sometimes when the first sergeant had equipment to turn in or pick up, he'd call on me to drive to Fort Carson for it, for which I'd receive a weekend drill's pay.

For the two-week summer camp in 1974, I went on the advance party with the supply sergeant and a couple lower-ranked men. In the field we'd set the mess tent, three GMP (general medium purpose) tents for the troops to sleep in, and a ten-foot tent for commander and first sergeant orderly's room. We lay irrigation pipe at the top of the field and also laid out water and sewer lines for the camp. Beforehand, the commander had the phone company come out and mark where the phone lines crossed our planned trenches. The phone men had marked the wrong places, though, and when we started digging in install pipes, we tore out all the phone lines for the county.

For summer camp in 1975, we went to Cheyenne, Wyoming. I and the supply sergeant and a few troops went on advance party to set up camp. Early on the last Friday of camp, we loaded the truck and returned to Montrose around 8 p.m., locked the truck in the armory and went our separate ways.

An hour later I went out dancing with Diane Smith, one of my friend Ross Smith's girls, and Donna Spurlock, whom I dated off and on. Around midnight I started shaking. We went to the hospital and the doctor said I had a stress attack and gave me 0.5 mg of Valium. I'd take a pill in the morning and pass out for twelve hours. I'd take a pill in the evening and I'd pass out for twelve hours, and my front door would be wide open. So, I stopped taking the Valium.

Donna Spurlock's dad Paul ran a fruit farm for a farmer who lived in Hotchkiss. The middle of July, Paul asked me to haul sour cherries to the cannery, and I wouldn't even have to pick them.

I went back the next Monday and helped Nancy's brother Jim put canvas on the cherry pickers. The pickers were built on ten-square-foot four-wheel frames. We threaded cotton rope through the canvas' eyelets to secure them to the frames

The frames would be placed at the bottoms of the trees. At the bottom of one frame would be a conveyor belt. On an adjoining frame was a mechanical arm run by a two-cylinder gas motor. The arm would shake the tree and the cherries would fall onto the canvas and roll down to the conveyor belt, which carried the cherries to tanks on the bed of a truck.

We had to take the small motor apart and replace the piston rings. After that, Paul told the owner he wanted me to maintain the pickers. So, the owner had his nephew take my place driving the truck hauling cherries.

We got done with the cherries in the middle of August and then we started harvesting apples.

I drive the apple truck, a five-ton flatbed truck. The farm grew red and golden Delicious apples. Pickers of the golden Delicious apples had to wear cotton gloves so not to bruise the apples.

I was only supposed to haul two loads a day to the packing shed, but I usually did four. Then I hauled six loads to the cannery where they made sliced apples, apple butter, apple sauce, apple cider. The bins for the truck were five square feet, and I could load two bins wide by four bins long by three bins high.

***

I got behind on my payments on my Ranchero, and eventually the bank found me to repo it. After that, I bought a 1962 Nash Rambler flat head eight cylinder for $150.

I was working fourteen to sixteen hours a day at $2 an hour.

I was taking emptied bins to Hotchkiss and bringing full ones back. One day I was driving back, and about a half-mile up the road I saw two dogs running back and forth across the road. I got up to where they were and one of the dogs ran in front of me and splat, I hit him. I stopped and carried him out of the road. Just then the owner pulled up, so I told him what happened and he understood.

I was hauling apples all over, putting them in four storage sheds. That year's yield was a bumper crop, bigger than usual. By the time I put the last load in storage on Monday before Thanksgiving, I had hauled in more than 600,000 tons of apples.

***

Mom had moved in to a rest home by this time. She'd been fighting cancer for about nine years, and she couldn't get up and down the stairs to her apartment.

I think the name of the care home was New Horizon. The manager was Mr. Hughes, my old senior bookkeeping teacher. She enjoyed embroidery, rug making, and ceramics.

Sometime in late spring Mom fell and broke her hip. She had to be taken eighty miles to St. Mary's Hospital in Grand Junction. They replaced her hip and she was there a month. I visited her a couple times but what touched my heart was that the care home employees cared enough for mom that on their days off, they would drive eighty miles to go see her in the hospital.

Grandma and Grandpa were still living in Delta at the time, and Uncle Howard had remarried and had another boy and girl.

***

I left Delta headed for Chattanooga, Tennessee, to see my sister Donna. The trip there would take a week, but I ended up staying a while.

I put studded snow tires on the car at the bottom of Loveland Pass because the highway patrol was enforcing the chain law, stopping everybody without snow tires or chains from going through. When I got to Denver, I stopped to spend Thanksgiving weekend with Donna Spurlock and her kids.

At Junction City, Kansas, I stopped to see Mary and the kids – but I didn't let them know in advance because I was two years behind in child support. I stayed a couple hours then told her I was going to get something at the store and left before she could get mad and call the police.

I arrived in Chattanooga about 9 p.m. At a service station I called Donna, who said she'd meet me in ten minutes to lead me home. She led me across a bridge, turned right, and went through a tunnel to Red Bank, to their three-bedroom house.

Donna's living situation was odd. She lived in a house with her boyfriend Arlen, Arlen's ex Helen, Helen's boyfriend Jerry and Helen's son. It was funny to see Jerry stand next to Donna because he was six-feet-six and she stood four-foot-two.

Around 11 p.m. Donna had to go to work. She worked at a factory out in the sticks that made big cardboard spindles for industrial thread.

I managed to get back to downtown Chattanooga for dinner with little problem, but getting back was trouble. I got across the river but finding the tunnel was impossible. I didn't find my way back through the tunnel until 5 a.m. On my drive I saw dancers from a go-go club outside protesting. It was December, and all they were wearing were panties and bras.

I stayed with Donna's group for a couple of months.

Normally the night temperature didn't get below twenty-five degrees, but I put a small battery charger and an electric dipstick on my car all night. If the car didn't start after the second time I turned the key, it would need a jump start. Pretty soon my Nash Rambler quit running so I junked it and bought a 1964 Pontiac.

I applied for work at a chicken processing plant, but they said I was overqualified. I found a job driving a truck route delivering supplies for a restaurant supply warehouse.

Just over the hill from Donna's place, I found a one-room furnished apartment for $50 a week. The building had six apartments. I lived in a bottom apartment.

One night I wrote a check and put it in the landlord's mail box. A bit later a woman named Charlotte Scheer knocked on the door and handed the check back to me.

My sister Donna and I visiting in the 2000s.

"You shouldn't leave the check in the mailbox because my husband Bill or brother-in-law James might steal it," she said.

I thanked her.

Charlotte and Bill lived in an upstairs apartment. Her sister Ann and husband James and four kids lived in another. Charlotte and Ann worked in a small sewing shop that made T-shirts.

Charlotte's brother Lee and sister Marlene were both blind. Lee attended a school for the blind in Nashville, while Marlene was married with kids and a seeing-eye dog that was an Irish setter.

A couple days after I met Charlotte, one of her uncles brought Lee for a visit. Nobody took Lee out much because of his disability. I started talking to Lee. I'd never had a long discussion with a blind person. He said he could only see the difference between light and dark. His other senses were heightened, particularly his hearing and memory. He could meet you once, not see you for months, and then you'd see him and say hi and he'd call you by name.

I took him to Pizza Hut. He ordered one with ham, mushrooms, black olives and onions. When they brought his pizza I asked for a second plate for him so he could have a slice cooling while he ate. I put a slice of pizza in front of Lee and had to pull my hands away quick because he would chew on them.

After pizza I took Lee out to a club on Fourth Avenue and got him dancing with some girls. He had a good time, and we hung out regularly from then on.

After a couple months taking Lee to the dance club, Charlotte and I started dating. It turned out her husband Billy drank quite a bit and worked only occasionally. He blamed his job situation on having epilepsy, but I think it was due to the drinking. He and Charlotte broke up, and he moved in with his parents.

I paid for Charlotte's divorce from Billy then she and I got married in the fall of 1976. She was ten years younger than me.

My divorce from Mary was final after ninety days but we went ahead and held our ceremony within that time then later had a justice of the peace marry us legally a second time.

***

Charlotte had four children, but the Welfare Office had put them in foster homes. Every month Charlotte had one-hour visitation with just two of the kids. One month she saw Margret and Geraldine. The next month she was to see Rebecca and Michael. But, every month Michael and Rebeca were supposed to visit, they couldn't come.

We petitioned the court for custody. Bill went to court with us and told the judge he didn't mind if we took custody of the kids. We got them.

I had never met Michael and Rebecca, and so at first I was afraid of how they would feel about the situation.

Charlotte and I took custody of them just before school started. I told the kids that after school started during the week they had to have all their school work done before 8:30 then they could watch TV till 9 then go to bed. But after 9 they would continue playing. I whipped them a couple times, but they still played. I knew I had to come up with a punishment they didn't like but would respect. So, I made them do their multiplication tables twenty times, then they started going to bed.

***

It's funny the details you remember from past jobs. I recall some of the places from my restaurant supply routes pretty well.

There was a school on one route that was run by a church group, and had kindergarten to twelfth grade and college. Twice a week I'd take them eight to ten pallets of food, a pallet of five-gallon cans of egg yolks, and a couple pallets of dry cereal.

Another route went up Lookout Mountain to the trolley station restaurants and store.

Usually we moved the pallets into the business, watched an employee check and sign for the items, and then we left. Sometimes there was a situation like one woman working at a place and she was busy so we'd put twenty-five dozen cases of eggs in the cooler for her.

There was a man who owned a motel and restaurant that was about three blocks from our warehouse. He'd always tell, not ask, the driver to load the frozen food into his cooler for him.

"Put the French fries up or take everything back," the man would say. He did me that way couple of times. I don't know the last time his cooler was cleaned out, but you had to stand to the side when you opened the door and hoped nothing fell on you.

His stop was the last stop on the route before heading back to our warehouse.

One Friday I purposely left his order on the truck except three cases of french-fries. He told me to put the French fries in the cooler

"That's not our job," I said, "and your jerk-wad account won't break us if you cancel over it."

I wheeled the fries back out the door and loaded them on the truck and went to the warehouse.

He sent his assistant to the warehouse to pick up the order.

It was the end of the business day, and Felix the warehouse manager wouldn't let him have the supplies and because we were closed Saturday and Sunday, Felix told him to come back Monday morning for them.

Felix asked me what happened and I told him. I never delivered there again, but the other drivers said that man never asked them to put the fries up again.

***

At the restaurant supply warehouse, once a month we'd get a railroad car of supplies. We went to a sugar plant to pick up ten pallets of sugar, to a vinegar plant to pick up ten pallets of vinegar. The warehouse had a cooler-freezer section for the French fries, butter, eggs, frozen fish, chicken, hamburger, meat.

After the first year the company started offering health insurance, for which we'd contribute $75 a month. During the winter Charlotte would often get a bad case of sore throat. After we had this insurance a couple months, she went to the hospital for her throat. We sat for five hours to see a doctor; finally we saw a doctor who told us her tonsils were swollen. They put her in the hospital for a week to remove them. It still cost us $1,000 over what the insurance covered. After that she didn't get sick much.

Felix the warehouse manager was around sixty years old but he could high step and speed around the warehouse. Some of the new hires were younger and couldn't outdo him.

We'd hired one man as a driver, but he couldn't drive a stick-shift truck. We sent him to pick up ten pallets of sugar, and when he got back most of the bags of sugar were leaning against the back door, having slid all the way back. We almost couldn't open the doors. We had to re-stack the bags on other pallets as we unloaded. When Felix sent him to pick up vinegar, Felix told him to stack two cases high on the floor. On his return, the floor was covered with two cases.

He was hired to run the route that had the big school stop. I helped him load the truck and we put nets between each order. I rode with him to help teach him to shift the gears. Starting out he had the clutch in, put the truck in first, pushed on the gas, popped the clutch, jerk stop, jerk stop, jerk stop. Once he got the speed going, he wasn't a bad driver but the company let him go.

***

In 1976 I joined the 278th Mechanize Infantry Company in Lenoir City Tennessee.

Around that same time, I went to work doing deliveries for a Chattanooga furniture store called Jernigan's.

Old man Jernigan ran it with his son and daughter. Jimmy lived on Signal Mountain, his house fifty yards from the edge of a cliff looking down over Chattanooga.

It was a nice, open house. The cliff-side wall was glass so everyone could enjoy the view. The grand finale was in the master bathroom: two steps led up to the toilet and a two-shelf bookcase.

I delivered furniture to all kinds of people and places.

One man came in and bought a Thomasville dining room set, the two-piece china cabinet with large table. With the leaves in the table, it was five feet wide by ten feet long, with twelve chairs, a tea cabinet and a server.

We loaded this on a one-ton truck. Very early the next morning I took Charlotte to the warehouse, met my helper and got the truck on the road: Interstate 24 to Interstate 75 going to Knoxville. About twenty miles before Knoxville we took Interstate 40 east into the Smokey Mountains. At Highway 66, the Pigeon Forge Parkway to Pigeon Forge, I called the man so he could lead us to his house. It took us an hour and a half to carry in the furniture and set up.

On the way back on Pigeon Forge Parkway, a park ranger stopped me and gave me a ticket for having a truck in the Great Smoky Mountains National Park; we were on the parkway. We got home about 8.

I think as a driver I was making $5 an hour. We went to work at 7 a.m. and sometimes not finish delivering furniture until midnight.

Another time I had to deliver a sofa with queen size hide-a-bed. We tied the bed so as turn the sofa on its side so the bed wouldn't come out. The destination apartment building was built crazy. We carried the sofa in, lifted it over the rail, carried it downstairs, and at the bottom of the stairs we stood it on end, twisted it into the hall, but at the apartment we couldn't twist and turn it in. We had to take it back down the hall, twist and turn it to go back up the stairs, lift it back over the rails, carry it back out the door and put it back on the truck.

We drove around to the back side of the building. The apartment was one floor up with a balcony. We unloaded the sofa off the truck again and carried it below the balcony, then tied a long strap around the end of the sofa then pulled it up over the balcony and turned it through the door. We set it in the living room, made sure the bed work folded out, put the cushions on, and left.

Another time I delivered a crushed velvet living room set – sofa, loveseat and chair – and removed the old set. We arrived at the house. The woman showed us where she wanted the furniture. I saw five kids sizes four to ten running around.

I thought to myself: This woman is crazy for wanting this white crushed velvet set around these kids. Or she used plastic covers on the furniture or the kids stood in the corners while the adults sat on the furniture.

***

On a Friday night I joined Donna's group at the dance club until 3 a.m. then we went across the street to Johnson's Truck Stop and eat breakfast. It was about 4 a.m. when they were ready to call it a night and go home.

I couldn't. I had to drive to Lenoir City for guard drill. I got to the armory at 7.30 a.m. At roll call, two people were AWOL, so I must not have been the only guy out late.

I was weapons platoon sergeant. At the range, I had the three gun crews dig their firing positions. The position was a hole dug ten-foot around and four feet deep, with two rows of sandbags on the top edge.

Next they placed the 81mm mortar tube in the center. On the gun's three-foot baseplate the gunner they attached the bipod legs to the gun. At the top of the legs were directional knobs for aiming. The gunner then attached the sight to the gun.

The gunner and ammo bearer would take distance-marking poles down range to twenty-five, fifty and seventy-five yards. With me looking through the gun sight, we'd calibrate the poles by hand signal.

I have the gun crews practice fire mission and time them to see how long it takes to set up their guns and get off their first rounds.

When evening came the mess sergeant arrived and set up the chow line. The first sergeant would have one of the platoons furnish ten or twelve men for servers, standing behind the food containers dishing out. The milk, bread and pies were on tables to be passed out. Then half of the men from each foxhole would go to chow and when they got back the other half would go to chow.

After chow the commander called off training and the men got their sleeping bags out, ready to sleep. One of the men in the platoon didn't bring his, so I told him that when he was ready he could sleep in my car's front seat. I was going to sleep in the back seat; I unrolled my bag and got situated. I was tired as heck, having been awake since Friday morning, and I crashed hard.

The one guy got in the front seat a while after that, but then another guy opened the car door and I sat straight up wide awake.

"What are you doing?" I asked.

"I'm cold. I thought there was room to sleep in the car," he said.

When I sat up like a mummy wrapped in my sleeping bag, it sure scared the hell out of those two guys.

***

One weekend, Charlotte and I decided to take her blind brother Lee out bowling.

He was right handed and I was left handed. I took him to the line and helped him swing the ball back and forth. On the third forward swing I told Lee to release the ball. He hit five or six strikes and spares after about four games. From then on when we went out, he ended up scoring 90 to 100 with a few gutter balls.

Lee had a friend in Knoxville and asked if I'd take him there some time for a visit. I told Lee I'd take him on my next guard drill weekend.

The weekend of my drill, I took off work Friday at 5 p.m. Charlotte, Lee and I drove to Knoxville. We picked up Lee's friend about 8 p.m. and we all went bowling. His friend was also blind.

At the bowling alley counter, Lee and his friend were telling the clerk what size shoes they wanted, but the clerk said they couldn't bowl because they were blind.

"You shut up and watch," I told that kid.

He gave us all shoes and we picked a lane. I showed Lee's friend how to bowl the same way I taught Lee. By the last frame of our first game, his score was

105. Lee's score was 90. He was disappointed because he threw some gutter balls and he wouldn't bowl the second game.

We were about halfway through the second game before the people on either side of us realized that Lee and his friend were blind. Both groups congratulated Lee and his friend.

A guy from the right lane handed me $20 and told me to take them out to supper on him!

At the end of the second game, we turned in the shoes. I showed the score card to the kid at the counter.

"See, they can bowl," I said.

We went out for dinner and returned to the motel around midnight and went to bed.

While I was at the armory the next day, Charlotte and the boys splashed around the pool. When I returned from drill we went to eat then went swimming again until 10.

At the armory Sunday morning, the medics gave us a class on First Aid, what to do for heat exhaustion and heat stroke, splinting broken arms and legs, and dressing head, chest and stomach wounds. So my weekend wasn't all fun and games.

Charlotte and I got home around 10 p.m. It was a fulfilling weekend.

***

Once a month, Jernigan's had us load the featured furniture – bedroom sets, dining room sets – and go to a TV station to make advertisements. Mr. Jernigan's little granddaughter would appear in most of them.

One of our trucks broke down so Jernigan's sent me to rent a Ryder truck. I paid the $100 deposit out of pocket. One of the front headlights got cracked during the course of the rental. When I turned the truck in, Ryder kept the $100 deposit to replace the headlight; if I'd known that would happen, I'd have gone to Walmart and bought a headlight and replaced it myself.

Charlotte and I moved into a four-bedroom house three blocks from a train-switching yard. Clank bang clank bang twenty-fours a day, it didn't take long for us to get used to the noise.

Around the corner from the house was a small restaurant and bar. Charlotte started going there to dance. After four months the night waitress quit and Charlotte took the job.

It was about month until our first anniversary. It had been a pretty good year.

For our first anniversary in 1977, I bought Charlotte a pantsuit from Frederick's of Hollywood. She wouldn't wear it out of the house. I guess she thought it was too sexy. I returned it, and she picked out a pantsuit elsewhere.

***

In September 1979 I stopped working for Jernigan's. We moved to Macon, Georgia, where I went to work for the Fowler's Furniture, owned by brothers Tom and Jerry Fowler.

I delivered new and used furniture but mostly touched up and repaired used furniture. Dents, scratches and gouges I could fill in and cover so they couldn't be seen.

In February 1980, Charlotte and I got into a heated argument and I quit the furniture store and moved back to Chattanooga.

The Fowlers had their accountant call the IRS to audit me. The IRS said I owed around $200 in taxes. I tried to tell the IRS that January and February taxes would go on 1980's tax forms instead of 1979's, but you can't educate those fools.

***

I went to work with Charlotte's brother Cecil and brother-in-law James for a lumber company that made window and door frames. We were only there several months. We drove trucks.

The day before the Fourth of July, we were unloading a train box car of lumber. It was the company's policy that those working the day before and the day after the holiday would get paid for all three days.

Around 5 p.m. some other drivers received some materials and started loading them on their trucks for Monday shipments. At 6 p.m. the warehouse manager told us to help those drivers load trucks. We said no and clocked out.

The company fired us for leaving work early and didn't pay us holiday pay. We appealed it to the employment board and showed that the company was calling leaving at 6 p.m. "leaving early."

The company was forced to pay us our holiday pay.

***

I started driving a taxi for Yellow Cab. The company's parking lot was just across the river in Red Bank.

An old man named Joe owned the cab company. He furnished the car, expenses like gas and oil and the drivers received forty percent of a night's run. If you ran $50 in fares for the night, you received $20. We got paid once a week.

I worked the twelve-hour night shift, 6 p.m. to 6 a.m., so I didn't have to worry much about a lot of small two-or-three-block fares from an apartment to a 7-Eleven store for a beer run. Night riders usually needed rides to real destinations. After shift I usually ate at a Kristal restaurant.

***

The night dispatcher was a low talker and I had a tough time hearing him. A lot of the time I had to call him on a payphone. Mainly, we waited for fares at different locations. Chattanooga was broken down into zones.

If you dropped a fare at the airport, you went to East Ridge mall and sat at that stand for thirty minutes. If you didn't receive a fare, you moved closer to town to another stand. You kept this up until you were downtown.

One of these stands was at Market and Bailey streets, across from a go-go club. Half a block past Market, on the left, was a rough black bar. I sat at this stand about thirty minutes, and was about to move to another stand in front of a big hotel, when a cop drove past. Not three minutes later, a white guy came running out of the black bar being chased by a black man shooting at him.

That end of Bailey Street was a slum area, for about fifteen blocks. A few months later the city council renamed the street from Bailey to Martin Luther King Boulevard.

One night I was sitting at the hotel stand. I'd been there about thirty minutes when the dispatcher sent another cab to the hotel to pick up a fare going to the airport. I went in the hotel and called the dispatcher. "Why are you giving my $15 fare away?" I asked.

"I had you marked at another stand," he said.

"You sent me here twenty minutes ago," I said.

***

One night the dispatcher sent me to a house on Ringgold Road. A male crossdresser got in the cab. He was high. He directed me to an address up the road, but when we got there he said it was the wrong address. We drove around almost an hour. For that long we are to charge $20 for our time along with the meter; he'd run up $20 on the meter. I finally dropped him at a gay hotel. He gave me all the money he had on him, $50, and he was still short on what was owed.

I stopped for some coffee at a 7-Eleven. The dispatcher called to send me back to that last hotel for a fare. I called the dispatcher on the payphone.

"If that's the guy I dropped off, he's broke and I'm not taking him anywhere," I said.

I went back and it was two railroad men wanting to go to a train yard on Ringgold. The boss had contracts with some railroad companies to pick up crews and take them to hotels or from hotels to holding areas. Ringgold was thirty-five miles away, a flat rate of $50.

After Ringgold, it was time to report to headquarters. For the night's fares – $50 for Ringgold run, $50 for the crossdresser, plus the other fares – I turned in a total a $150. My share for the night was $35.

***

There was a woman who was a regular customer who lived on Lockout Mountain. Her fare was always $20 flat and she would write a check. She'd go from her house to town or back again. One afternoon I picked her up in town and it had started to snow. By the time we got to her house, there were two inches of snow on the ground. I helped with the bags then started back down the mountain. She was nice enough she called the dispatcher two or three times to see how I was doing.

Another time a couple went to the movie theater at River Gate Mall and had locked their keys in the car. They lived in Red Bank, so the round trip costed them $40 plus $20 for an hour of time.

Some other regular customers were a husband and wife named Blue. The husband weighed 280 pounds, the wife weighed 230 pounds, and they had a boy around seven years old who already weighed 100 pounds. They'd been to a Christmas party when I picked them up one night. They got in and the car leaned something awful.

I had to use my right foot to brace myself while driving to keep from sliding into the middle seat. The next morning I told Joe the cab needed new shocks and springs on the passenger side.

"What the hell did you hit?" Joe asked.

"Nothing," I said. "I took the Blues home."

***

Charlotte's dad Fred Sanders had moved from Signal Mountain to Dunlap, Tennessee. While we were going to Fred's one day, a truck hit my Pontiac and totaled it. The insurance paid enough to buy a Chrysler station wagon, but it broke down a few months later and cost too much to fix. I ended up buying an American Motors Gremlin.

Charlotte and I were granted custody of her kids during this time.

Around this time also, Charlotte and I separated. Fred let me stay with him. I went to Charlotte's to pack my clothes, Army mementos and collection of Don Pendleton's "Mack Bolan: The Executioner" book series.

When I returned to Fred's, he said the police had stopped by to tell me that one of my daughters with Mary back in Kansas was deathly ill in the hospital.

The next morning I asked Joe for a week off and a week's advance to go to Kansas. By this time the four-lane Interstate 24 had been built, connecting Chattanooga to Nashville to Paducah, Kentucky. From there I hopped Interstate 55 to Mt. Vernon, Illinois, to Interstate 64 to St. Louis and Interstate 70 to Kansas City to Topeka and Junction City. I went to Mary's and then the hospital.

It turned out that Tammy, our next to youngest kid, had her appendix removed and was recovering. By happenstance, the week before, Ella, the youngest, had her appendix removed, but her situation had not been as serious.

While I'd been away Mary had gotten rid of Georgy Porgy and married a man named Bob Cook. Mary's daughter Nora had also gotten married, to man named Jeffery Prafke, and given birth to a son. The previous May I'd received a baby shower card saying I would be a grandpa, but nobody said she was married.

After recovering, Tammy wanted to see her sister Loretta. I went to the house and knocked, and when she answered the door I was looking eyeball to eyeball with her. The last time I'd seen her, she was small.

That evening I was sitting talking to Nora, and Mary started to go in the kitchen. Not thinking, I stuck my lighter under her butt to give her a hot seat, and when she came back I did the same thing. It was something I did when I was home years ago. A few minutes later Mary's husband Bob went in the bedroom and closed the door. We heard banging, and I thought Bob was doing wood work or something.

Nora said no, that he was in there banging his head against the wall. Nora tells me that Mary told him she wanted to leave with me.

Things cooled down. A bit later, when Bob needed to go to work at the water plant, I offered to give him a ride so we could clear the air.

I told Bob there was no way I was taking Mary anywhere. That settled him down.

After a couple days I went back to Chattanooga.

Around this time my sister Donna and her husband Arlen divorced, and she and her friend Bill Goins quit the cone factory. Bill was a nice guy and we occasionally set each other up with jobs.

Donna started waitressing. Bill Goins had gone to work for Jimmy Rice's Moving and Storage.

With Charlotte and I separated, Donna lived with Charlotte for a month then left and I didn't hear from her for several years. When I ran into Donna again, it was a real surprise.

Chapter Thirteen

Hauling

A few days after I got back to Chattanooga, I applied for work at a trucking company wanting drivers.

There were about ten other people at the office applying. They gave us all an open-book test for Department of Transportation rules and regulations. After the written test was scored, they took two of us at a time on a road test. We did a walk-around inspection of the truck, tallied the wheels on the trailer, locked at fifth wheel, checked that the air and electrical cords were hooked, and then we got in the truck.

I climbed into the sleeper and watched as the applicant got in the driver seat, and the tester in the passenger seat. The driver released the air breaks and pulled out of the yard, got on Interstate 24 headed to Chattanooga's East Gate area. The tester had him turn around then stop.

The driver and I switched places, and I drove back. Back at the lot, the tester told me to back the trailer into a space about as wide as two trailers. I finally got backed in, and the tester told me that when I got a little more backing experience to come back to apply.

He would've had a fit if he knew that was the first time I'd driven a semi-truck.

After that road test, though, I knew how to do it.

***

I went to Jimmy Rice of Ricc's Moving and Storage, where I had briefly worked some time before, and started driving smaller trucks. The one I drove the most was eighteen feet long with a compartment that hung over the cab to the front bumper.

One job I went to, the house had three bedrooms and most of the furniture was new in boxes. We had to take the second-floor stuff from off the overhead deck. I loaded the sofa, loveseat, stuffed chair, ottoman coffee table, two end tables other small odd and ends. All the bedroom furniture, kitchen table, four chairs, a two-piece china cabinet were all in boxes. The people drove their car to our warehouse, and I drove it into the truck using the loading dock. I strapped the car down inside and drove the load to Memphis and unloaded at another warehouse.

Another time I took Charlotte and a helper David to Copperhill Tennessee, to pack and load a four-bedroom house and deliver to a warehouse in Panama City, Florida. We left Chattanooga around 2 a.m. We got to Copper Hill in the morning. The woman said that if we weren't done loading by 8 p.m. we'd stop for the night. I told her we'd be done before that.

I went through the house with inventory sheets and stickers listing all the furniture. I started in the front room so Charlotte could start packing.

There was an upright piano. I checked the bench for any dents or scratches. I don't see any so I put a red shipping sticker on the bench. I put a matching red sticker on the top inventory sheet, so it could be matched to the boxes, and marked the time at 10:11 a.m. Everything got a sticker and everything went on the inventory sheet.

Charlotte started packing books in a large box, but I stopped her and told her that because books are heavy, they are better put in small boxes so we can lift them. Charlotte worked through the front room packing books, lamps, sofa cushions. David worked in the kitchen packing dishes.

I finished inventory, and readied the furniture for loading. I took the legs off the piano bench, wrapped them in paper and placed them inside the bench.

After David was done packing the dishes we started loading. We took the sofa out to the truck, put pads on it, then the love seat, chairs, coffee table and end tables. We moved the piano out, padded it, and then we took out boxes, the washer and dryer.

We padded and stacked everything from the floor to ceiling and across the floor. About 6:30 p.m. we loaded the last things: the patio table and lawn mower. We shut and locked the doors.

The woman bought us all some fried chicken and Cokes and then we hit the road for several hours, got a room for the night, and then kept going. We arrived in Panama City about 7 p.m., got a motel room and splashed around in the pool. The next morning we unloaded at the warehouse and started back to Chattanooga.

***

Eventually, I told Jimmy I'd drive one of his semis over the road for him. He agreed.

It took a couple weeks to get a truck ready. The oil was changed and all that, but the most important things were leasing the truck (he leased the truck from Red Ball) and clearing the trip and fuel permits for Tennessee, Georgia and Florida. There around twenty trip and fuel permits altogether. He had my coworker Bill Goins give me the road test.

Our business used Red Ball dispatchers who'd tell drivers where to go and what to load. They had me load three shipments; I dropped them off in Kansas City, Missouri; Topeka, Kansas; and Fort Riley, Kansas. After unloading the last stop, I went through Junction City see Nora and Jeff. They had their own apartment, and Jeff was in the army too.

The next morning I went to a warehouse for four medium loads. Then I swept through Oklahoma City, Atlanta and New Orleans mixing and matching more loads.

I was getting to see more of the country than I had before, but for the most part spending only time enough to see warehouses and restaurants.

***

The dispatchers loaded me again going north and west to Detroit and Chicago. I came back through Topeka and Fort Riley, and picked up more shipments from an operation owned by a man named Dale Simpson. The dispatcher sent me to McConnell Air Force Base in Wichita, Kansas, and then south on Interstate 35 to Dallas, where I unload housewares.

From Dallas, I went up Interstate 30 to Texarkana, Arkansas; I put in town around 8 p.m. at a Union 76 truck stop. I went in the restaurant, and there was a short dark-haired waitress standing in the middle of the floor with her back to me.

I think it was my sister Donna, so I went up and poked her in the ribs. She whirled around ready to slap the hell out of me and then she saw who I was.

I hadn't seen her in about five years! After she got off work, we went out to a club and partied till 2 a.m. She dropped me off at my truck, and I slept till 7a.m. then and went back in the restaurant to eat again.

After tracing Interstate 30 to Little Rock, Interstate 40 to Knoxville and Interstate 81 to Hagerstown, Maryland, my truck was all unloaded. The dispatcher sent me to Pittsburgh, where I loaded one shipment of 15,000 pounds going to Chicago, where I receive $1,000 for that job.

After a drop in Topeka, I took a few days off to visit family in Junction City. I asked my daughter Loretta if she and her husband Bodine wanted to work for me. They said yes and packed some clothes.

We loaded four medium shipments at Simpson's in Topeka and three more in Wichita. Our first drop was Vicksburg, Arkansas. We took Interstate 35 through Oklahoma City, Interstate 40 to Henrietta, down Highway 69 to Texarkana and we stopped at the Union 76 where Donna worked.

We went in and ate, then waited until Donna was off duty and then went to a club until 2 a.m. Donna dropped us off and I slept a couple hours, got up and started driving to Vicksburg.

We arrived there around 1 p.m. and called a customer to lead us to his house. He had a lot of furniture and boxes of dishes and clothes. It took three hours to unload. We set up the beds and kitchen table, hooked up the washer and dryer. The wife wanted us to put the clothes in the closet and dishes in cupboards, but I told her we would only assemble what the packers disassembled. She would have to do the clothes and dishes.

We left there late so I rented us a room for the night. It was a nice break from all three of us sleeping in the truck. I had Loretta and Bodine with me about three months, and they were good help and company, but the partnership would end suddenly.

We took a shipment to Miami. After we went swimming at the beach, dispatch assigned us on our first load to the far north. We arrived in New York City after dark. All the lights made it look pretty.

We had to go out on Long Island over a toll bridge. It cost $2 per axle; my truck and trailer had five axles, three on the truck and two on the trailer.

The boss had said there was a truck stop on Long Island that would cash a com check, but the truck-stop had closed for Christmas and I didn't have any com checks. A com check allowed me to get money that was wired from headquarters. The boss had put $100 on the wire.

I didn't have enough fuel to get off Long island, so we pulled over to figure out a plan. A driver stopped and asked what was wrong. He was an off-duty cab driver, but was not in his cab. He said he knew where an open truck stop was, and offered to lead us there.

This truck stop turned out to be in the middle of Harlem. It was a dangerous place in the 1980s. The off-duty cabbie and I were the only light-skinned fools running around there at three in the morning. Loretta and Bodine stayed in the truck.

I bought a book of com checks so I wouldn’t have the problem again of not being able to get money off the wire. I cashed one for $50 and we got a five-gallon can of diesel.

The cabbie led us back to Long Island, and I gave him $20 for his help. Loretta, Bodine and I slept in the truck. The next morning, a Saturday, I filled up the truck and tried to call the customer. It turned out he was out of town until Monday, two days later.

I decided the time would best be spent going to Boston to deliver another shipment we had on board.

Interstate 95 took us 250 miles northeast to Boston. We arrived just before sundown. That night we checked into a motel room. The next day I called the Boston customer to lead us to his house. By the time we finished it was dark, and we found out the hard way that the famous Massachusetts Blue Laws were in effect. These laws descended from laws passed by the state's early religious settlers like the Pilgrims, who believed no work should be done on Sundays except worship.

The law pertaining to us was that no bars or service stations could be open or commercial trucks on the main highways from sundown Saturday to sundown Sunday. Just before we got out of Boston, a patrolman stopped me and issued a $25 ticket.

On Monday, after paying all the road tolls again, I landed us back on Long Island. As we were unloading and carrying everything down two flights of stairs for the customer, Bodine twisted his knee. He was out of commission. After the job was done I took him to a hospital, where they gave him crutches and pain pills and told him to stay off the knee for two weeks.

The truck was empty, so I called the dispatcher. He ordered me to go to Pittsburgh, Pennsylvania, 400 miles straight west, for five shipments to load. At a warehouse in Pittsburgh I loaded four shipments: three 4,000-pound shipments of furniture and a La-Z-Boy-style easy chair.

Then the agent led me to a house for the last pick up, a baby grand piano that was billed as a 1,000-pound shipment. Bodine and Loretta couldn't help load it. Luckily, there were two men working on the street outside and were on lunch break. I gave them $20 to help. We flipped the piano on its side on some pads, removed the legs and wheeled it out the door onto the truck. I strapped it to the side wall. I wrapped the legs in pads and we were done.

Our first drop was Knoxville. Then I passed through Chattanooga and drew some of my money out of the bank to pay what I owed Loretta and Bodine. I put them on the bus to Kansas so he could recuperate.

My next drop was the baby grand piano in Atlanta. I stop at a Truck Stop of America to see if there was anybody I could hire to help unload the piano, but I didn't see anybody. I called a couple moving companies. They offered to send a man to help for $20 an hour for a minimum of four hours, or $80 total. I said no.

I saw a man and woman hitchhiking with a German shepherd dog.

"Where are y'all wanting to go?" I asked.

"We want to go to Mobile, Alabama."

Their names were Steve and Kelly.

"If you help me unload this piano at Atlanta, I'll take you to Mobile," I said, "but we also have to go to Macon, Georgia."

I called the Atlanta people to tell them I was on the way to unload the piano. I backed into the driveway to a twenty-foot walkway. Steve and I unstrapped the piano, wheeled it down the dock board and along the walkway up a six-inch step into the house. We re-attached the legs, flipped the piano upright, and had the customer sign for it. Altogether, we were back on the road in thirty minutes.

We got on Interstate 75 to Macon, about 90 miles south. We unloaded that job's two chairs and a few boxes ten minutes then hit Highway 96 straight west to Montgomery then southwest on I-65 to Mobile. That was a full day's drive.

Eglin Air Force Base is in Mobile. We were unloading when the base transportation showed up to inspect and told me to come back in the morning for two loads: one to Chicago and one to Detroit.

While in Mobile, I received word from my boss Jimmy that he was looking for another driver. I told him that my hitchhiker Steve was a good loader and could drive a semi. Jimmy said to bring him in when I got back to headquarters. So instead of staying in Mobile, Steve and Kelly and their German shepherd kept on the road with me.

We ran up Interstate 65 to Chicago, unloaded, went Interstate 80 to Detroit and unloaded the rest of the trailer.

The boss said to come in.

We got to Chattanooga around 5 p.m. on a Saturday. I dropped off the trailer, and headed to motel down the street. I got a room and Steve and Kelly got one too. Steve planned to talk to my boss about the job offer.

I took Sunday off to drive to Pikeville, Tennessee, about an hour north, to see my ex-wife Charlotte and her kids.

On Monday I loaded four military shipments to Missouri. One of the shipments had come from Germany.

What I learned from hauling shipments to military bases is that most of them were entertainment centers or weight-lifting sets.

Soldiers, sailors, airmen, it didn't matter; they'd all buy four-piece entertainment centers. They'd move in or out of three-story buildings, invariably on the top floor. Each section of the entertainment center was too high or wide to get on the elevator, so I'd have to lug it up or down the stairs.

As for the weight sets, they'd buy those at Walmart and ship them wherever they served. At purchase, the clerk would wheel the barbell weight set out to their car and put it in the trunk. The guy would set up the weights at home with two 50-pound weights on the bar and they'd stay like that for the next two years until the movers loaded it.

At Junction City, I got my daughter Nora's husband Jeff to ride with me. One night we went up Black Mountain in Kentucky with two inches of snow on the ground, and more falling. The truck lost traction. I got pads out of the trailer and put them under the tires. Jeff watched made sure they were in position while I started picking up speed then he picked them up and got back in the truck. We made it over the pass slowly.

While I was gone, my boss Jimmy and coworker Bill Goins talked to Steve. Bill gave Steve a road test, and Jimmy hired him. The dispatcher sent him out to Eglin Air Force Base, back at Mobile, where we'd been.

He was on base starting to load when the base's transportation officer showed up to inspect. He saw Steve in the trailer smoking and told him he couldn't do that while loading. The inspector talked to someone then went out and saw Steve smoking in the trailer again. The inspector told Steve he wasn't authorizing the shipment to leave base.

Steve drove the truck to a truck stop, parked and called Jimmy. Steve said he was quitting. Bill had to go get the truck.

When I called for my next haul, Jimmy told me what happened. I felt bad. Sometimes you just can't count on guy you met hitchhiking.

I unloaded at Carlisle, Pennsylvania, and headed to Pittsburgh on the Pennsylvania Turnpike, the toll road across the state. At that time, trucks paid over $20 in toll fees so it should have been a super smooth highway. Instead, it was riddled with potholes.

I pulled over along the road looking for something in a compartment I could only access from outside the truck. I'd pulled stuff out of the compartment, including my trusty briefcase, which I sat it on the deck. I thought I put everything back in the cubby hole when I was done, but I forgot the briefcase and it fell off the truck. All my paper work was in it.

Fortunately, a driver picked it up off the road – which would have been tough on the Pennsylvania Turnpike because drivers ignore the speed limit. He mailed my briefcase to trucking headquarters.

My boss Jimmy surprised me when I called in one day, and he said he had it.

At Pittsburgh I loaded a shipment out of a warehouse then went to a town back along the highway to load a shipment out of a house. I hired a guy to help. We hit town late, got a motel and loaded the next morning.

After that, the shipping agent had another one to go. We went to the fourth-floor apartment of an old Mormon man. He was supposed to reserve the elevator for that day but he didn't. I sent him to the apartment office to reserve the elevator for the next morning.

I drove the helper back to the shipping office and told him I'd pick him up the next morning at 7:30. I returned to the man's apartment to inventory his stuff.

The next morning we used the elevator and loaded up the shipment. I paid the helper and left.

The old man had said he was moving to an apartment house in Miami. I told him that he'd have to reserve the elevator. He said he'd be signing for the apartment on July 5, so I told him to reserve the elevator for the morning of July 6. I thought I made my point clear.

All the shipments were going to Florida except one. I left Pittsburgh on Interstate 70 to Somerset then Highway 219 to Hagerstown. Truckers try to run the interstate highways; even though they may drive a lot of miles out of the way, it's often faster than taking a two-lane road through a bunch of small towns where you have to slow down to a thirty-mile-per-hour speed limit.

I continued along Interstate 81 to Knoxville then I-75 to Chattanooga, where I stopped at headquarters. I picked up my briefcase. Jimmy gave me the name and address of the man who mailed it back, so I wrote him a thank-you letter and enclosed $20.

I stayed at the office most of the day filling out paperwork, like sending invoices to Red Ball Trucking so I can finish getting paid for hauling shipments. When I first loaded a shipment I'd receive twenty percent of total payment for travel expenses via wire. For example, if I took a $1,000 load from Chattanooga to Nashville, as soon as I closed the doors of the truck I'd call the dispatcher. He'd send a wire for $200 that I could claim at any stop connected to the wire service. If I needed money for diesel fuel or to have the oil changed, I could get the money off the wire.

I returned to the road, taking Interstate 75 south to Macon then Interstate 16 to Savannah to drop one shipment. I took Interstate 95 South all the way to Miami.

During the summer there'd be a several-week period that the state was infected with an insect they call love bugs, clouds of them flying. My truck was white; by the time I reached Fort Lauderdale to unload, the truck and white trailer were black with those bugs.

I arrived in Miami the evening July 5. At 7.30 a.m. July 6, I was at the moving and storage agent's office to get the old man's apartment address and pick up a guy to help unload. We arrived at the apartment building, found out the old man's apartment number from the complex manager, and I knocked on the old man's door.

"Good morning," I said. "Are you ready for your furniture? Did you reserve the elevator?"

"No, I didn't think you'd be here on the sixth," he said.

There was nothing for my helper and me to do. I made sure the old man rode down in the elevator with us to the office to reserve the elevator. I took the helper back to the agent's office, and said I'd pick him up the next morning.

I went to a motel, settled in and called my dispatcher to ask if I could charge the old for an extra day because he'd pulled this same stunt in Pittsburgh. The dispatcher said no.

We unloaded the next day, using the elevator.

For my next assignment, the dispatcher sent me to a moving company in Miami for three small loads. At the moving company, we went into the warehouse to get the shipments out from the storage area. I checked the inventory sheets and made sure there were no new dents or scratches. After loading the three, there was plenty room left, so the dispatcher sent me to Ochopee, plum across the state.

I took Highway 41 west to the agent's warehouse, and loaded up. There was still room on the truck, so the dispatcher then told sent me to Fort Lauderdale.

I backtracked to Miami, and turned north on Interstate 95 to Fort Lauderdale. This shipment was a big table and chairs at a high-rise office building. A helper from the shipping agent's office went with me to the office building. I inspected the table and chairs for dents, tears, and scratches, and inventoried the items. We flipped over the table and removed the legs. The table was five feet wide and ten feet long. We took the twelve chairs down, wrapped them and stacked them.

As we moved the table into the elevator, it became apparent it was too big to fit, so the two of us lugged the table down five flights of stairs. Down at the truck, we put pads around the table but had to lean it at an angle because it was too long to put flat.

I now had five shipments on the truck and it still wasn't quite full.

The dispatcher directed me to Waycross, Georgia, for a four-bedroom shipment. From Fort Lauderdale, it was straight shot north on Interstate 95 to Jacksonville then Highway 1 to Waycross.

When I called the people to tell them I was there to get their furniture, they said I was a week early. I called the dispatcher, who he told me to come in for a week. So I went to Chattanooga for a week get the truck checked out to make it was in good shape. I went to Pikesville to see my ex-wife Charlotte and her kids for a few days.

The night before I returned to Waycross, I did a little shopping on Chattanooga's Fourth Avenue, and went to a laundry-mat to wash my clothes. In the laundromat parking lot, I started the truck, letting the air pressure build and filling out my logbook. Ready to go, I turn the wheel left and start off when a woman comes running across the lot waving her arms and yelling.

I stopped and got out. My truck's front bumper had caught on a guy's back wheel. I used the laundromat phone to call 911 and get connected to the police dispatcher.

"I need to report an accident," I said. I told what happened.

"That man gets in and causes traffic problems on Fourth Avenue all the time," the dispatcher said. "Don't worry about it. Just go on."

"Hell, no," I said. "You get somebody out here to fill out an accident report. I'm not having that man's family suing me and my company for a hit-and-run accident."

Five minutes later a police car arrived, and he took statements from the woman and me.

The next day I arrived back in Waycross. I hired a man to help load the truck. Finally, after this stop, the trailer was filled.

I weighed the truck: 12,000 pounds. The dispatcher said it was time to deliver. From Brunswick Georgia, I drove Interstate 95 north to Washington, D.C., west on Interstate 66 to Hagerstown to drop one of the small shipments. I took Interstate 66 to Toledo, Ohio, then Interstate 75 to Detroit to unload the big shipment.

I went across Interstate 94 to Chicago, and unloaded the big conference table and twelve chairs into another high-rise office building. Luckily, the table fit in the Chicago elevator. The office was on the eighth floor. A helper and I carried the chairs and legs in. I reassembled the table, we flipped it right-side up, and they signed for it.

Down Interstate 55 to St Louis and across Interstate 70 to Kansas City, Kansas, I took I-35 south to Wichita and McConnell Air Force Base, picking up my son in law Jeff to help. We unloaded that a couple days before Christmas, so I took a week off.

The holidays made me generous. I paid Jeff $200 for working, and told Mary I wanted to take the kids to Walmart so they could get some clothes. She said she had to go with us. I unhitched the trailer across the street from Mary's house and everybody got in the cab of the truck. It had snowed and there was about two inches on the ground.

In Walmart, I told the kids to pick out a couple blouses and skirts and Alvin a couple shirts and pants. While waiting, Mary and I were standing by a rack of bedsheets and she mentioned that Loretta and Bodine needed some.

“I’m not buying any damn sheets,” I said. I bought Loretta and Bodine a quart of Jack Daniel’s and a dime bag of pot, but Walmart wasn’t selling either of those at the time so I bought them elsewhere.

The kids found the clothes they wanted and we checked out. Back in the truck heading out, I did three or four donuts in the snow there in the Walmart parking lot. The kids liked that.

I dropped off Mary and the kids, and went to a Dillions grocery for some lunchmeat, bread, soft drinks and a carton of cigarettes. The next day I told Mary I wanted to take the kids to a pizza buffet. I picked up Jeff and the kids in the truck while Nora picked up Mary and her husband Bob.

“Kids, eat all the pizza you want,” I said.

“No, no,” Mary said. “Don’t eat more than two.”

But, she and Bob put their own hog bibs on, and had six or seven slices apiece.

Nora took Mary across the street to a shop while Jeff and I took the kids next door to an arcade. I gave the four girls a $20 roll of quarters to play any games they wanted. Alvin, Jeff and I played Pac-Man. Jeff and Alvin played it for a long while without losing. I didn't know Alvin knew how to play, but he spent about $15 in quarters.

At Mary’s house, one of the kids took my four work uniforms so Mary could wash them. A day later, they brought the four shirts out.

“Where are my pants?” I asked.

They said they didn't know.

I asked Mary where the pants were. She said she didn't have them.

“The kids brought in four light blue shirts and four dark blue pants, now give me my pants,” I said.

I was sitting in the recliner and she went to the wall phone to call her shyster lawyer. The secretary answered, and I could hear Mary telling her that I was making her nervous. I walked out.

I started the truck, building the air, when a cop pulled up.

“You can’t park here,” he said.

“I'm just leaving,” I said.

I stopped at Dale Simon's Moving and Storage for a shipment going southeast. Next the dispatcher said to go to Oklahoma City for two shipments and Dallas for two more shipments. All were going to Tennessee and Illinois.

I hopped on Interstate 40 to Music City, then from Music City on I-24 to the warehouse at Tullahoma, Tennessee. The last four shipments were going to Illinois, two to Louisville on the west side of the state and two in Lexington on the east side of the state.

I was getting tired of the business, mainly, what I felt was the lack of route planning.

Since I was already in Tennessee, I drove to Chattanooga and told Jimmy I was turning in the truck and quitting.

Chapter Fourteen

Back in Kansas

After several years in the Chattanooga area, I returned to Junction City and went to work for Midwestern Trucking out of Fort Scott, Kansas.

Midwestern was a firm where a driver leased a truck from them and eventually would own the truck.

After applying, I had to take an open-book test for the Kansas Department of Transportation and a road test. They hired me and sent me on the road for two weeks as co-pilot to another driver, named Larry. I think we were around Detroit when the dispatcher told me to come in and get my truck.

I caught an express bus to Fort Scott, arriving on a Saturday. I inspected the truck and signed for it. It felt like a new beginning for me.

The trailers were fifty feet long, longer than some states such as Missouri allowed. We had to stay on Interstate 70, and were advised not even to take off ramps to truck stops to use restrooms.

The dispatcher sent me to Longview, Texas. On the two-lane Highway 69, at a certain speed the truck died. I started to go a-ways farther and it died again. I nursed the rig along like that until I finally passed a small truck stop. From there I called the dispatcher to update him and he said to have the local mechanic look at it. The mechanic at the truck stop diagnosed that the fuse to the governor had burned out. He replaced it for $10 and I was on my way again.

I arrived in Longview a couple hours before sunup, and got in line with the other trucks waiting the warehouse to open. I slept a while. A couple hours later I opened the back doors and backed up to the loading dock for ten pallets of new aluminum soda cans. I delivered them to a soft-drink factory in Memphis.

The dispatcher sent me to a warehouse for 11,000 cases of KOTEX tampons going to a Safeway store in Dallas. I hopped on Interstate 40 to Dallas, where I arrived around 10 a.m.

I discovered the Safeway only received shipments between 3 a.m. and 6 a.m. so I went to a Truck Stop of America and called the dispatcher with an update. While there, I installed my new forty-channel CB radio and mounted the antennas on the mirrors. I also went in the store and bought a 15-inch color TV, which I hooked up in my sleeper compartment. I did my laundry while there and ate in the restaurant. Back in my truck, I watched some TV and went to sleep.

I woke up at 2 a.m. to drive back to Safeway. I lucked out being the third truck in line. The guard checked my paperwork and I backed up to the dock to unload my tampons.

Most of the shipments hauled for Midwestern didn't require the drivers to load or unload, which was a nice change from my previous trucking experience. But, I did have to unload the tampons myself, stacking the different types and brands on pallets. At least, it was easier than carrying furniture.

The dispatcher sent me to Waco, down I-35. There I was told to go to a farm. I found the farm and the farmer's crew loaded 300 bags of coffee beans, each weighing 100 pounds. The farmer told me to stay in the truck while they loaded. It took a little over an hour. Something interesting they did was they blew smoke into the trailer before closing the doors. They said the smoke was to kill any bugs.

Those beans were going to Chicago. I took I-30 to Little Rock, I-40 to Memphis, then I-55 to Chicago. The warehouse workers unloaded the coffee.

I next went to a steel-wire manufacturing facility with an open furnace. They loaded twelve huge rolls of wire down the middle of the trailer. They were each two feet high and three feet around. They blocked the spools so they wouldn't roll. I went to a truck stop to weigh the trailer; those twelve rolls of wire weighed six tons.

The route I took to Savannah, Georgia, was I-65 to Louisville, I-64 to Lexington, Kentucky, I-75 to Macon, then I-16 to Savannah. A couple of spools had shifted out of line making the trailer's left front corner dip lower.

The dock to this factory was on the back side. The turning area to get into the dock was eight feet long and forty feet wide ending at some railroad rails. My trailer was fifty feet long and the semi was fifteen feet long, so my rig altogether was 65 feet long. After some maneuvering, I finally got the back of the trailer heading into the dock. I was able to get the trailer within two feet of the dock but no closer. The dock guys placed a ramp across the space to unload.

The dispatcher sent me go to the Scott Paper Company for cases of paper towels going to Philadelphia. This was an easy route straight up Interstate 95. After being unloaded at Philadelphia, I was sent to the Lipton's tea and soup factory then headed to Kansas City, Missouri. I took I-95 to Washington, D.C., crossed I-66 west to Strasburg Virginia, the down I-81 to Lexington, Kentucky, across the state on I-64 to St Louis, and finally I-70 to Kansas City.

About eighty miles before Kansas City, was a Missouri Department of Transportation truck weighing station. I ran across the scales. Two highway patrolmen came out with a measuring tape and measured the truck from its front bumper to the rear bumper of the trailer. It was sixty-five feet. They had me park.

I went in the office and they gave me a ticket for being over length. They had me walk across the highway to the scale office with my shipment invoice, logbook, driver's license and vehicle registration. I called the dispatcher to give him the ticket number and he sent the $125 for the fine.

I did the walk of shame back across the interstate, started the truck and continued to Kansas City to unload. It was a Friday afternoon. I updated the dispatcher.

"I'm unloaded," I said.

"Where do you live?" he asked.

"Junction City."

"Drive home and call us back in five days."

It was company policy to send drivers home once a month. I wasn't used to that.

***

One tool a driver used back then included a road atlas to plot the course from one city to the next and calculate how many miles so you can figure how long the drive would be. Now, smart phones do that in a few seconds. The Department of Transportation required drivers keep logbooks, and keep them filled out. You couldn't be eight hours behind on it.

At that time a driver could only stay on the road ten hours a day, unless you had a fixed route, in which case twelve hours was acceptable. The rules have fluctuated since then. Now, I believe, a driver can drive for eleven hours of a fourteen-hour shift but then has to rest for ten hours before driving again.

For cruise control, I had a two-foot rod with an adjustable lever. I'd put the end of the rod on the gas pedal and hook the lever under the dashboard. I believe this is now illegal, but most big rigs now have cruise control built in.

I also had a radar detector that was legal in most states. But, in Pennsylvania I had to unplug it and put it out of sight. If a patrolman caught you with it, he'd take it from you and ticket you.

***

With all the driving I was doing, I'd think about the history of the areas I'd go through.

Do you know why St. Louis is called the Gateway City? Most of the frontiersmen and settlers would join wagon trains there to head west. It was very fitting that they built the Gateway Arch there to commemorate that heritage.

I'd think about how at one time France claimed all the land from Canada to the Gulf of Mexico and west of the Mississippi River to the Rocky Mountains. If President Jefferson hadn't made the Louisiana Purchase in 1803 buying that region, we'd probably have to use passports to drive from St. Louis to Denver because we'd be passing through another country's territory.

***

Back in Junction City a few days, I stayed with daughter Nora and her husband Jeff.

When ready for duty again, I called the dispatcher. He sent me to a feed factory in Kansas City for sixteen pallets. The scales said the weight was nine tons. I headed to New Orleans, south on Interstate 49 through Fort Smith, Arkansas, made famous in the 1890s by Hanging Judge Parker.

On down through Shreveport and continuing down to Lafayette, I hopped on I-10 into New Orleans. Downtown in the French Quarter, the streets were narrow. I had fun trying to get my eight-foot-wide, sixty-five-foot-long vehicle through there.

A cop stopped me to ask what I was doing. I said I was trying to get to the feed factory. He guided me to a larger street and over to the factory.

A man in the plant told me to unhitch from my trailer, and they'd move it. Unfortunately, my trailer was sitting right over a spot where the factory had replaced a water line two weeks before.

The trailer's left dolly sank down into the ground, bending the dolly. I had to get two wreckers to lift the trailer so I could back out. We removed the bent dolly after I was unloaded, and I called the dispatcher. He said to take the trailer to Slidell, Louisiana, to drop at a trailer factory. It cost me $100 for the two wreckers plus $200 to replace the dolly.

At an Indianapolis paper mill, they loaded my trailer with forty big rolls of paper. The rolls stood around five feet high and weighed around 1,000 pounds each. The last rolls were on the trailer floor's guide line, maybe an inch over. I weighed the truck at twenty tons.

I ran Interstate 70 down across Missouri, arriving at the "Scales of Hell" around midnight. Of course, they stopped me for being over length but they also claimed I was over weight on the rear wheels.

I slid the trailer as far forward and the rear wheels as far back as I could. The scales worker asked why didn't get in the trailer and move the contents around. I told him it was big rolls of new paper.

They made me walk across the highway and call the dispatcher, and they held my driver's license. They shut me down.

I was wondering how I would take off one roll of paper so I could take the rest to Kansas City. I lay down to sleep a couple hours. On waking, I looked around. The scales were closed down.

With no one watching me, I threw the truck in gear, slid onto I-70, and waited until I was a half mile down the road before I turned my lights on. That next morning the paper company unloaded me, and I drove back to the scale to get my license.

The dispatcher then sent me to the Scott Paper Company for a load to Dallas. From I-49 to Joplin then 1-40 into Dallas, I arrived at the warehouse.

Afterward, I ate at a Truck Stop of America about 7 a.m. The dispatcher sent me to a washer-and-dryer factory for a load to El Paso. Interstate 20 took me south. The factory sat on the border of Texas and Mexico.

I looked across the border and saw a truck trailer like mine sitting over there. I could make out some faded lettering that said Midwestern. The wheels were off and several Mexican families were living in it.

"What happened there," I asked a worker.

"A driver got loose in Juarez and the Mexican police seized the trailer," they said. "Midwestern is trying to get the trailer back through the courts."

I ended up leaving Midwestern soon after that. The truck grind still got old for me, even though Midwestern was a better company than where I'd previously worked.

Chapter Fifteen

Taxi Driving

Back in Junction City I stayed with Nora and Jeff, and started driving a taxi for Bell Cab.

The town may have had a hundred city blocks, and hadn't grown much since I left Fort Riley in 1964. The Grandview development added a few blocks. Yellow Cab had seven or eight cabs and Bell Cab had ten or twelve. Then there was a new company called Robbins that had eight to ten cars.

In my early days at Fort Riley, from 1961 to 1964, I caught Bell and Yellow cabs frequently to get to and from town.

Like in Chattanooga, I drove at night from 6 p.m. to 6 a.m. The fare changed frequently: $1.25 then $1.35 from Junction City to Manhattan airport, $25 to $30 into Manhattan.

From Junction City to Custer Hill was $4.25. If you picked up four people at the same place, say the post exchange store, and they all got out at the theater, the fare was $4.25 plus a quarter each for the other three, so $5 altogether.

After a month the cab company needed another driver so I got Jeff a job. I'd also gotten my junior-high-aged son Alvin a job there washing and cleaning out the cabs.

I was the oldest of the six night drivers. Around one or two in the morning, we'd all wait at a cab stand or office for a call. To kill time we'd toss quarters at a wall; whoever tossed a quarter closest to the wall without hitting it won all the quarters.

Around 10 p.m. one night, a young gal called saying she and her friends wanted to go to a club on Grant Street, the main street going to the post. I picked them up on Chestnut Street. They were smoking a joint and gave me a couple hits. By the time I got back to the office I had enough of a buzz that I told the dispatcher I was going to catch a few winks and to yell at me when it was my next turn came up.

Fort Riley instituted a new rule that if a soldier kept getting into minor trouble, the company commander could give them an Article 15, giving them two-week restriction at the stockade at Camp Funston, about 10 miles away. It wasn't uncommon for us taxis to drive the soldier and the escorting CQ to the stockade.

The soldier worked and trained in the company during the day, ate supper then packed his duffle bag, uniforms, TA-50, and pillow, sheets and blankets the CQ delivers him to the stockade. From the time he'd arrive until 9 p.m. he'd do PT and dismounting drill, then make his bunk, hang up his uniform, lay out his TA-50 field equipment for inspection. After inspection he'd put his TA-50 on top of the wall locker, take a shower and go to bed. At 5 a.m. he'd be wakened, get dress and do thirty minutes of PT, pack his equipment and get picked by the escorting CQ in a taxi and return them to the company.

The military had changed from paying once a month to twice a month and privates by that point received a lot more than I did. I got $67 month, and these guys were getting around $300.

The Friday and Saturday on a payday weekend, a soldier could get a six-hour off-post pass. We taxis would pick up a couple of them at a time and run them into town to Safeway or Dillions to cash their checks. The stores required them to spend around $30 before they'd cash checks. (That was a fair amount of groceries at that time; a cartoon of cigarettes was $6.)

***

Around the beginning of December, eight inches of snow fell during the day. I was up on Custer Hill, and picked up five troops at their barracks. They wanted to go to Church's Chicken in Junction City and return to the barracks. I charged each one $10. It was a good price mark up.

We'd get forty percent of the fare. We got paid once a week.

During the snow, one of the night drivers strayed off the cleared roads for a short cut and got stuck. We other drivers tried to pull him out but we only had one-inch straps and they broke. We had to call a wrecker to get him out.

The next night another driver got stuck, so all the taxi owners said no night drivers could go on post due to risk. I told the man who owned my cab that if he let me run on post I would pay the tow bill if I got stuck; he agreed and I ran a little over $200 in fares that night.

Say I picked up four people on Custer wanting to go to town. I reported to the dispatcher that I had four going to town on regular fare, but I'd write down for myself that I charged them $5 apiece. By morning I'd run around $200. I gave $100 to the company to get my commission and bonus then kept the rest. That week I ran around $800 total.

***

I called my second ex-wife Charlotte to see if she and her kids wanted to move to Junction City. She said yes, so I took a week off to drive to Pikesville, Tennessee, where she and the kids were living in the attic of her dad Fred's house. I rented a small U-Haul trailer, and we packed in their beds and clothes, a sofa, table and chairs. Back in Junction City, we moved into a two-bedroom house two blocks from the school on Fifth Street. My first ex-wife Mary and our kids lived around the corner on Sixth Street.

Instead of letting Charlotte's kids go to the school two blocks away, I enrolled them in the school at the south end of town so there'd be no problems with my kids or Mary. Mary still walked my kids to school: Ella was eleven, Tammy twelve and Nancy fourteen, and Alvin was fifteen and in high school. Charlotte's kids were Gerald (Jerry) was seven, Rebecca eight, Margaret nine, and Michael ten. I didn't want Mary even close to walking Charlotte's kids to school.

On the mornings I was on a run on post and couldn't take the kids to school, my dispatcher had another driver drive the kids six blocks to school and charge me $2.

Charlotte took a job at a liquor store from 2 p.m. to 10 p.m. Some Friday or Saturdays nights that Charlotte was off, we'd go to a little neighborhood bar to drink and dance.

I told my kids they were welcome to come over to play or stay overnight. Ella and Tammy came over all the time.

I lived two blocks from work, and I stopped by home one night around 6:30 to find Nancy, one of my daughters with Mary, standing in my living room with Charlotte's kids Jerry and Becky crying.

"What's going on," I asked.

They said Nancy was picking on them and slapping them.

"Nancy, you're welcome to come over, but you can't slap the kids," I said.

"Go f— yourself," she said. "I don't have to mind you."

Mary let the kids get away with that talk, but I wasn't going to. Nancy had just gotten out the last word and I slapped her across the face. She cussed me so I took off my belt and whipped her butt. Nancy marched out the door still cussing me.

I followed her out, and slapped her mouth and whipped her butt again in the middle of the street. Mary was standing on the corner watching all this so she called the police. They went over to Mary's house and she made out a complaint of child abuse.

The next night when I went to work the dispatcher told I had to talk to a detective at the police station. I walk around the corner to the station and talked to the detective.

"Does Mary have custody of the kids?" he asked.

"Yes," I said.

"Did you whip Nancy last night?"

"Yes," I said, "and here's why: Mary lets the kids cuss and slap at her, but I don't put up with my kids cussing me and telling me they don't have to mind me without getting their butts whipped."

He didn't have any more questions.

I went back to work.

There was a bus stop on Washington Street left of Mary's house. Across the alley was the Bell Taxi stand on the corner of Sixth and Washington. The Yellow Taxi stand was straight down Sixth on a corner.

Sometimes new troops would arrive at the bus station and I'd pick up two or three of them, drive down the alley, turn right then turn right again and drive by Mary's honking the horn.

I'd turn right on Washington Street, run up to Grant Street and on to the main post. I'd drop my fares at the replacement company then go up on Custer Hill. I did this one night and had to cross the river, but while on post the dispatcher told me to return to the office.

"I'm about to deliver some troops to the replacement company," I said. "Bring them and return to the office now," he said. "There's a policeman in the office."

When I got there the cop asked me, "Did you honk the horn in front of Mary's house?"

"Yes," I said.

"Mr. Cook, quit honking the horn in front of her house," he said.

"Stop right there," I said. "I'm Babcock, not Cook, and don't call me Cook."

***

Charlotte, her kids and I stayed in Junction City around a year. There was too much family drama with Mary. At the end of the school year, we rented a U-

Haul saying we are making a move there in Junction City, but we headed out going back to Tennessee.

We stayed in the attic of Charlotte's dad Fred for a week until I found a single-wide trailer home that had three bedrooms. It was about a half mile from Fred's, but it didn't have inside plumbing. For water to wash clothes or take a bath there was a little pond twenty feet from the door. For water for drinking and cooking, we filled plastic gallon jugs at a neighbor's trailer.

I took a job as night watchman for a strip-mining company.

This strip-mining operation used D-8 caterpillars with blades and front-end buckets to scrape off the topsoil and keep scraping the dirt until they hit a coal vein. They trucked off the coal, eventually making a big hole or pit.

I worked the summer then got on with a man with a small sawmill. We cut six-by-six ten-foot-long planks for underground mines then I'd haul them to an underground mining company.

When this work ran out I went to Chattanooga and started driving for Arrow Trucking, a flatbed trucking company. They had a docking yard on the river where they'd unload river barges of rolled steel or rail steel.

The first truck of theirs I drove was a long-nose semi. Most of their trailers were forty feet long. They had one stretch trailer. A foot behind the fifth wheel was two pins, one on each side of the rails; you could pull these pins and stretch the trailer to forty-five, fifty, fifty-five and sixty feet. The frame of the trailer was bent a little. Sometimes when opening or closing it, I had to chain the trailer bumper to a pole and pop the truck's clutch until I got the trailer to stretch to the full sixty feet.

To close it, I had to ram the end into a cement wall. Even with its quirks I liked to use this trailer because the bigger size meant it paid more per load.

For a month I'd make two round trips per week from Chattanooga to New Orleans. Most of the time the tires on the vehicles were used or retread. On one trip I had thirteen flats or blowouts.

I left Chattanooga down I-59, dropped off two coils of rolled steel in Birmingham, then kept on to New Orleans when one of the trailer chains came loose and wrapped around the rear trailer.

I didn't see this until one of the tires blew. I stopped and had the tire man single it out on I-10 to Slidell and New Orleans. He removed the dead tire and left the remaining tire next to it alone.

In New Orleans for reloading, I stretched out the trailer to sixty feet. I start out of town. I tried to get into the right lane to go over the high bridge but a car was there and wouldn't open space for me. I turned the wheel and forced him to the side of the road. A cop stopped me and asked if I'd seen the car. I claimed I didn't see it until I was already in the right lane.

Around ten miles outside Tuscaloosa, that single tire I had blew out along with two more trailer tires and one tractor tire. I called the office that I was having all these flats and blow outs and I asked them to send the mechanic with tires. They referred me to a nearby tire shop.

The local guy put used and capped tires on, and as I was turning into the truck stop, one of his tires popped. I called the manager and told him I was at the truck stop, and that I'd paid his tire man and one of his retreads had already popped. He said he'd send one of the mechanics out with some tires. It was around 2 p.m. By 7 p.m. the mechanic still hadn't shown. I called again and they said the night mechanic just walked out the door in my direction.

The night mechanic brought two used tires and neither one fit the semi he singled out the tire on the semi, replaced the trailer tire and put the other tire in the tire rack. I was finally ready to drive. The mechanic followed me for a few miles to make sure I didn't have any more tire trouble.

I arrived in Chattanooga around 9 a.m., unloaded at the steel mill and then drove to my company's truck yard.

The Chattanooga police, six or seven car loads of them, and the FBI were there. It seemed that one of the managers, the shop foreman and two of the truck drivers had stolen a semi-tractor and brought it to the shop, took that semi-tractor body off and replaced it with one of our truck bodies, put the stolen truck body in a company dump truck and drove down Interstate 59 just across the Georgia state line. They were going to dump it in a draw, but they backed up too close to the edge and as the dump truck bed rose, the truck body and dump truck went over the edge.

The police arrested the manager, shop foreman, and the two drivers. They posted bail. Three of them were on probation for something else.

***

I was staying in a small motel downtown, and I happened to see that Charlotte's other ex-husband, Billy Scheerer, was also staying there.

***

That afternoon I went to our company yard by the river and loaded I-beams that are used for trailer-house frames, and planned to leave the next morning

I arrived back at the yard at 4:30 a.m. I had to move the other tractor from the trailer and hook up my semi. I lowered the trailer dollies then backed up my semi to the trailer but the trailer wasn't high enough to get over my back tires. I had the night mechanic use a small forklift to lift the trailer high enough for me to hook up.

I pulled out of the yard, and caught I-75 north to Knoxville. About twenty miles outside Cleveland, Tennessee, a tire blew. I called the night mechanic and he brought a tire to change it. I was on the go again up I-75. A little before Knoxville, I hung right on Interstate 40 through the Smoky Mountains past Pigeon Forge. I started up Black Mountain. Before starting down the mountain, there was a weight scale that I didn't know how to get around so I had to stop for weighing. They said I was over weight on the drive wheels. They fined me $125, so I paid.

As I entered Greensboro in the early morning, two more used tires blew. Since there were no truck stops or tire shops nearby and no one was in our office to wire me any money, I nursed the rig along to a truck stop and rested until around 7 a.m. Then I got up and went in the restaurant and ate. When the tire shop opened I asked if they had any to fit a semi. He didn't.

I called my manager with the situation. "This tire man has to order the tires from Raleigh," I said.

"Go to the next truck stop," the manager told me.

"The tire man says the next truck stop is Raleigh, forty miles away," I said.

I handed the phone to the tire man to let him haggle with my manager over price on cheap tires that wouldn't quite fit my rig but would get by temporarily.

They came to an agreement: $300 per tire plus $40 for two inner tubes, $50 labor and $50 for shipping, total $740. The manager wired the money, and hours later I was back on the road.

I rolled into Durham and found the destination, a tobacco drying plant. The guard told me to go down the hill and they would unload me. Going down the hill, I heard a loud pop.

At the bottom they unloaded the chimney sleeve I had for them, and pulled my truck to the side.

I called the manager to tell him I was unloaded but the drive shaft was broken.

He pledged a drive shaft the next morning. Another driver arrived with the drive shaft and another chimney sleeve. He brought the tools we needed to replace the drive shaft ourselves then we swapped trailers. He went to Florida. I went to a brickyard to load eight pallets of bricks and headed back to Chattanooga.

Back at base, the shop foreman told the owner and the manager that I was popping the clutch and jerking the truck and that was why the drive shaft had broken.

When I arrived in Chattanooga, I unloaded at the brickyard and went to the river yard. While the truck was being loaded again, I went to our parking lot.

The manager and owner came over to me to talk about me popping the clutch and twisting the drive shaft.

"No," I said. "I know how to drive. The shaft has been cracked a long time."

I showed them the shaft where the crack was rusted across its whole length.

The manager took me out of the CMC truck I'd been driving and put me in an International.

I'd be taking a load of I-beams to a trailer factory in Valdosta, Georgia. I arrived at the yard at 5 a.m. I checked over the International, hooked up to the trailer and hopped on Interstate 24 through Chattanooga, over the ridge into East Ridge, then I-75 straight south.

I'd gone about thirty miles when I got my first shock and realized that piece of junk truck would not go 55 miles an hour unless I was going down a steep hill.

I settled in for a long drive. It took me eleven hours to reach Valdosta. After unloading, I called home. The manager told me to go to a mulch factory for twelve pallets of mulch.

I started the long trip home. Driving through Atlanta, I got another shock: this piece of junk was a gas guzzler. It was eating one gallon of diesel every five miles. I had to put in $30 of diesel to make the last hundred miles from Atlanta to Chattanooga.

In Chattanooga I go to a Walmart to unload the mulch. At the company lot, I parked the truck and went home for the day. My log book was all messed up due to driving a regular distance at a slower speed for longer than DOT allows. The allowance was ten hours of driving, eight hours for loading or unloading, and then eight hours for rest.

The next morning I told the manager I wouldn't go to Valdosta or Waycross in that truck again because it would only go fifty miles an hour and get five miles to a gallon of fuel. I'd run short hauls, but not long ones.

The manager told me he was going to take two of my paychecks for that $125 over-weight fine and $700 to pay for all the used and retread tires blow outs he was paying for on my loads.

I kept my mouth shut for the time being. I was able to get the money back later by claiming false blowouts.

The next morning the river yard boom operator put four coils of rolled steel on my trailer from a river barge. I chained them down and drove thirty miles to Cleveland, Tennessee, to a stove manufacturer. I made eight round trips like that.

Around 5 p.m. the forklift operator loaded three coils of steel for my trip the next morning for Union City, just below Atlanta. I left the lot around 5 a.m. and ran down Interstate 75 to Atlanta, then Interstate 85 another twenty miles to Union City. I arrived around 9 a.m., so it took four hours to drive a 150 miles. Ridiculous.

After unloading I drove to the brickyard for sixteen pallets of bricks, and then started the four hour drive back to Chattanooga. After unloading at the Chattanooga brickyard, I went back to the river yard, where the forklift operator loaded I-beams for the next run.

***

It was early November and the weather was growing cold. The truck's heater and defrosters were bear-ley putting out any heat. In fact, my own huffing and puffing was getting the cab warmer.

When I had the mechanic check them out, he said the heating coils and fans were working fine.

I took matters into my own hands. In the front of the radiator were metal fins that could shut, blocking airflow through the radiator and causing the thermostat to open and the water to get hot. I didn't close these. I ripped a small plastic tarp into strips, placing these levers above the radiator. I then wrapped a sheet of cardboard in the plastic tarp and wire it to the front grill. Any other truck blocking that much air flow would cause the engine to overheat and burn the motor up, but not this truck.

***

Thanksgiving arrived and the company gave every driver a turkey. I took a week off to go Kansas to see my kids.

I was driving a Ford by this time. I threw my suitcase and the turkey in the trunk and hit the road. I was almost through Missouri when the car started backfiring. There were no truck stops or garages open. It being 4 a.m. on Thanksgiving, I knew I couldn't get a motel room, so I parked and slept in a garage's parking lot.

The next morning I was waiting for the garage to open. It finally did and the mechanic found the problem: the bolt holding the distributor in place came loose, letting the distributor turn and the timing was off. The mechanic readjusted the timing and the car ran better than it ever had been.

I arrived in Junction City around 3 p.m.

My daughter Tammy was staying with a military couple. The husband was a sergeant first class, a helicopter crewman at Marshall Army Airfield. I gave the turkey to them. While it was thawing, I made a couple pumpkin pies. The wife and Tammy prepared the turkey. It was the first turkey that Tammy ever helped bake.

***

Back at work, I loaded two coils of steel going to a factory. I ran down Interstate 59 to Birmingham and unloaded. My manager sent me to a blast furnace plant. I stretched the trailer to fifty feet and the forklift driver loaded six I-beams on the trailer, which I chained down. I jumped on Interstate 59 north and raced back to Chattanooga at fifty miles hour.

The next day I took the load of I-beams to Birmingham and unloaded at a trailer manufacturer.

For a load of railroad ties, the forklift operator told me most drivers take 100 ties. Not knowing how much a railroad tie weighed, I said OK. After I was loaded and chained down, I weighed the load: 50,000 pounds I was ten tons over weight.

There wasn't a weight scale on the road to Chattanooga, but there was one spot where Georgia DOT would set up a portable scale. The time was around 9 p.m. and DOT shouldn't have been out, but I still took a side road around. I successfully carried through and unloaded at Walmart.

Running short jobs, with a load out and a load in, made me the highest paid driver in the company. Many times I was getting paid for two shipments a day.

But even on these short trips, I'd still have a flat tire or two. I called the manager on a blowout and I needed $75 to buy a retread tire or $150 for a used tire at a truck stop. I'd go through their pile of blown tires and find one the size for my truck or trailer.

Doing this got me all my money back that the manager took out of my paychecks.

***

One day I delivered a load of coil steel on the south side of Atlanta. One DOT rule about Atlanta was that trucks without a shipment downtown couldn't take I-75 through town; all semis had to make the I-185 loop around Atlanta.

After unloading, I called the manager, figuring he'd send me to the brickyard. No, he told me to come back empty.

Back at the yard, I saw younger driver waiting. The manager told me to take this driver to Nashville to the Pilot Truck Stop and see the ex-manager turned shipping agent.

We arrived around 3:30 p.m. The agent told us to hook up to one of our trailers parked there then go to an address to pick up the tracks, boom, and bucket of a crane.

The weather was icy when we reached the yard where the crane was. The men there wouldn't load so we returned to the Pilot and told the agent. Instead, he had me pick up two coils of steel at a plant then wanted me to come back and see him. I got the coils then returned to the agent, and he gave me the shipping orders to a place that received shipments until midnight.

There at the Pilot, I overheard some other trucker's wife standing around complaining about going to work at a bar when there's freezing rain and the roads are icing up. The agent told this woman to call in to say she couldn't make the five or six blocks to work because the roads were icy. Yet, he told me to take a semi-tractor trailer with twenty tons of steel to Lenoir City, ninety miles away.

From the truck stop I took Interstate 24 east to the junction of I-40 north. The first fifty miles was freezing rain and iced roads. I had to stop once to scrape the windshield. The next forty miles had snow-covered roads and sleet. I arrived in Lenoir City around 11 p.m. and got to the plant. While they unloaded me, I hooked a charger to my batteries because I knew they were low. It wasn't a night to have dead batteries.

I took I-75 south back to Chattanooga. I stopped at the mechanic shop and had the mechanic charge the batteries again. I left there to get on Interstate 24 toward Nashville. Going through Monteagle, hail started falling off and on the rest of the way to Nashville. We got back to Nashville around 6 a.m. and ate at the restaurant. At 7:30 a.m. the agent told me to load another round of coils for Lenoir City. I did and returned to the Pilot.

At this point, I called my manager that I had a load for Lenoir City but that I'd been up twenty-four hours. He authorized me to turn over the driving to the young driver with me. Just before we go to the truck, we the announcement that the highway patrol closed the interstates.

I called the manager back and told him the highway patrol had closed the interstates, and he told me to get a room. The next morning the agent told us to return to Chattanooga.

We had two trailers to take back to base. We cleared the snow out from under them, lowered the dollies on both and unhooked both semis. I backed the long-nose under the loaded trailer and the junk one under the empty trailer. I locked both axles to pull.

I had the kid drive my truck I told him to stay a half a mile behind me and to keep his speed up going uphill. The weight of the load gives me traction. We got on Interstate 24 east to Chattanooga. Even though the interstate there was open, there was only one set of tracks each way; everybody stayed in the same tracks.

We crested Monteagle, and when we got to Jasper I noticed one set of tires dragging. I called the mechanic. While waiting for the mechanic to show, I sent the kid on to the yard.

The mechanic arrived and lifted the tires off the ground and pulled the chain out of the ground. He jacked up the wheels and took off the axle hub to see that the brake shoes had come apart. He fixed it.

The next morning I delivered the coils to Lenoir City and returned to Chattanooga. The following morning the manager sent me back to pick up the crane parts. I arrived and the crane operator wanted to load the two sections of the boom on the floor of the trailer then the tracks on top of the boom.

"No," I said, "Load the tracks on the floor then the boom and bucket. That way it's not top heavy."

***

Another time I went to Nashville in a long-nose truck with the stretch trailer for a load of pipe three feet in diameter and sixty feet long.

I chained it down and returned to Chattanooga to get over-load permits. The shipment was going to St. Louis. This was on a Friday. The agent called the client and the client said that if I could be there the next morning, he could load me with a shipment to Columbia, South Carolina. The agent told him I'd be there in the morning.

After the agent hung up, I told him I didn't get my $50 for expenses; he handed me $50 and said go.

On I-24 headed west, at Clarksville, Kentucky, I knew Exit 1 had a DOT scale. I had to sneak around for time constraints but I made it around. My heater quit working so every twenty miles I stopped at a truck stop for a pot of coffee and to chip the ice off the truck. I drove on. At Eddyville, Kentucky, was another DOT scale, but I sneaked around it too.

At Paducah, I crossed the river into Illinois. Just before I reached Interstate 57, I took the two-lane Highway 37 to Marion, Illinois, to avoid the scales just before there. I get back on Interstate 57 at Mt. Vernon, hung a left onto I-64 going west and there were no more scales. (Though, at O'Fallon going east, there were scales.)

I got into St. Louis and found the shipper's yard. The time was around 6 a.m. The truck that I was driving didn't have a sleeper so I wrapped a couple of small plastic tarps around me and curled up on the floor for a nap.

A couple hours later, the shipper and his forklift operator unloaded the sixty-foot pipe. The operator loaded regular six-inch by thirty-foot pipe for the return trip. I chained it down and went to a truck stop for $30 in fuel and started back to Chattanooga.

I had no trouble going across DOT scales with those smaller pipes. Around 4 a.m. I stopped at a Truck Stop of America in Nashville for a pot of coffee, chipping off ice and napping a couple hours.

I started out again and got on Monteagle. Between the first and second exits there I ran completely out of fuel, so I called the shop for some fuel and $20 for more fuel to get back to Chattanooga. The mechanic said the agent was there at Mont-eagle and would get me going. The agent picked me up and we bought five gallons of diesel and went back. We did this several times until I had around twenty gallons of fuel.

The truck wouldn't start back up. It seemed like it wasn't getting fuel to the injectors. Then the battery went dead while we tried to start it. The agent radioed for a wrecker. He put an air hose into the gas tank and blew fuel into the injectors then he hooked a charger on the battery and blew air into the air-starter. All that did the trick, and I was finally on my way.

After getting to the shop, I had the mechanic check the truck's heaters. It turned out the heating elements had burned out.

The next morning I traded trucks and headed off to Columbia, South Carolina. Heading south on I-75 too Atlanta, then across I-20 to Columbia got me there. I returned to Chattanooga with plywood. With plywood unloaded, I took coil steel to Bristol, Tennessee, got a load of bricks there and came back to Chattanooga.

On I-75 South, I passed through Cleveland, Tennessee. Halfway between there and Chattanooga was a sharp S-turn. I was running seventy-five miles an hour when just before I started into the first curve, a trucker behind radioed that he thought he could see my right tie rod dragging the ground.

I stopped to check it out, and, sure enough, the tie-rod was dragging. I wired it together and eased through the S-turn. At a store, I parked on the side of the road and went in to call the shop to request the mechanic bring a passenger-side ball joint and get me off the highway.

Chapter Sixteen

Tennessee National Guard – 1981-83

I joined another Tennessee National Guard unit, the 181st Field Artillery based in Dayton, Tennessee. I was assigned to C Battery.

The company commander told me he couldn't double-slot me as a sergeant first class so he'd have to reduce my rank to buck sergeant, but that I would start earning my rank back.

They didn't have an armory, just an arms room. With all my experience with different weapons – M1, bar, .30 cal. and .50 cal. machine guns, M79, M16 Al, M16 A2, M16 A3 – I took over the arms room.

A couple months after I joined, the battalion went to summer camp. We went to Camp Shelby near Hattiesburg, Mississippi. To get there I drove down Interstate 59 through Gadsden and Birmingham, Alabama, and even passed a convoy of the battalion's jeeps, trucks, two-and-a-half-ton trucks pulling 155 towed cannons.

At the main gate to Camp Shelby, I showed the guard all my paperwork from my DD form to my pink ID card. He handed me a map showing the barracks area that the battalion was in. I found the building and claimed a bunk. I hung my uniforms and assembled my pistol belt with first-aid pouch and two ammo pouches, rolled the poncho onto back of the belt, and made my bunk. I got all that done by the time the company commander and the truck convoy arrived.

I took six men to the supply truck and trailer, and had them unload the lockers and racks of weapons: the individual weapons M16 A2, M203s (M16 with tube under the barrel to fire the smoke flare and high-explosives rounds), the six .50 cal. machine guns, the twelve M60 machine guns. I counted all the weapons, making sure I had everything that was shipped down. It was all there.

The summer camp was just like being back in the military. The next morning, Monday, everybody got up at 0600 hours, dressed in PT uniforms (T-shirts, shorts and running shoes) and did our stretching exercises (bending, reaching, squatting, pushups, sit-ups, deep-knee bends, and leg-raisers). We formed up and ran then showered and dressed in our fatigues for breakfast.

At 0800 hours, the first sergeant called a company formation. All the people in the tree gun platoons, FOS (Forward Observers) and their radios operators, the TOC personnel (Tactical Operations Center, the people who determine our course of action), and the three-gun crews loaded up to go to the range for practice setting up and firing.

The people who didn't go to the field stayed with me for weapons classes: M16s in the morning (zeroing, firing, disassembling and assembling) and M203s in early afternoon. At 1700 hours we cleaned the weapons and I locked them in the racks. We made final formation then ate and scrambled into downtown Hattiesburg to find a bar. We returned to the barracks around 0000 hours for shut eye.

Tuesday was more of the same. Awake at 0600 hours, physical training, shower and shave, breakfast. At 0800 hours the first sergeant formed up the battery and the gun platoons headed to the range.

That morning I taught the class on the .50 cal. machine gun, which I set up on the table at the front of classroom on a tripod. The .50 cal. gun by itself weighed 125 pounds plus thirty pounds for the tripod and ten pounds for the spare barrel. It was either mounted on a vehicle or in a defensive position.

***

Each soldier is assigned a V-shaped sector of fire to be responsible for. The center of your sector is where your barrel is pointing straight ahead. Let's say a house 2,000 yards in front of you is your main target. Swinging the barrel all the way left with the barrel aimed at, let's say, a tree 2,000 yards away is your left sector. Swinging the barrel all the way right gives the right sector, maybe a road junction 2,000 yards away. Drawing yourself a range card showing these targets helps you engage at night.

The ammo is heavy duty. The .50 cal. lead bullet head is one inch around and one-and-a-half inches long, and the shell case holding the gunpowder is one inch around and four inches long.

That afternoon I gave the class on the M60 machine gun, which replaced the old .30 cal. machine gun. It was the baby version of the .50 cal.; it looked the same, with the head-space and timing the same but weighed only thirty pounds. On the M60 the head space and timing is preset, you just flip a lever on the right side of the barrel. The maximum effective range was 11,000 yards.

For the middle weekend of summer camp, several of us went bar-hopping together in Hattiesburg. There was a black guy with us and we thought it would be funny to stop at a country-western bar. Unfortunately, a few rednecks wanted to fight so we left.

We went on down two-lane Highway 26 to Gulfport, where we stopped at a little go-go club. They charged $8 for a bottle of beer. The club had the dancers in a three-girl set: an ugly one, a fat one, and a pretty one. By the time that three-songs set was done, in ten minutes, you were supposed to be done with your beer ready for another $8 bottle. We didn't stay long.

Next we hit a club where some women were that would dance with us, and we stayed until closing. We rented a motel room, and didn't stir until 1100 hours. We got up, ate, splashed around at the beach, and ate supper around 2100 hours. When the club opened up, we went back for another night of partying, and ended up closing down the club again.

We returned to Camp Shelby late Sunday evening. At 0500 hours the first sergeant woke everybody and the day started. After breakfast, I issued M16 rifles to everybody and we headed to the zero and qualification range for annual qualification. Afterward everybody cleaned their M16s and turned them in.

That year battalion command decided to fire all the M60s in the arsenal. There were eight M60 machine guns per battery, and five batteries in the battalion.

We took those guns to the range on Wednesday.

Arriving at 0800 hours, we lined up people three guns per battery at a time. We set up the zero targets to calibrate the sights then we set up the qualifying targets.

Thursday morning the first sergeant assigned me five men to clean all the M60s. I placed a tarp on the ground then went to the trash behind the mess hall and found four one-gallon cans. I filled each half full of cleaning fluid then we started disassembling the guns.

Under the barrel is the gas circular with the gas piston. I took the ends off the circular and placed those parts in a can of cleaning fluid. Next I took the forearms off, then the feed covers, removing feed trays, placing these parts in cleaning fluid. I removed the trigger group and put those parts in fluid. I removed the butt plate, took the buffer apart, and removed the bolt and operating rod, spare the rod and bolt. I took the bolt apart, removing the firing pin.

The men were in T-shirts and shorts so I had them take the barrels and receivers into the showers and clean them out. We applied a light coat of oil on these pieces.

The first sergeant walked by and saw all the pieces lying out and he went crazy.

"Can you put the guns back together?" he asked, starting to sweat. He'd never had a trained armorer before.

"Yes," I said. "I can put the guns back together."

The next day, Friday, we started loading up the trucks. We got paid for summer camp, a day's pay for each day's training rather than a full day's pay for every four hours training.

Early Saturday morning the commander led the truck convoy out the gates of Camp Shelby, up Interstate 59 headed back to Dayton, Tennessee. I took off the same way, passing the convoy, running through Meridian and Birmingham, stopping in Gadsden for food and arriving back in Chattanooga around 1600 hours. A few hours later I hit the old dance club on Fourth Avenue, dancing until closing then going home to sleep.

Early Sunday, I found the strength to wake up, dress in my fatigues and drive to Dayton to unload the battalion trucks. I put the weapons and racks back in the arms room, made the final weapons count, accounted for everything, locked the arms room and set the alarm.

By 1630 hours all trucks were unloaded and everything put up. The first sergeant held retreat formation and dismissed everybody. Summer camp was over.

Chapter Seventeen

King of the Road

Returning from Tennessee National Guard camp, I was back to trucking. One order of business was that I moved out of the motel near the trucking operation to a one-bedroom trailer house along the Tennessee River.

A week before Christmas, my manager asked if I would go to Nashville to pick up a trailer of wooden chairs and deliver them to Buffalo, New York.

"If I have to drive my junky International, then no," I said, "but if I can drive one of the GMCs, then yes."

The manager let me take a GMC.

Early the next morning I got on I-24 West heading to Nashville. I arrived at a Pilot truck stop to talk to the shipping agent and get the paper work. I hooked up the trailer and took I-65 North toward Bowling Green, Kentucky, on up I-65 to Louisville and through Cincinnati, Ohio, to Cleveland, then I-90 the rest of the way to Buffalo, arriving late in the evening.

I got a room for the night at a Truck Stop of America, but was at the store for delivery at 8 a.m. They unloaded all the chairs, and afterward I called my manager. He sent me further north to Wendelville, New York, to pick up bags of fertilizer. Just before I got there, I called from a stop and the manager said to turn around for Buffalo because the fertilizer deal fell through.

I got back to Buffalo and called the manager for an update and he said go back to Wendelville again and pick up the fertilizer. I pulled into the Wendelville fertilizer plant around midnight, and they loaded the trailer.

I left for Atlanta, Georgia. After that, I couldn't joke about traveling across the country dragging crap behind me.

From Wendelville, I took I-90 down to Cleveland, I-71 to Cincinnati, I-75 through Knoxville down to Chattanooga. While in Chattanooga, I left the truck in the yard to get a shower and spend a good night of sleep at my new trailer.

When I arrived, the landlord told me she hired a young woman to help take care of her wheelchair-bound brother and sister. The landlord said the woman was named Shirley. I thought to myself that it seemed like I'd actually met Shirley a couple years earlier.

It turned out I was right. Over the next few months we got to know each other. The only day she had off was Saturday, and once in a while we went dancing at the club on Fourth Avenue.

The next morning I drove the rest of the way to Atlanta to deliver the fertilizer to a lawn and garden business.

***

Around this time, the shop foreman and two drivers who had been arrested for stealing a truck finally went to court. They were given three years in prison. The company's ex-manager turned shipping agent was also supposed to go to court for the case, but he lifted anchor on his twenty-foot sailboat and made a run for it down river. He didn't get too far before the Tennessee Highway Patrol caught him and locked him up until his court date. He was sentenced to five years.

***

I was nearing the end of my run with the trucking operation on the river.

One day, the manager reamed me out. "Our two accountants say that International truck you been driving gets ten miles per gallon instead of the five you claim," he said, "and they say it runs seventy instead of fifty-five coming down Monteagle.

I'd been driving that piece of junk for seven months. "Listen," I said, "you tell those accountants to bring their computers and calculators, and have the yard load them up with I-beams for the factory in Valdosta, have them deliver the load. It'll take them a minimum eleven hours at fifty-five miles an hour. They'll use half a tank of fuel just to unload and start back. If they don't put in at least $20 of fuel between North Atlanta and Red Mountain, the mechanic will pick them off the road."

The next day I made my last hauls for them. My last load out was an order of sixty-foot I-beams going to a construction site just off I-75 in downtown Atlanta.

It had started to snow when I left for home the night before, and by the time I was back at work there six inches on the ground. I started the truck and as I headed through the gate, the guard asked where I was headed.

"Atlanta," I said.

"Good luck!" he said.

The snow had covered the highway all the way there. I was raised in Colorado so driving in snow didn't bother me, but those Georgia drivers weren't even good at driving in the rain so I had to stay aware.

As I was going through East Gate off the road between the four lanes, near Ringgold and the DOT scales on the northbound lanes, I could see one car rear end another car. A hundred yards below that, south bound, three more cars were off the road. The DOT scales were closed and the Ringgold police weren't even sitting along the interstate in their Mustangs and Thunderbirds.

I was running fifty miles an hour, trying not to slow down to where my tires would start spinning. Entering Marietta on the outskirts of Atlanta, I saw people trying to push cars up small hills in eight inches of snow.

After tire trouble under the I-285 overpass, I trudged on and finally got into Atlanta on south I-75. At the construction site, the forklift operator tried to unload me but all he did was slide and spin around. I called my office to see if I could return to Chattanooga, but the guard answered and told me to get a hotel room.

The next morning they unloaded the I-beams and I went to the brickyard for a load of bricks going back to Chattanooga.

Chapter Eighteen

Used Cars

I saw the advertisement in the newspaper for a small used car dealer named Ralph Anderson needing a few men to go to Florida with him to pick up some cars and return to Chattanooga.

Six of us drove down in two cars. Ralph drove two guys and I drove the second car with the other two drivers. We headed south on Interstate 75 through Atlanta on down to Macon left on I-16 to Savannah, hopped on I-95 straight to Jacksonville Florida.

We went around to two or three car dealers and Ralph bought ten cars. We had to tow several of the cars so we hooked up tow bars, chains and lights for the ride back to Chattanooga.

After that, Ralph had me start washing and cleaning cars for the dealership.

And so I started my career as a used car salesman. Ralph paid me $90 a week. If I sold a car I got a $25 commission.

Ralph's wife June served as the business's notary public, and as a backup, he also had me get certified as a notary public. He paid the $50 fee for my notary license and seal. A notary at that time was needed to sign vehicle titles and validate vehicle sales contracts. When one of the other salesmen sold a car, I could notarize the sale. When I sold a car, June notarized it.

I was also in charge of having spare keys made. When a car was sold, I'd take the car keys across the street to Ace Hardware and make another set that we would tag and place in a key box – and if the customer got behind on payments, we took that set of keys to repo the car.

On Friday and Saturday people came in to make their $75 car payments. I took the money and wrote receipts. Sometimes I'd go to one of the banks Ralph used and make deposits. I regularly made $5,000 to $10,000 deposits in his accounts.

***

I still attended monthly guard drills In Dayton.

There was one guy who'd been in the unit about four years and he decided to take the six-month Officer Candidate School (OCS) course. He became a second lieutenant. Book-wise he was smart, but commonsense-wise he was dumber than a box of rocks.

There were and still are four ways of becoming an officer: OCS, military academies, college ROTC programs, and battlefield commissions. Receiving a battlefield commission is pretty rare, and the most famous case of it was Medal of Honor recipient Audie Murphy during World War II.

Summer rolled around again, and I took two weeks off work for guard camp.

The Tennessee National Guard commander decided that some of his ordnance personnel should go to Camp Shelby for summer camp to supervise. (If weapons needed repair, they were sent to ordnance.)

Around 1600 hours on a Friday, the company commander arrived at Camp Shelby with the convoy. I counted the weapons and placed them in lockers and racks and locked them up. A buck sergeant walked in and said he was from state ordnance and was ready to inspect my weapons.

"Get the hell out," I said. "There's nothing wrong with my weapons and they are locked up."

The next morning the first sergeant told the supply sergeant that we had to take all our M203 rifles to ordnance personnel who would be giving classes. That buck sergeant looked at my weapons and saw that they were clean and oiled and all working.

In his class were all five of the batteries' supply sergeants and arms-room people. As the sergeant was demonstrating rifle disassembly (basically the same class I gave the previous year), his assistant walked around the room helping the supply sergeants and armorers who were having problems. The weapons from the other armorers were dirty so they had to be cleaned and lightly coated with oil. We broke for lunch, and afterward they continued cleaning weapons.

For another class on another day we took in our M60s, tripods and spare bags. Again, my weapons were clean and ready.

The buck sergeant disassembled and reassembled the gun for the class. Then he explained how to make a range card. He placed the gun on the tripod mounts and set the T/E mechanism, explaining the traversing scale and elevation scale. His assistant moved around helping the supply sergeants and armorers draw range cards.

The following Wednesday all the supply sergeants and armorers went to the firing range. We took all the .50 cal. machine guns in the five batteries. I set the head space and timing on all my battery's guns, and to save time as the other batteries arrived, I had my men bring me their guns and I set the headspace and timing on all the guns.

One battery brought two jeeps, another brought a truck and one had an APC (armored personal carrier). I mounted guns on these vehicles then mount the rest on tripods. We fired twelve rounds to zero then set the targets diagonal right and down, horizontal, diagonal left and up.

During this, our guard unit's new lieutenant, who was dumber than a box of rocks, was making a nuisance of himself. His platoon sergeant sent him to ordnance to get a .155 cal. cannon barrel extension. There's no such thing, so he searched a good long time. When he returned, he was sent to get a box of grid squares, the protractors you place on the maps to figure azimuth and distance.

The buck sergeant who taught the classes told me he'd repaired the .50 cal. guns but had never fired one. I put him and his assistant on a gun and told them to knock their socks off.

The next day, Thursday, while we were cleaning the .50 cal. guns, my pain-in-the-butt buck sergeant came in and thanked me for helping. We shook hands and parted company as friends.

On Friday we loaded the trucks to depart early the next morning for Dayton. Sunday we unloaded and put up everything by 1630 hours and were dismissed.

***

I drove to see my ex-wife Charlotte to ask if she wanted to get back together. She said yes.

I found a three-bedroom trailer house, paid the deposit and one month rent, paid the deposit on electricity, and rented a U-Haul trailer. We loaded her and the kids' clothes and things and moved easily enough.

We stayed the night at our new place. Then, the next morning she went back to Pikeville, to a guy named Malcom Thurston.

I couldn't believe it.

I called the lawyer. I had filed for divorce the year before but didn't pay the fee, so I sent him $250 to finish paying the fee and thirty days later I was a free man. There'd be no more patching up things with Charlotte.

I left Chattanooga to return to Junction City.

Chapter Nineteen

Kansas Army Reserve School – 1987-89

Back in Kansas, I joined the Kansas Army Reserve training school as an instructor.

There are differences between the Army Reserve and the National Guard. The Reserve is under control of the federal government and can't be called into domestic service. The National Guard evolved from state militias and can be called to service by the federal government or state government. National Guard units are often called to service by governors to help with relief following natural disasters. In recent years many Reserve and National Guard members have served on active duty in Iraq and Afghanistan.

I was assigned to the training school in Topeka. The school had two functions. The first was PLDC (Primary Leadership Development Course) to prepare a specialist fourth class to become a buck sergeant, and the BNOC (Basic Non-commissioned Officer Course) to prepare the buck sergeant E-5 to become staff sergeant E-6.

The second function was training MOS military work number 11B40: infantryman, grunt, or ground-pounder.

This group was where I was assigned.

On a regular weekend drill, we instructors just drilled on Saturday but received full pay, four days' pay of $360. We taught MOS classes for $360, and also received one day's pay of $90 for prep like making lesson plans. We would go to a Guard unit on its weekend drill: eight hours Saturday and eight hours Sunday to teach infantry formations and tactics then our monthly drill. Travel expenses paid 75 cents per mile for gas, $40 hotel expenses per night (usually two nights), and $2 per meal (usually six meals). Altogether, I made about $1,600 for a month of training. At the end of summer camp the trainees had two MOS skills.

***

In spring 1987 the 1st Infantry Division at Fort Riley started expanding Marshall Field, which was the helicopter area.

I went to work for a company installing the water and sewer lines there. I made $9 an hour.

We started our water line around four feet from where the main water came on to Marshall Field. We dug a trench down four feet, putting us a foot below where the ground can freeze in winter. Lining the bottom with gravel, we then lay eight-inch-diameter by ten-feet-long PVC pipe. We glued the pipes together, running to the barracks, hanger area and maintenance shops. After we laid the pipe on the gravel we covered the pipe with a foot of gravel then replaced the dirt. Inside the buildings' foundations we packed the dirt down added more dirt on top. We branched off the main eight-inch pipe with two- and one-inch pipes for showers and water basins, cutting them off three feet above ground.

***

I spent two weeks at the Kansas National Guard summer camp.

A commander during this session thought he'd float an APC (Armored Personnel Carrier) across a river instead of going over a bridge. You can float a steel APC but you have to put in the drain plugs, and he didn't.

The river was extra high and the APC filled with water and sank so far down that only the top foot of the vehicle's nine-foot radio antenna was above the water. All the people got out and swam to shore except one man who dog-paddled to within three feet of shore then drowned.

***

After summer camp, I returned to Junction City to find the construction company had replaced me.

In another career change, I went to work making and delivering pizza.

We'd roll the dough to sizes of ten, twelve and sixteen inches and place them on thin tin pans, spread tomato paste on the dough, and add the cheese and toppings. The pies were placed in an oven for ten minutes, removed, cut in slices, boxed and placed in an insulated bag for delivery in thirty minutes or less.

I did this for a month before switching jobs again.

***

The Junction City school district needed bus drivers. I had a Class D driver's license, and landed a job there.

Drivers were paid for four hours a day: two hours in the morning rounding up the monsters and delivering them to school, and two hours in the afternoon returning the monsters home to their parents.

My first bus was eighteen feet long. My route ran from the bus barn at Sixth and Chestnut up Washington Street, across the river to Camp Forsyth where I pick up a first grader. I placed him in the seat right behind me and let him play with his toys the whole ride. I never heard a peep out of him. The rest of the kids were junior- and high-school monsters. They sat in the back and didn't bother the first grader.

On Trooper Drive just to the left of the paved road, I could see the stream bed that had been a tank trail to Custer Hill when I was stationed at Fort Riley from 1961 to 1964.

I drove through the three housing areas. The first was along Trooper Drive, the second was along 1st Infantry Division Road, and the third was at the fork of the road 1st Infantry Division Road and Ammo Drive. Below the housing areas, the road forked again and one went by the hospital the other ended at Camp Funston.

After I picked up the kids I drove down 1st Infantry Division Road to Kansas Highway 18, turned right, went around the circle and buffalo corral, across the river and off post on Grant Street then left on 14th Street to the junior high and continued on Ash to the high school. From there I went back to the bus barn until afternoon and then reversed the route.

The bus drivers could also volunteer to drive students to ball games.

For my second year as bus driver, I was assigned a twelve-foot bus to drive a rural route.

I drove around fifteen miles east of Junction City to pick up about sixteen monsters, some of whom were related to each other. Leading to Christmas vacation, I told the kids to bring money and a list of what they wanted me to pick up for food as long as they put the trash in the trash bags. The day before school was out, I told the kids they could have water-gun fights as long as they stayed in the back of the bus and didn't shoot anybody up front.

Just before school ended, six of us drivers went to Manhattan for a district bus rodeo. We drove an obstacle course, and backed the buses to within a foot of a metal bar. I took second place in the district.

***

That summer I worked a month for Dale Simmons Moving and Storage in Junction City. It was a business I'd stopped at many times during my trucking days.

Dale and his brother-in-law owned a farm outside of Dalhart, Texas, and they needed me to help deliver a grain trailer and a combine. I drove a longnose International semi-tractor that had two four-speed transmissions hooked one behind the other. It had sixteen gears and could easily run 80 miles an hour.

I followed Dale to the ranch and dropped the grain trailer. Then we drove to Mount Vernon, Illinois, where Dale's brother-in-law lived, and we loaded the combine on a lowboy, a flatbed trailer. We took Interstate 64 to St. Louis, I-44 to Oklahoma City, I-40 to Amarillo then up state Highway 87 to Dalhart.

Dale and his brother-in-law drove the combine while I and another driver operated two trucks and the grain trailer. We hauled eight loads apiece per day. At night we stayed in a motel. We finished hauling wheat in two weeks. We took the combine back to Mt. Vernon, and I went back to Dalhart to pick up the grain trailer.

Back home, drive one of Dale's moving trucks out state for him on a job. I took a shipment to Pittsburgh, unloaded half the trailer, drove to Chicago, unloaded another shipment at a warehouse then the trailer was emptied except the deck. The agent said he had a shipment of 5,000 pounds at a house. A warehouse worker tried leading me to a house on a street that had a nine-and-a-half-foot high underpass, but my trailer was thirteen-and-a-half feet tall. I backed up to where I could turn on a side street. I told the worker to get me to the house using a street with no overpasses and he did.

I took inventory of the furniture, checking for dents and tears. The shipper told me he had a twelve-foot chest freezer in the basement. I opened the freezer lid to see it was full of meat.

"You need to unload the freezer," I said.

"The man at the warehouse said I didn't have to unload it," he said.

"This is Friday, and after I load I'm headed to Junction City," I said. "It's going to sit all weekend thawing out."

He unloaded the freezer and gave the meat to neighbors. To get the freezer up the stairs, I had to remove the handrail going to the basement. Once outside, I loaded it on the floor of the trailer and stacked the washer and dryer on top. I filled the trailer and still had to find room for the picnic table and chairs. I strapped the table to the outside of the back doors. I stuffed the lawn chairs and tools in the truck. I strapped three bikes behind my cab.

After I got loaded I weighed the truck. Instead of 5,000 pounds, it weighed 10,000 pounds.

***

That summer my next-to-oldest daughter Loretta married a man named Evans. A Baptist preacher did the ceremony. They got married at a friend's trailer house at Milford Lake, near Junction City. I think Nora, Nancy, Tammy, and Ella were there.

Their mother Mary was there and started running her mouth. Instead of arguing and fighting with her, I walked five miles back to town.

Just before Christmas, my next-to-youngest daughter Tammy got married to a man named John Buck. They had the same Baptist preacher as Loretta, but rented a church.

I walked Tammy down the aisle. It was a proud day for me.

***

After the first of January, Dale Simmons took that International truck we used for harvest and put a dump-truck bed on it and change out the rear axles.

He asked me to drive to Orlando, Florida, to take the truck to sell at auction. I told the superintendent of the bus drivers that I was going out of town for three days.

I got in the truck at 4 a.m., and headed out Interstate 70 East. With the truck's rear end changed out, the air drag cut its speed from eighty to fifty-five miles an hour. Around 5 p.m. I was passing Lambert Airport in St. Louis when one of the axles broke.

I called Dale, who said to have a wrecker tow it to an International dealer. It took three days to fix, by which time I should've been back to the bus barn. Around noon Thursday, I picked up the truck. I needed to be in Orlando by noon Saturday.

I continued on I- 64 to Mount Vernon, I-57 to Carbondale, hung a left on I-24 through Chattanooga, a hard right on I-75 South to Macon, hopped on I-16 to Savannah, and a hard right on I-95 into Orland. I drove it all at fifty-five miles an hour, only stopping for fuel and an hour's sleep.

I arrived in Orland around 10 a.m. Saturday. I washed the truck and drove to the auction field. A construction company from Gaum bought the truck. They took it to the railroad yard and shipped it to Galveston, Texas, where it was loaded on a ship to Gaum.

Dale met me at the auction and afterward took me to a bus station to head home. The only one leaving was the slow bus that stopped at every cow pasture. It was a four-day trip to Junction City.

The school bus superintendent was going to fire me for being gone so long and not letting him know my status, but I got to keep my job.

***

Keeping that bus job wouldn't really have mattered. With no National Guard MOS classes to teach at this point and only four hours a day driving the school bus, I was starving.

I went to an Army recruiter and told him I wanted to go back on active duty.

Back in the Army, I could make as much as I had been without switching jobs every few months.

The recruiter would have told me no due to my age, but he looked at my DD Form 214 and saw my Silver Star Medal, the third-highest award given by the Army.

The recruiter had to send out police checks to Wenatchee, Washington, where I was born, and Delta, Colorado, and Helena, Montana, where I was raised. Police checks were also sent to Junction City and Chattanooga. I'd gotten speeding tickets in North Carolina and Alabama, and they had six months to send police reports.

I went to an induction center for a physical. I was drawing ten percent disability for hearing loss, but didn't think that would matter. The sergeant major at the MEPT (Military Entrance Processing) station called me later and told me to clean out my ears with a cleaning rod and retake my hearing test. I then passed it.

The recruiters didn't receive all the police checks back in six months and had to send them all out again. The reports all came back in time for the recruiter to place me in a standby unit.

The reports showed I had a bad-check charge and twenty-eight days of lost time (jail time) for an obscene literature charge from the Department of the Army. The secretary of the Army signed my waivers.

It wasn't until February 1990 when I was able to enlist back into the Army.

***

I headed to the MEPT in Charlotte, North Carolina, driving an empty trailer for Dale, which I'd fill up on the way home.

"MOS?" the sergeant major asked at the MEPT.

"I'll stay a grunt," I said.

"You can go back through basic or sometimes not worry about it," he said.

I wanted to have gone back to basic. As a forty-eight-year-old corporal combat veteran, I could have helped the drill instructors. If the day's training was something I didn't want to do, I wouldn't do it.

With my spit-shine boots and military creases (two razor-sharp creases in the shirt front and three razor-sharp creases in the pants, extra heavy starched razor-creased pant legs), what would they do? Bend my dog tags and send me back to Vietnam?

I was excused from basic. In the long run, it was better I didn't go through it because it had become co-ed. With women in the same barracks, that would be like putting a fox in the hen house. I'd have been in trouble all the time.

"I want to go back to Fort Carson," I said to the sergeant major.

He typed it in the computer. When he tried to enter my birthday, January 14, 1942, the computer laughed at him.

He had another recruiter try to type in my birthday. The computer still wouldn't accept me.

They finally tried to enter my birthday as January 14, 1953, making me thirty-five years old. Then the computer accepted me for an infantry slot at Fort Carson.

Enlistment appeared complete, and I took off for home.

I was driving a Peterbilt with a big motor that made hauling seven tons of furniture feel like an empty trailer. I loaded a shipment out of a warehouse bound for a soldier's house in Leavenworth, Kansas. I couldn't find anyone to help me unload, so I called the soldier to say I'd go through Junction City to pick up a helper. He wanted his furniture sooner than later, so I went straight to Leavenworth and he helped unload the heavy stuff.

***

Knowing I was returning to active duty, I went to the Marlow White military clothing store in Leavenworth to order a set of the Army dress blues, for formal parties or traveling. These uniforms are issued to the honor guard and band members, so anybody else who wants a set can buy their own.

There were three styles to choose from. I chose the style with the full-length jacket that is like the Army green uniform.

"I'm going to be spending some money," I told the clerk. "First, I need seven gold stripes to put on the uniform." One stripe represented three years' service, so seven covered my initial service plus my National Guard and Reserve service.

They measured me for the coat, size 38. While trying on one coat, the clerk remembered one in the stock room, and returned with a coat with seven stripes just like I wanted. They tucked in the sleeves, made two tucks in the back and, like magic, it became a perfect fit.

All that was left were the corporal stripes. I added a fancy white shirt and cuff links, a pair of patent-leather shoes and a blue dress hat. The cost for the uniform was $300. To this I started adding my miniature medals:

Oak leaf showing second award of the medal - 95 cents,

Silver Star Medal - $10.95,

Bronze Star with V and two oak leaves - $10.95 plus 95 cents for each device,

Purple Heart with two oak leaves - $15.95,

Army Commendation Medal - $10.95,

Good Conduct Medal - $10.95,

National Defense Service Medal - $10.95,

U.S. Vietnam Service Medal with one Silver Star and two Bronze Stars for seven different campaigns - $10.95,

Vietnam Campaign Medal with 1960s device - $14.95,

Armed Forces Reserve Medal - $10.95

RVN Gallantry Cross - $13.95,

RVN Civic Action - $12.95

Total for miniature medals - $160 dollars for twelve medals.

While I was back on active duty for my second round, 1990-1998, the Army changed awards. I added the following medals:

Army Achievement Medal

Armed Forces Expeditionary Medal

Air Force Achievement Medal

Army NCO Professional Ribbon

Army Service Ribbon

Army Overseas ribbon

When you are in a unit in war the unit receives a unit citation and can wear those unit citations. I have the following unit citations:

Presidential (blue)

Army Meritorious (red)

RVN Gallantry Cross

RVN Civic Action Medal

Korean Presidential

Two Bronze Stars

Legion of Merit

This last medal, the Legion of Merit, isn't ranked highest but it's one of the most valued. It's usually received at retirement by officers ranked at colonel or above when they've commanded a battalion division. Some sergeant majors and first sergeants will receive the Legion of Merit. Of the twenty-two people who retired in my group in 1998 – one warrant officer, six or seven sergeant majors and first sergeants, eight or nine sergeants first class, two or three staff sergeants – there was one Legion of Merit awarded, twenty Meritorious Service Medals, one ARM. One of the first sergeants had applied four times for the Legion of Merit and was turned down four times. I was the oldest retiree in the group, at fifty-six years, and had the youngest wife, thirty.

Chapter Twenty

The Next-To-Last Haul

My next to last trip driving a big rig for Dale Simmons was a trip to Miami, Florida.

I'd bought the Florida trip and fuel permits and they sent the wrong trip permit, but I didn't realize it until it was too late.

I reached the Florida DOT scales at Pensacola, drove across the scales then pulled off to the side, handing the DOT clerk my paperwork and permits. The man returned from the office.

"One of your permits is wrong," he said. "Circle around and cross the scales again. Then park and come back in the office."

The shipment weighed 18,000 pounds. I went in the office.

"For not having the correct permit, you are being fined $650," the man said.

I called my boss, Dale. He said he wouldn't pay the fine.

I had to do some quick thinking. The clerk didn't take my truck keys.

"A patrolman will drive you the twelve miles into Pensacola to a motel," the man said.

While I waited for the police officer, I made the first step of my plan. I went out to the truck and unplugged the trailer lights. I returned to the office to wait for my ride.

From the motel office in Pensacola, I called the permits office. A cab took me there, where I picked up the proper permit. I hung around the motel ate at a restaurant, waiting until dark.

I hitchhiked back to the scales.

I started the truck and built up the air in the lines. The DOT people were too busy to notice and couldn't see me due to trucks blocking their windows.

Under cover of night, I slowly drove a mile down the road then stopped to plug in the trailer lights. Going around some side roads, I finally got back on I-95. At Miami, I unloaded in a warehouse.

"If you wait until Monday, I can fill the truck for the return trip," the agent said.

Knowing my status with the DOT scales, I declined. "The boss wants me back sooner than later," I said.

Again, I waited for dark then ran like hell back up I-95. When I crossed the state line into Alabama around 3 a.m., I pulled over to sleep a while. If the Florida DOT had caught me after I left the scales, they would have put me under the jail.

***

When my youngest daughter was fourteen, she was placed in foster care with a military family. They moved to Hawaii.

She came of age and married a GI. They moved to Juarez, Mexico. She gave birth to a boy January 10, 1990, four days before my forty-eighth birthday.

I tried for a year to get her phone number and address from my ex-wife Mary. She wouldn't give it to me. When I'd ask Nora, Loretta or Tammy they'd end up arguing with Mary too. I finally got the address and wrote my daughter a letter. She never responded.

***

My last trip for Dale Simmons took me to Fort Huachuca, Arizona. From there I drove to El Paso to try to see my youngest daughter, Ella. She wouldn't see me.

***

By early 1989, I'd been going with a woman bus driver named Sylvia Rodriguez. She had two daughters and a boy. The daughters, Ellen and Desiree, lived with her, and the oldest had a baby boy. Sylvia's son lived in Hawaii. Sylvia was four years younger than me, born in 1946.

Around Valentine's Day, I rented a church and had the same preacher that Loretta and Tammy. Sylvia and I tied the knot.

For the gowns we had to go to Manhattan, Kansas, to a shop for formal wear. I think Sylvia wanted a little pink dress. Desiree picked a pale blue. Ellen wanted white, but the shop didn't have a white dress in Ellen's size, and had to order it from Chicago. The shop got it the day before the wedding, however, the shop, in trying to make another sale, let another woman try on the dress. When we picked up the dresses, the salesperson told me they'd let somebody wear the dress. I was angry about it because I didn't want to buy a used dress, and if there been time before the wedding, I'd have made the shop replace Ellen's dress.

In addition to the same preacher, the funny thing that Loretta's, Tammy's and my marriage had in common was that after about five years, all of us got divorced.

Chapter Twenty-One

Return to Fort Carson – 1990

On February 9, 1990, my Army recruiter called to ask if I was ready to go to the induction center at Kansas City. I said yes. I had to be ready to get on the bus at 6 p.m.

At 5 p.m. I took a shower. By 5:30 p.m. I'd put on my Army class A uniform and Sylvia and I got in the car to drive the five blocks to the bus station. My recruiter was there. He handed me a ticket.

I sat in the middle of the bus. All I carried were my briefcase and garment bag, inside of which was my Army Dress Blue uniform. It was a short ride to Kansas City.

There a bus clerk announced that everybody going to the induction center should go to door number one. There were six of us, two young women and three other men, all carrying small suitcases. As the van driver called our names, we got in the van. He took us to a hotel.

"By 0500 hours dress and report to the restaurant for breakfast," the van driver said. "At 0600 hours, be here in the lobby to leave in van for the ride to the MEPS (Military Entrance Processing Station)." Then the clerk assigned rooms: Ronda and Betty, room 205; Jones and Richard, room 206; Sims and Roberts, room 207; Babcock room 208.

Two kids maybe 18 years old stood there chattering like chipmunks, looking lost and uncertain what was going on.

I shook my head and asked myself if I was ever that young and dumb.

Everybody got on the elevator ride to the third floor then back to the second. After finding my room and hanging up my garment bag, I went down to the bar for a rum and Coke. I visited a bit with the young barmaid, and after a couple drinks I went to my room.

I woke up at 4 a.m. and made use of the two-cup coffee maker. After showering, I took off the blue infantry rope and combat infantry badge from the green uniform and put them on the blue uniform. I turned in my meal ticket for a big order of coffee, toast, hard-fried eggs. It reminded me of fishing and hunting with grandpa. He had a frying pan with two inches of grease that he'd use to fry the bacon and over-easy eggs.

We arrived at MEPS in Kansas City by 0630. The doctor pulled out our tongues, hit us on the knees, felt our chests to see if we're still alive, and pronounced us fit for duty.

The recruiters set us down to go over our enlistment papers. Mine typed in my birthday, January 14, 1942, and the computer takes it. Duty field: [11B20] infantry. Duty station: Fort Carson Colorado. Everything was correct, and I signed the enlistment papers.

After everybody signed their enlistment papers, we were taken in a room. An officer told us to raise our right hands and repeat after him, "I Corporal Russell A. Babcock solemnly swear to defend my country against all enemies foreign and domestic." We're in the Army now, not behind a plow.

I signed out on ten-day leave. I asked when I could get a bus ticket back to Junction City.

"You're on leave now. We can't give you a bus ticket," the recruiter said. A recruiter from Topeka offered me a ride as far as he was going, so I called the recruiter in Junction City to pick me up in Topeka and get me home.

While waiting on the Topeka recruiter to leave, I stood around watching. There was an Air Force full colonel with three ribbons glaring at me. I flipped him off.

One recruiter was talking to a young woman, something about SPC-4 or E-4. I asked, "What does a corporal E-4 get paid?" He didn't know.

Finally the Topeka recruiter was ready to go. It was dark when we reached Topeka. My Junction City recruiter was there, and he got me home around 7 p.m.

Because Sylvia and the kids hadn't been to Colorado, I planned to take them with me for a few days. We took Interstate 70 West to Limon, Colorado, and State Highway 24 to Colorado Springs. We passed Fort Carson to Pueblo on I-35 South then headed west on State Highway 50 to Royal Gorge National Park.

We entered the east gate. If the year was dry, with little rain, the park rangers would sell small bags of alfalfa pellets to feed the deer. As you drive through the park, the deer stand next to the road and move their hooves up and down telling you to stop and feed them potato chips and peanut-butter sandwiches.

In rainy years, when there's plenty green for the deer to eat, the rangers post signs telling tourists not to feed the deer, but the deer and the tourists don't pay any attention to the signs. The deer will eat out of your hand then shake hands thanks.

Just before you left Royal Gorge Park, you paid $5 to drive across the world's highest suspension bridge. From the bridge straight down to the Arkansas River is 955 feet. We drove across, returned to Highway 50, turned right and went back to Fort Carson.

I rented a room for us in a guest house, and went to the PX for some shopping. That evening we went to the movie theater. We got there before the doors opened. It was cold and lightly snowing so we went into the bowling alley. I saw a black man talking to someone, and I knew I knew him but didn't know where from. After he finished talking, he came up to me. He was my first sergeant when I was at Fort Carson in the 5th Infantry, 1966-67. He told me that less than a year after I'd left, he'd retired because of gambling and drinking problems.

The next day being Monday, I signed into the replacement company. Sylvia and the kids started the drive back to Junction City. I had a duffle bag, a B4 garment bag in which I had my set of dress blues, white dress shirt, two sets of Army dress greens two long-sleeve shirts, two short-sleeve shirts, eight sets of heavily starched fatigues. I had my patent-leather low-quarter shoes and two pairs of jump boots. I'd stopped using shoe polish to shine my boots like glass in favor of a rubber-like paint that made them look like patent leather. My fatigue cap I sprayed six coats of starch, blocked to stand up like the old Fidel Castro caps. Before entering a building, usually you'd take your cap off but I couldn't roll mine up put it in your pocket because of the starch. I hated the Fidel cap, but I guess I starched it to mess with officers and high-ranking NCOs.

In my Samsonite hard-case briefcase that I bought at Carson in 1971, I carried a copy of my enlistment papers and my original certificates. I made copies to place in my new 201 file. The first sergeant let me copy the certificates and then I bought frames for the originals. I had my Silver Star plus orders, Bronze Star/V-device plus orders, three Purple Hearts, and my jungle bunny (jungle expert certificate).

The first sergeant wouldn't let me wear my uniforms until I went to the quartermaster store. I went on Friday afternoon and got a complete issue of uniforms: four sets of fatigues, two sets Army dress greens, two short-sleeve shirts, two long-sleeve shirts, one pair low quarter shoes, two pair combat boots, two black ties, one service cap, two fatigue caps, rain coat, long dress overcoat, two towels and wash clothes, six T-shirts, six pairs of boxer shorts, six pairs of boot socks, three pairs black dress socks.

Monday morning we ate a nice breakfast of fried eggs, bacon, and coffee. We went to the hospital for health check. The nurse did blood pressure and took a blood sample then told me I had high cholesterol, but it was partly from the greasy food and stress.

At 0800 hours we arrived at Personnel and Finance. At Finance I started a checking account so I could get paid twice a month, and turned in leave papers to be paid for leave. Next we went in Personnel three at a time.

A staff sergeant MP who looked capable was at the first desk, but I got the middle desk with a green female SPC-4 clerk. All she could do on my 201 was type my name, age and rank.

"Do you have any certificates you want in your file?" she asked

I started flipping the certificates in a circle on the floor. While I did this, the soldier next to me also had a copy of a letter from President Nixon that the MP was looking at. His clerk was a smart-ass who said that unless the certificate signed by a general it wasn't going in. The MP asked the clerk if the commander in chief would be OK. The clerk said yes and shut up.

The MP saw my stack of paper and asked, "Do you have your letter from Tricky Dicky, too?"

I opened my briefcase and held up my original. That was the first time those young people had seen letters like that.

My green clerk told me I would have to come back for personnel to look at my DD-214 and said she didn't see a discharge or enlistment paper for one four-year period. I'd have to get a copy from the military.

Until my actual military time could be verified, my first month's pay was $850 for corporal E4 with zero years of service. I made an appointment at finance to have somebody figure how much time I had with twelve years active in five different Guard and Reserve units in addition to Army time. It took the woman about forty-five minutes.

"The best I can figure you have twenty-two years ten months," she said.

I told her, "That's close enough for government work."

They couldn't place me at the rank I was when I left in 1973. They put me back at the bottom, but the maximum time for a specialist E4 without earning promotion was ten years, or you were discharged, so due to my time they made me a corporal. The salary of $1,070 meant that as a corporal I was making $270 more than the $900 I made as a sergeant first class E7 with twelve years' service.

I was assigned to the 2nd Battalion 8th Infantry Regiment. The 4th Infantry Division was at Fort Carson. The first sergeant driver took me to headquarters. I unloaded all my bags inside by the door, turned in my orders and filled out a bunch of papers. They were going to assign me to Charlie Company.

While I waited for somebody from C Company to come to get me, a sergeant major poked his head out his door and told me to come and see him the next morning.

Two men showed up to help carry all my stuff across the field. At the company commander and first sergeant offices, the first sergeant told me I'd be in second platoon. The company barrack was fifty yards across the basketball court. It had three floors: ground floor for 1st Platoon, second floor for 2nd Platoon, third floor for 3rd Platoon.

They assigned me a room with a man who was TDY (temporary duty) with another unit. The next morning I talked with the first sergeant.

I told him, “I'm forty-eight and I have eight years to retire, which means I’ll be fifty-six to hit my twenty-year minimum, but that’s one year over the fifty-five mandatory retirement age.”

He couldn't figure it out.

“I have the Silver Star, which exempts me from the age cutoff,” I said.

The sergeant major wanted to see me, but was busy for several days. When he did meet with me, he said, “I want to bring you into S-3 intelligence because you have too much experience to be in a squad and basic. You can get away with anything but murder.”

A couple days later at PT, the platoon gave me a PT test because of my age. I think I had to do twenty pushups and twenty-two sit-ups to receive a passing score of sixty percent. The minimum for the two-miles was thirty minutes, but I ran it in fourteen-and-a-half minutes. I passed the PT test.

At this time I still had eight inches or so of hair on top of my head I use to comb my hair forward with a cowlick to the left. If we weren't wearing caps for PT, my hair would wave at everybody.

Every Thursday the platoons could do different training. The squad did a five-mile road march. I wore a pair of the new boots and got blisters on my feet but completed the march. The next week the company was going to run an obstacle course with live rounds firing over our heads. In the basic obstacle course, we crawled under barbed wire two feet off the ground with the machine gun on a four-foot stand. For running under it, the gun was mounted on a six-foot stand on top of ten-foot hill.

I wouldn't have had to run under the gunfire, but there were supposed to be VIPs watching and the platoon sergeant was short of men so he asked me to run the course. Afterward, as we were in the tent, the commander came over to me he asked when I last went through basic training. I told him three weeks in 1961. It was before he was born.

A couple weeks later the company went to the field to complete some tasks to see which squad was the best in the battalion.

The company commander and first sergeant didn't say anything but I could see in their eyes, "You dumbass, you're too old for this."

The first task, we left company defense camp, marching eight miles. Along the way, smoke and M80 fire crackers were thrown to see how we reacted to artillery fire.

The squad leader yelled, "Right 50,", which means run to your right side for fifty yards, make sure everybody is there then continue on. I was leading the squad, we completed the eight miles in less than two hours. We ranked first in battalion on that event.

After that, the first sergeant, CO and other officers and NCOS kept their eyes on us.

The next event was firing live ammo from an armored vehicle. I was the track commander and in firing on the moving targets I hit the most targets and scored the highest in the battalion. My squad took first place again.

The third event was defensive live fire. Each squad broke down to pairs, each placed in bunkers. A target would pop up at different ranges from twenty-five yards to 300 yards, and we fired every time we saw a target. Our squad again hit the most targets in the least amount of time, first place again.

The last event was to attack an enemy defensive position. We drove our APC 400 yards from the objective, a hill. We turned and went into a ravine, stopped the APC, dropped the ramp, dismounted and charged for the hill.

I had an M203. When we got close to the concertina wire, I fired a smoke grenade to simulate a wire breach. Before I left the track, I'd put my sleeping pad rolled up between my pack suspenders and my back. The bed mat must've fallen out during our repeated firing and moving over 400 hundred yards. We were ten feet from the wire when I reached for the mat, and realized it was missing.

I figured, OK, we'd do this the John Wayne way. I held my rifle vertical, ran to the wire and fell over the wire so the other men of the squad could run up and jump using my back to bounce over the wire. My helmet forced my head down, putting my nose against my gun barrel, splitting the skin. When I rolled over the wire and got ready to catch up with the squad, the company commander grabbed my arm to have me wait for a medic. The medic put a bandage on my nose.

Again our squad scored the best time. We were the best squad in the battalion, for which the battalion gave the squad leader an Army Commendation Medal.

Once every month the battalion commander had everybody go to the theater to talk about upcoming events or present awards,

A week after the competition the sergeant major, named Martinez, called a meeting for all NCOs about an extra guard detail and talked about other events. Then he asked if we had any complaints after fifteen minutes of meeting.

Sergeant Major Martinez had me stand and tell the NCOs a little bit about myself.

"Well," I said, "I first enlisted in July '61, spent four years at Fort Riley. I earned the EIB in '64 as a SPC-4 made sergeant. January '66 went to Fort Carson. The 5th was activated June '66. I made staff sergeant E-6 June '66. Went to Vietnam September '67, in October '67 I received three Purple Hearts, the Silver Star and Bronze Star. November '70 was back to Vietnam as advisor up north at Hue. Left the army November '73, played in the Guard and Reserve nine years enlisted back in the Army February '90. I'm forty-eight years old."

***

Because I was a combat veteran, I could wear either the 25th Division patch or the MACV patch on my right sleeve, and I could wear either the EIB or CIB over the left pocket. On one uniform I had the 4th Infantry Division four-leaf patch on the left shoulder (the unit that you're in at time), and above left pocket the CIB

25th Division tropical lighting patch. Another uniform had the 4th on left shoulder and CIB over left pocket, MACV right shoulder. The next two uniforms had MACV patches on right shoulder. All four sets of my Army greens had 4th patches on left shoulder, and the CIB or EIB were medals I placed above all the Army ribbons: blue infantry disk on collar brass, blue rope on right shoulder, two 25th Division patches on right shoulder, two MACV patches on right shoulder.

***

My battalion commander Colonel Dees and Sergeant Major Martinez were not combat veterans. My brigade commander was a combat veteran who fought with the 25th Infantry Division. The brigade sergeant major fought with one team of MACV. I had both of those patches.

The next month when everybody went to the theater, Colonel Dees talked about new events and old events. Our squad was seated in the first row of seats. Colonel Dees named us the overall top squad in the battalion, and we walked up on the stage for Colonel Dee to present the squad leader with the Army Commendation Medal with certificate and a battalion certificate for top squad.

Then Colonel Dees presented me with an Army Achievement Medal with certificate, battalion certificate, and he presented battalion certificates to the rest of the squad. The division sergeant major plus the brigade commander and brigade sergeant major came across shaking hands.

Colonel Dees announced the top squad in assault of objective. We marched on stage for battalion certificates and more handshakes.

Next Colonel Dees announced best squad in defense, and handed us the last round of certificates. During handshakes, Sergeant Major Martinez jabbed the division sergeant major in the back and pointed at me and told him, "That SOB is 48!" That brought the curtains down.

We were dismissed to return to our companies, and got the rest of the afternoon off.

***

After the board they figure up all the points and come out with your promotion points you have to have high enough points to be promoted. How do you get these points company commander representation up to 200 points PT test up to 50 points, weapon qualification, up to 50 points education points up to 100 points military education up to 100 points, promotion board 400 you add all these scores up for your promotion points you see what the department of the Army says you have to have to be promoted to next highest rank.

My score: company commander 200 points, PT test 50 points, weapons qualification 50 points, high school education 75 points, military education 50 points, promotion board 380, total points 800. The Department of the Army said the points I needed to be promoted to staff sergeant was 998. The qualification didn't drop below 998 for two years.

About eight months later, Sergeant Major Martinez moved up to S-3 intelligence.

I became Colonel Dees' track commander and was placed in charge of the other drivers.

***

As soon as the kids' school was out in May 1990, I drove to Junction City. I told Sylvia and the family to pack up to move to Colorado in a couple days.

While they got ready, I hot-footed to St. Louis. It was time to get my missing military records.

The National Personnel Records Center, at 9700 Page Boulevard, was where all military records were kept. They'd had a fire in one section that burned many records from WWII, Korea and Vietnam, but I hoped they had what I needed.

A guard called upstairs with my name and rank. A few minutes later a woman came down and took me upstairs, where she handed me two folders about three inches thick. One folder was the twelve years of active duty and the other was all the Guard and Reserve service. I told the woman I needed a copy of everything except pay vouchers.

They sent me downstairs to a cafe to wait. I ate then read a Mack Bolan book for around two-and-a-half hours, until they brought close to 500 pages documenting everything.

I thanked them and left. I got back to Junction City early in the morning. We loaded a U-Haul and drove to Fort Carson. I rented a room in the guest house for a week, until we found an apartment out Gate 5 in Fountain, around nine miles from the company. I sorted through all the papers by dates: July '61-August '64; November '64- November '67; November '67- November '73; January '74-November '76 in the Colorado Guard; December '76 - October '79 in the Tennessee Guard; January '80-'83 in the Tennessee Guard; September '87-December '89 in the Kansas Reserve; February '90-May '90 in the 4th Infantry Division.

I bought a fireproof filing safe to keep everything in.

I called Personnel and told them I needed an appointment to fix my 201 file. Personnel said to be there at 0900 hours on a Wednesday. I talked to a staff sergeant.

"Finance has to figure how much time in the service you have," he said.

"I've already done that," I said.

"Come back next Wednesday," he said.

I went back the next Wednesday.

"You were right," he said. "We've already calculated your service time."

I called him a dumbass.

A female staff sergeant clerk sat down with me and scanned my records. She started typing across the first four lines:

Fort Riley, Kansas: A Co. 28th Inf. RFC. December 1961,

SPC-4 August 1962

C Co. 2-12 Inf. February 1963

Honorable discharge August 1964

She figured my service at around 103 months. Then she started filing down. After about two hours of typing, flapping our gums, scratching our heads, checking over the papers, we decided we had everything we needed and were as accurate as we could get. I thanked the woman and put my papers in my briefcase.

***

The apartment complex where we were staying was around five miles from Colorado Springs Airport.

One Saturday afternoon a Boeing 727 developed engine trouble and couldn't make it to the runway. There wasn't enough open land for the pilot to glide in for a landing, so the pilot plunged the plane into the ground. It was buried so far in dirt that just a small part of the tail was above ground.

I heard the noise, and opened the front door. Just a hundred yards – one football field – from the door was a big hole in the ground with smoke coming out.

The FAA came to investigate. Some post engineers set up lights and started marking, digging, and removing plane parts and bodies.

***

It was rumored there were pockets of Bloods and Crips gang members in the area. The girls started school. Ellen was in high school and Desi was in grade school. They had several friends who would come over and stay the night. On a Friday night I heard some noise. I went outside and saw two black guys beating out the windows kid's parent's car.

I called the police. When they arrived I told them what happened and that one of the men had entered a second-floor apartment.

The next weekend somebody fired a gun in the archway.

I'd gotten my sergeant stripes so I put in for housing on post.

Before we moved, one more incident happened. Sylvia's girls were staying overnight at friends. Sylvia and I went to bed around 1 a.m. Not long after, a squad of police knocked the door down. I woke up and see two men in my bedroom door. I jumped up to get tough with them and they yelled, "Police!"

I was in T-shirt and shorts and Sylvia was in bra and panties. The police handcuffed and took us to the living room. The front door lay across the recliner in front of the doorway. The police said some of the girls' friends were Crips and sold drugs, so they searched the dresser, closet, shelves, and phone records. They didn't find anything.

Evidently, friends of Sylvia's daughters were connected to gangs, and someone once saw them come in our apartment and turned us in. We moved on post as quickly as we could.

A month later, Sylvia received word that one of her nieces was moving to Fort Carson. Her husband was a sergeant first class in the signal corp. He was from the Solomon Islands. Things would not turn out well with them.

***

At the base one day, I walked in a tent and saw a captain and a two-star general standing there. I yelled attention and walked up to the general to salute and report.

"Where is everybody?" he asked.

"Out on maneuvers," I said. "Sir, I noticed you have a MACV patch."

"I was Team l, 1970-71," he said

"I was in Team 3, same years," I said.

The general's name was Jacob, and he was the 4th Infantry Division's new commander.

***

After we returned from Fort Hood in February, Sergeant Major Martinez, decided to hold an enlisted formal ball. He rented the Air Force NCO club because it was bigger than our club. The NCOs that had dress blues wore them, and all other personal wore dress greens.

Staff Sergeant Napoleon Johnson, who'd been in the 3rd Infantry Honor Guard at Arlington, wore his dress blues with his full-size medals, all highly polished.

Sergeant Major Martinez placed a thirty-gallon pot on the table in front of him.

"The forefathers of our unit used to make a special drink to the following generations," he said and then poured in two quarts of rum, then two quarts of vodka, two quarts of Jim Beam, two quarts of Mad Dog 20/20, two quarts of tequila then started mixing in a bag each of cherry, orange, grape, and lime Kool-Aid flavoring, and finally three gallons of beer.

"Staff Sergeant Johnson will now add the final ingredient," Martinez said.

Staff Sergeant Johnson started slowly marching around the room with both hands above his head, holding a new white pair of women's bikini bottoms. Reaching the table, he dropped the panties in the pot and stirred the grog with a long-handled spoon. He poured a glass and tasted it. "I pronounce the grog ready," Johnson said.

Everybody marched up for a glass and returned to their places. We supplemented the grog with pizza, and the banquet lasted a couple of hours. I was able to drive back to my barracks room, so maybe I didn't have as much fun as some other soldiers did.

***

At the start of August 1990, Iraq's President Saddam Hussein sent his military to invade the neighboring country of Kuwait.

As with Vietnam, most Americans didn't know anything about Iraq or Kuwait.

What we knew is that America's President George H.W. Bush said, "This aggression will not stand," and the United Nations Security Council gave Hussein a deadline for his forces to leave Kuwait, which he ignored.

What we didn't know is that the only reasons our government was concerned about Kuwait were oil and a possible risk to Saudi Arabia, which is on the southern border of Iraq and Kuwait. Experts later said it's also likely that British Prime Minister Margaret Thatcher convinced Bush to intervene because of her country's investments in Kuwait.

Anyhow, over the next few months the United States and coalition nations started building up troops in the area for impending action. This was called Operation Desert Shield.

Then on January 16, 1991, U.S.-led aerial strikes commenced, followed by a ground campaign the next month. These actions started Operation Desert Storm.

I'd finished thirty days of training and went to Tennessee and back to Fort Carson. After we got back to Carson, they asked for volunteers.

"I want to volunteer," I told the first sergeant.

"Shut up and sit your old butt down," he said. "Let the younger guys go and get their CIBS."

So for me, Desert Shield came and Desert Storm went.

Not so for my oldest daughter, Sergeant E-5 Nora Fay. Her MOS 88-M placed her driving semi-trucks and trailers. She was in a transportation unit at Fort Riley, then chased through the Middle East desert carrying fuel, bullets and beans.

The conflict didn't last long. Saddam saw where the cards were falling and surrendered at the end of February.

***

In April I received orders going back to Korea. This time I flew instead of making big circles in the ocean on a troop ship.

I shipped via whole baggage four Class A greens, eight fatigues, three pairs of low quarters and boots. I turned in my TA-50. Transportation picked up our household things and delivered them to Junction City and shipped my whole baggage to Korea. I made sure my medical, personnel, and finance records place were all together in my legendary briefcase.

Something happened to our car, I don't recall what, but Sylvia's niece and Nephew drove us to Junction City. About a week before my thirty-day leave was up, I finally got a twelve-month back-pay check from Finance $3,500. I put $1,000 down on a 1970s Chrysler New Yorker.

To catch the plane for Korea, I had to go St. Louis's Lindbergh Airport. We drove there the day before.

My orders said to travel in Class A greens or Class B greens. I knew that we could travel in dress blues, and that's what I did since I loved to mess with officers and senior NCOs. We stopped in Alaska for fuel and we had to deplane, and several first sergeants and sergeant majors asked, "Man why are you in dress blues?"

"To mess with you," I said.

It's around eighteen hours flying time to Korea. When we hit the International Date Line, we lost a day. At Seoul, they took us from the airport to the replacement company. The NCOs spot-checked the bags. As I was putting up my bag, a female staff sergeant yelled for me.

"Why are you in blues?" she asked.

"To be different," I said.

An hour later, about 1800 hours, we arrived at Camp Casey, the same base I was at in the 1960s. The NCOs at the replacement company showed us our bunks and wall lockers. We changed clothes and walked a couple blocks to the NCO club.

I only planned on having a couple rum and Cokes, but I started dancing with the go-go girls and the guys were buying me drinks so I don't remember much more about my first night back in Korea.

Chapter Twenty-Two

Return to Korea – 1992

I was back in Korea in April 1992. I was curious what changes had been made and if it was better or worse. From 1965 from 1992 was twenty-seven years.

For one thing, there were more trees and they were larger. When the North Koreans and Chinese came down in the 1950s, they destroyed the forest. In the '60s, the trees were around four to six feet tall and scattered, but they'd grown to forty to fifty feet tall and filled out.

Another thing was that in 1965 the twenty-some miles of road from Seoul to Dongducheon, the village outside Camp Casey's front gate, was two lanes for vehicles and four lanes each way for walking, bikes, and ox carts. In 1992 traffic had grown to four lanes for vehicles with only an occasional bike rider or water buffalo on the side.

I recall that in 1965 the only electricity was on post and down the main street shops and bars of Dongducheon, none in the outlying villages. The people used kerosene for light and charcoal bricks for heat. Houses and stores were not over two stories tall because the Koreans built them out of any material at hand: paper, wood, plastic.

Since the 1986 Olympic Games in Seoul, all the towns have electric and three-story buildings, even high-rises. There's six-lane highway from Seoul to Panmunjom, a town on the DMZ, the De-Militarized Zone, thirty-five miles to the north.

I'd changed too, and my second tour of duty was a lot different than the first.

During my first tour I was young, full of piss and vinegar and hard charging. During my second tour I didn't have to make rank or worry about much.

At the end of my first night back, after the rum and Cokes, they got me back to the barracks and poured me into bed, where I had to place one foot on the floor to keep the bunk from spinning.

Around 0400 hours I woke up. There was no place open on post to buy any coffee. After a long night, I solved that problem in the afternoon. After we finished in-processing for the day I went to the PX and bought an electric coffee pot, an extension cord, coffee and sugar.

We first started in-processing turning in our leave forms to receive our leave pay and travel allotments, we turned in our greenbacks for military pay scrip (paper nickels, dimes, quarters, half dollars, $1, $2, $5, $10, $20. Next we went to Personnel to turn in our medical and 201 files, and Personnel assigned us to our unit. Around fifteen of us went to the same battalion, with seven or eight going to the same company.

After we cleared Finance and Personnel and the medics said we're alive, the replacement cadre took us to the quartermaster to be issued our TA-50. Someone in D.C. decided us grunts needed something other than the regular field pack. They issued us grunts full-size duffle bags with two carrying straps, about half-down the bag was a zipper where we placed our rolled-up sleeping bag, helmet, pistol belt, ammo pouches, suspenders, shelter half, two wool shirts and two wool pants and two field pants, rain suit, over-boots, and something new, a bear suit (a two-piece dark brown fuzzy suit).

We were at the replacement company a week before going to the 503rd Infantry headquarters.

The 503rd Infantry was nicknamed The Rock. During World War II a lieutenant fighting on the island of Corregidor in the Philippines picked up a rock and carried it all over Corregidor. They display the rock at battalion headquarters today.

***

Battalion sent eight of us to Bravo Company. At Bravo the CQ assigned us to two-man rooms. Two rooms shared one bathroom with shower, sink and commode. The rooms had built-in double-wide wall lockers with foot locker on bottom. The bunk beds had wooden head and foot boards with mattresses that were wider than a twin but smaller than a full. There were two small writing desks with chairs. Besides my coffee pot, I bought a small microwave. The barracks were four floors high and air conditioned. On the first floor were the commander's and first sergeant's offices, supply/arms room, mess hall, day room. The second floor housed the first platoon. The third floor had the second platoon, and fourth floor the third platoon. We also had Korean soldiers living with us as part of KATUSA, Korean Augmentation To the U.S. Army, a program started by General Douglas MacArthur.

Our barracks were all the way to the back of Camp Casey, with our motor pool behind the building. The bus came up the main road, turned around at the end of the building, went up a half mile, hung a left and went to Camp Hovey.

The company went to Camp Greaves near the DMZ for field training. Everybody had a week's oration. E-6 and below stayed in the leadership school's barracks. At 0500 hours we got up, dressed in our PT suits, signed out rifles, grabbed our duffle bags and went to the leadership school. We put our duffle bags in bay and waited outside for the armorer so we could lock up our weapons.

I heard a sergeant first class tells a corporal, "I've been in the Army seventeen years and have forgotten more about infantry than you'll ever know."

The corporal said, "Talk to Pop," referring to me.

I turned to the sergeant and said, "I won't f— talk to you."

The armorer finally showed up and we marched to the PT field. On the way the sergeant first class asked how old I am.

"Fifty," I said.

At PT, for a nineteen-year-old to receive 100 points he has to do around eighty pushups in two minutes. I got down and knocked out sixteen pushups and stood up. The instructor looked at me, "Ah, you sure you want to stand up?" I told him I got sixty points. I knocked out eighteen sit-ups for another sixty points. I ran two miles in fourteen-and-a-half minutes, and completed PT with a total score of 200.

***

The company was up country training in the field while we doing class on base. One of the first days we qualified with our rifles on the school's firing range. Some people from the company had come down to base for appointments and they heard rumors about me and went back up country and told the company about an old antique buck sergeant in the company, saying I was from Fort Lewis, Washington.

Others who served with me laughed and said, "No, you're talking about Pop."

The last day of orientation was a Friday morning. The brigade commander and Sergeant Major Hendricks stopped to welcome us. The colonel asked, "How many of you have been to Korea before?"

Several of us raised our hands. The others answered, 1986, 1988, 1989, 1990.

The colonel asked me.

"Sir, '65-'66," I said. It turned out I was there when his father was a commander.

Sergeant Major Hendricks and I talked and we figured out we were two little peons in the 31st Infantry Battalion. He arrived in '64 leaving late '65 and I arrived in '65. Sergeant Major Hendricks had twenty-nine years in the service, and spent over half his career in Korea. He'd married a Korean woman and planned on retiring there, but the Department of the Army said, "No. Go to Fort Hood." I think that after he retired he did return to Korea.

Sergeant Major Hendricks laid down the law to us. If we pulled courtesy patrol in Tongducheon, the village out the back gate where the sergeant major lived.

If we called for reinforcement from the MPs at the front gate to deal with drunks or something else, we'd be locked up too. The thinking was we should be able to handle it ourselves. For the most part, we returned to our barracks rather than raise hell in town.

That weekend the company returned to Camp Casey. We met the commanding officer and first sergeant.

***

For the first field duty I did with the company, the platoon sergeant told me to take my study materials because he was going to send me to the next promotion board.

We arrived at Camp Greaves for a live-fire exercise. The company commander called the platoon leader to his position, and issued the patrol order, "At 0700 you will be at coordinates N 1251 O 2178 and engage the enemy."

The platoon leader returned to the plat area and took out his map. The compound was located at coordinate D 0511 R 2841 so then the lieutenant had to figure how to get from point A (the compound) to point B (the target coordinates). The platoon leader told the platoon sergeant to issue water, rations and ammo (blank for the time being).

The lieutenant studied his map and saw we had to travel ten clicks, or ten miles. He called in the plat sergeant and squad leaders and issued his patrol order. At 1800 we left the compound for coordinates N 12510 2178, then the squad came back to tell us we'd attack the hill at 0700 in the morning.

We drew our weapons from the arms room, inspected them and prepared our backpacks, the ones larger than regular issue. We packed a couple sets of fatigues, a pair of boots socks, T-shirts, shorts, one C-ration, seven twenty-round boxes of blanks. We zipped up our sleeping bags in the bottoms of our duffles. At 1630 hours we ate in the mess hall and at 1730 we suited up: helmet, camouflaged face and hands, put on harness with straps, poncho rolled up on our back, pistol belt with ammo pouch (we had two ammo pouches, each holding six twenty-round magazines).

The plat leader inspected us. At 1800 we walked out the gate in a column of ducks. Our back-duffle packs weighed a hundred pounds, and we marched with them for three miles to the river.

We paddled across the river on rubber rafts, loaded on a Hummer and rode thirty-four miles to a helicopter, flew in circles for fifteen minutes, landed a half-mile from the bottom of the 300-foot mountain, or yama, as locals call it. We walked single file because it was dark, and started up the yama. Nearly reaching the top, we circled around to the other side instead of going over the summit because our silhouettes would have been visible. We started down, went across the valley, up a yama, down a yama. About 0400 we came to a wide stream. We waded across, waist deep.

On the other side we stopped to change out of our wet clothes. We'd been making go time so we rested for forty-five minutes. By this time my butt was starting to drag the ground.

We got up and went another 100 yards to the road for the last two miles to the range. The squad leader asked if I wanted him to carry my ruck. I said no. I spotted a solid four-foot sapling that I broke off at the ground and used as a walking stick.

Finally, we were getting to the range. The last 400 yards had an incline the ground. To get up it, I had to use the butt of my rifle and the stick like ski poles to get up the grade. I made it to the tent, and everybody had dropped their packs and were sitting around. I dropped my pack and my butt.

The range personnel had the lieutenant and plat sergeant bring us to the edge of the range to see how the targets were set up. Then the range personnel had us go in the tent to hear safety rules. They gave us a twenty-minute break and I got to go out of the tent and I was bent at a ninety-degree angle at the waist.

"Pop, lay down by the packs and guard them," the platoon sergeant said.

After the platoon completed the live-fire exercise, we were trucked back to the compound. We ate and cleaned weapons and turned them in. We slept for a couple of hours. When we woke up, we hung out our wet clothes to dry. That afternoon another platoon prepared to go to the live-fire range.

Friday we mounted up on trucks and returned to Camp Casey. Tuesday afternoon the platoon sergeant told me to be ready in the morning for the promotion board, 0900 at battalion headquarters.

At 0700 I shaved and showered and got dressed. I combed my hair forward with a cowlick to the left, put my pants on and my patent-leather low-quarter boots on, and put on my short-sleeve shirt, clip-on black tie. I hung up my green dress jacket and measured a half-inch from the right collar's edge to place the shined US disk pin with blue background. I did the same on the left collar for the infantry crossed-rifles pin, and for the combat infantryman badge on left side of jacket, and the rack of ribbons (six rows of three ribbons).

On the right side of the jacket, from the center-top I measured down two inches to place my regimental crest, the 9th Infantry crest. Next I placed my six presidential unit citations, then my name tag on pocket flap. I put the infantry blue rope on the right shoulder, the two green NCO tabs with the 503rd Infantry Regiment crest on the shoulder strips.

I walked out the door and down the block to battalion headquarters. I noticed I was the only sergeant in the battalion going for staff sergeant. The other fifteen were SPC-4 going for buck sergeant.

At 0850 the battalion sergeant major who was president of the board called everybody into the board room to explain how the board would run: "You knock on the door. When you hear 'enter,' you go in, march to the center desk, stop at attention, salute stating 'Sergeant So-And-So reporting to the board.' You stand in front of that first sergeant. He inspects and can ask you a personal question, then move to the right next first sergeant, go around the sergeant major to the last three first sergeants then back in front of the sergeant major. Salute. He tells you to sit. He tells you that you'd better look over your shoulder as you back across the room to the chair. You miss the chair, you fail the board."

The sergeant major asked me what time I had.

"0855, sergeant major," I said.

"No, you don't. You have 0857. In three minutes, at 0900, knock on that door."

Everybody marched out. At 0900 I knocked on the door. "Enter." I did. I saluted the sergeant. "Babcock reporting, I said then moved to the right and that first sergeant.

"Why do you have more ribbons then me?" he asked.

"I have more years than you, sir," I said politely. I moved through the other sergeants and backed up to the chair and answered the sergeant major's questions.

I passed the board.

***

The second time I went to the field, all field duty was done at Camp Greaves.

Camp Greaves was two miles below the DMZ. It was closed in 2004 and the United States turned it over to South Korea.

It was maybe the strangest camp I was ever at. All night every night the North Koreans had English-speaking women broadcasting over loudspeakers. They played Dick Clark's American Bandstand, Soul Train, and even hillbilly music. They'd say, "Hey, GI, come over to our side. You no have-y to work-y. You get two pretty women who wash-y you four times a day, massage-y six times a day, you drink-y all day."

These women would even know our names and address their statements to us individually. "Sergeant Babcock, you be treated like king over here."

For this round of field training, at around 1800 hours we marched out the gate in two columns. We'd march four miles, stop and move off the road. We'd get in a perimeter, a big circle. According to the original plans, we were to stay there until 0400 hours, ten-march another five miles and set up a temporary base camp.

Weather got cold at night. We took off our field jackets and put on our bear suits top, put our field jackets back on, removed our field pants and put on our bear suit pants, put our field pants back on. After 30 minutes the CO had everybody move on to the road. We started marching again. We marched four or five miles until we came to a medium tent, which was the site of our temporary base camp. I and my two sergeants placed the squad in five two-man positions. Just after sunup, I poked my head out the sleeping bag and told the team leaders to check on the troops.

Around 0900 I got up to go see if the company medic had a back brace. "No."

"Do you have any pain pills?"

"No."

He gave me seven Aspirin. "Take two now, two more in a couple of hours, and call me in the morning," he said.

The mess sergeant arrived with morning chow. I drank a cup of coffee while the squad went through the chow line. I made sure everybody stayed five yards apart. When the last man went through, I got another cup of coffee, powdered eggs, two strips of bacon, and two slices of toast with strawberry jam.

Around 1600 hours the platoon leader, Second Lieutenant Anderson, issued the defense orders to the squad leaders. About the same time, the mess sergeant arrived with the evening meal. After everyone ate we started getting ready to move.

At 1800 we moved up a hill, turned left along the ridge, down the hill. Moving up the hill, I held two sticks ski-poling. I got to the top and everybody was gone ahead. I turned left and started plodding along, and slipped and slid to the bottom of the hill.

We went across the valley, up the next hill, and dug in.

Sometime between 0500 and 0700 we would be attacked.

The squad was set up in three positions of three men. I drew an overlay of the squad's position and fields of fire. I sent my B-team leader, Sergeant Briggs, to the platoon sergeant to check on the delivery of our three sleeping bags. A while later we got word they'd been delivered to the bottom of the hill. Sergeant Briggs and a PFC went down to get them. Sergeant Briggs started cussing. He'd put the wrong markings on his bag and it was dropped at another platoon's area. They returned with just two bags.

The platoon sergeant called to ask what happened. I told him.

"Will it cause any problem?" he asked.

"No," I said. "Two men can sleep with one on watch."

At 0530 everybody was awake, ready for the attack. Our platoon's section was not hit, though.

We ate our MRE then at 0800 we received word to move to the bottom of the hill. We stacked the bags and readied to march three miles to load on helicopters and fly to another area. My energy was flagging and my body ached. The platoon leader told me to stay with the bags and go back to Camp Greaves.

When I arrived I went to the battalion aid station. The doc gave me some Tylenol #3 and a light-duty slip. He said he'd talk to the sergeant major about me going to the field.

The next morning the first sergeant sent me back from Camp Greaves to Camp Casey on the supply truck. At the end of the week the company returned.

The third and last time I went to the field, around 1800 hours we marched out the gates of Camp Greaves in a column of twos along the road for three or four miles, then merged to single file and climbed up and down yamas most of the night. Finally, we stopped and camped during the day. That night we were going to climb some more yamas before making a daylight attack.

Before the evening meal, I told the platoon sergeant I wasn't going to try to go on, that I'd take the mess truck back to Camp Greaves.

I hated to admit I couldn't keep going, but marching for miles in rough terrain with a hundred-pound pack is not a game for most fifty-year-old men. I was glad I was able to make most of the marching and earn the respect of the younger soldiers.

***

Compare me in Korea in 1965 to me in Korea in 1992.

Camp Casey, South Korea, 1992. The barracks were no longer Quonset huts.

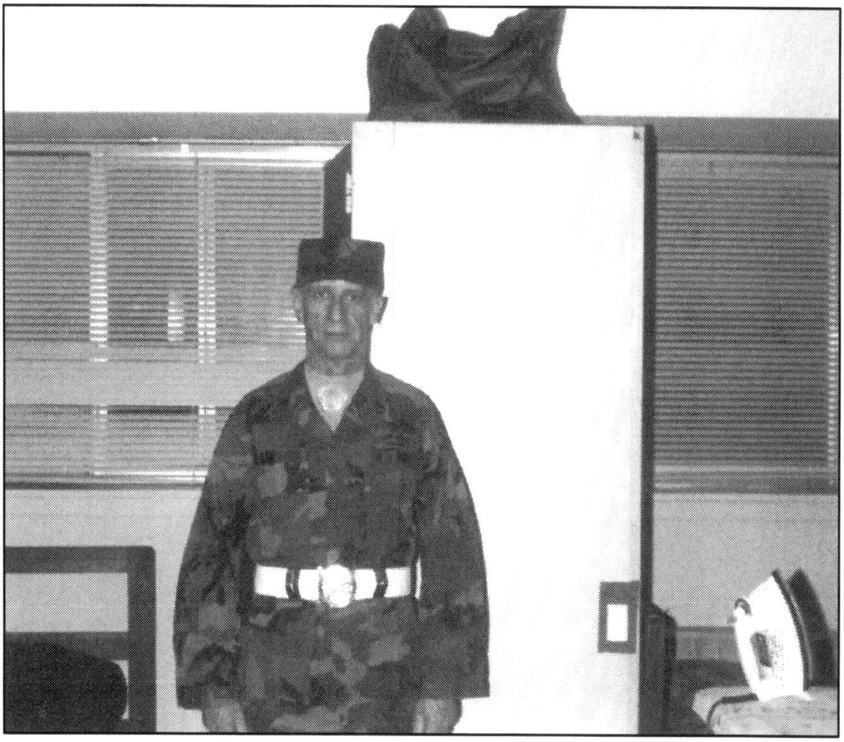

My bunk area was luxurious compared to my first time at Camp Casey.

Above: Camp Casey, South Korea, 1993, I was promoted to staff sergeant E6, a rank I'd held during my previous stint in the Army.
Below: I visited the United Nations complex in Seoul, South Korea, as part of Division Honor Guard.

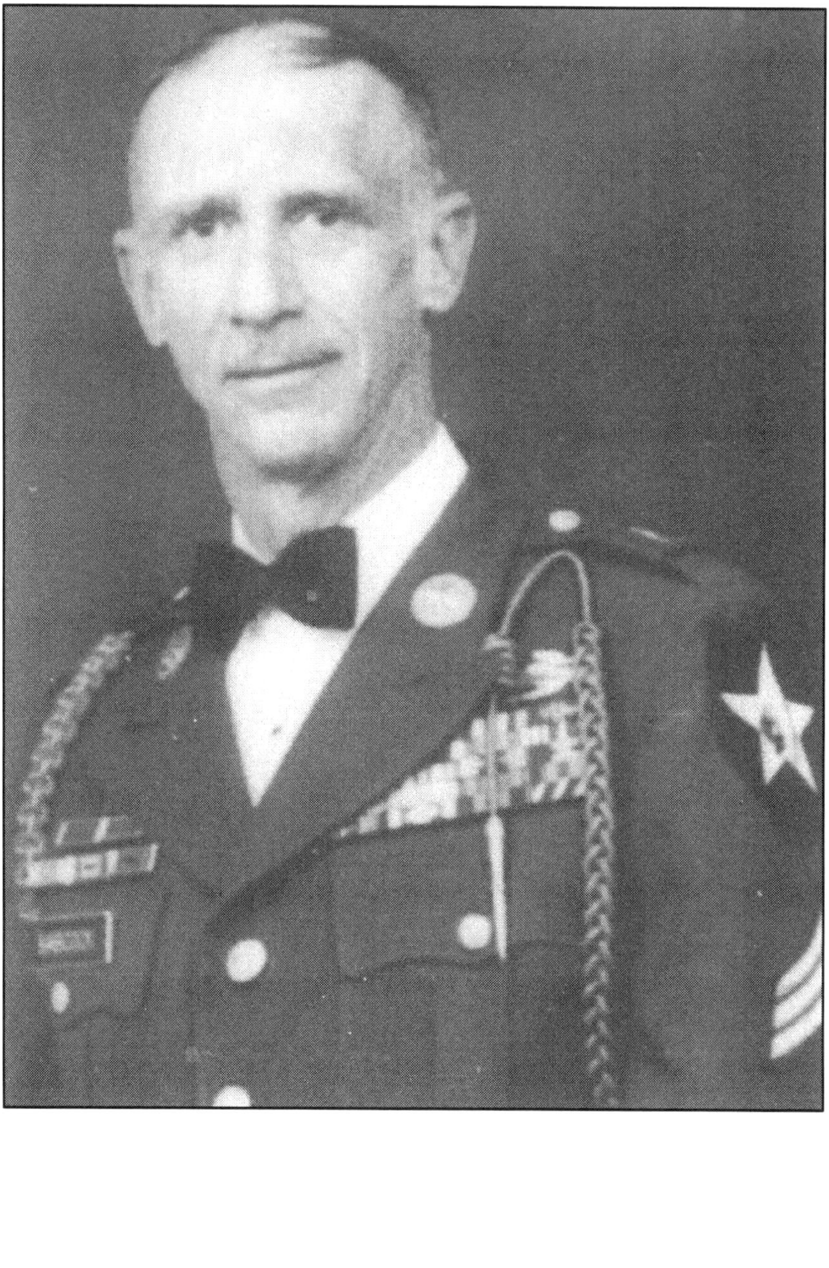

In December, the Department of the Army posted the cutoff scores of all the MOS designations: for 11B20 infantry buck sergeant to 11B30 infantry staff sergeant the cutoff was 750 points; 12B artillery 800 points, 31M radio repairman 850 points; 76Y30 900 points.

Sergeant Jones and Sergeant Briggs had been to earlier promotion boards than me. We all made the cutoff score but none of us had been to BNOC school (Basic Non-Commissioned Officer school) to train us in the duties of being staff sergeants. Because there wasn't an infantry BNOC in Korea, personnel called DA to find out what to do. In two months Sergeant Jones was rotated back to the states so when he got to his next unit he'd go to BNOC, and he'd be promoted if he passed. Sergeant Briggs was married to a Korean and had extended six months so he had to wait until he returned to the states for BNOC.

DA looked over my records and saw I had been a sergeant first class E-7, higher than staff sergeant. They sent my promotion orders without requiring me to attend BNOC.

The promotion boards I'd been through included: 1965 for SPC-4, December 1968 for sergeant first class, 1990 for buck sergeant at Fort Carson, and 1992 for staff sergeant in Korea.

***

In early November I went to the post cleaners' sewing shop to order a tailored formal dress white uniform with white jacket and black tuxedo pants. It was an optional uniform for the most part (required in some tropical locations), but I thought it looked elegant. The white uniform was most often worn by officers to formal events. The Army replaced it with a different uniform in 2014

The jacket was available in three styles: a long coat like the Class A greens, a short "Ike" jacket like General Eisenhower wore, and a short jacket with tails. The jacket with tails went out of style in the 1940s, so I definitely wasn't interested in it.

I decided to order my jacket made Ike style. The uniform came with staff sergeant insignia and eight sleeve strips on each sleeve. I ordered a white MP hat to wear with it. The bill was $300.

I was able to wear my new uniform to Thanksgiving dinner, and it was a big hit.

There was a photographer in a neighboring village, and I decided to have him take my picture in my various uniforms. We decided we could do a triple-exposure that could show me in all my uniforms in one picture. It took two-and-a-half hours to make.

First, he took my picture in the Army green uniform then the blues and finally the whites. In the end, we had three versions of me.

I ordered six of the eight-by-ten pictures and eight of the five-by-sevens to give to my kids and grandkids. The photographer made a couple eleven-by-fourteen pictures for himself. He put one in the front window of the PX on Camp Casey and one in a photo shop in the village.

***

In February the company posted me to the commissary (food store) six days a week for a month. My job was to check ID cards of military personnel and their dependents. Two SPC-4s worked with me.

If a person bought more than $400 in groceries, they had to show their ID card to one of the SPC-4s, who put their name on a list with the amount purchased. If they returned to the commissary within thirty days, they'd have to talk to the military police for suspicion of black marketing.

Just after we started working in the commissary, we were given a short list of lost or stolen ID cards. A few days before we were done with the detail there, a Korean woman walked in and showed her ID card to me. I noticed it one of the cards that was reported lost or stolen. I alerted the manager about the woman. He called the MPs.

After she went through the checkout, the MPs moved her to the side and asked where she got the card. She said her husband had taken her to Personnel and had a new card issued. The MPs called the lieutenant she claimed to be her husband and he had to come down and verify that she was his wife.

***

A local photographer near Camp Casey took a triple exposure of me in, from left, dress blues, dress whites, and dress greens. He liked the picture so much he put a copy in his shop window as an advertisement.

A new sergeant first class named Chavez joined the company. He took over third platoon, and we hung out together.

I bought a black winter coat with a dragon design on the back. I had some writing sewn on it: "65-66 Korea 92-93" on the back left, the 2nd Infantry Indianhead patch on the right sleeve, American and Korean flags, and on the front left side I had sewn "Sexy Swinging Grandpa," which was my CB radio handle when I drove trucks.

***

The 2nd Infantry was detailed to send a platoon to the United Nations compound at Seoul to serve in the honor guard there. My company was the first to go. We stayed for three months.

The units that made up the U.N. Honor Guard included one squad from Thailand, one squad from the Philippines, one squad each from South Korea's navy, air force, marines and army, three squads from the U.S. and a platoon of US Army Band musicians. The barracks for honor guard and band was on a hill behind the United Nations Headquarters.

This was some nice duty. The unit did parades once a week plus guard duty on different people and property. One of our squads would have guard for a week, with the SPC-4s doing two-hour shifts guarding the U.S. Army commanders. Our plat sergeant, Sergeant First Class Chavez, two other staff sergeants and I didn't have to post or check on the guards. For my squad's week of guard, I'd start and stop the work day by firing the cannon for reveille in the morning and retreat in the afternoon.

I went by a lot of different names in the honor guard. The U.S. commander and first sergeant called me Pops, the Korean Army sergeant major called me Brother because we both were fifty, and the Thai sergeant major called me Dad.

The SPC-4s were restricted to the barrack during guard week, but the squad leaders weren't. Sergeant First Class Chavez and I joined a group of officers and NCOs to act like fools twice a month. We'd meet at a point and break into two groups, the hounds and the hares (rabbits). The hares would follow a course through Seoul, and the hounds would have to chase them, and at the end of the route we all drank beer.

The hares would leave the starting point running or taking the subway through Seoul. Maybe they'd go through the large underground market, a park or another location. About fifteen minutes after the hares took off, we hounds started chasing. We ran, took the subway or cabs, or rode bikes but mostly ran. Once everybody got to the destination point, the partying started. The first-time runners were each given a can of beer. Once you opened the can you had to drink the whole can; if you didn't, the rest was poured over your head. Next, the fastest person from the previous run and the fastest person from the current run would stand. The winner from the previous run had a rope tied on around his neck with a dried squid hanging on it, and he/she would take a bite off the squid and pass it to the current winner to take a bite and have to wear on the next run, then they'd drink a can of beer. Finally, all third-time runners would stand and each drink a can of beer.

The sixth-time runners were given running names. They'd have to stand out of earshot until the group decided their names. One band member's name was Peck-a-low (she played piccolo). Another gal's name was Twin Peaks. When I made my sixth run, I was named Polly Gripper because I had dentures.

Our last week there, another platoon from another battalion arrived. There was a change of command ceremony as our commander turned over his post. My squad had guard. They moved our platoon to an empty barracks as the new platoon moved into our old barracks.

There was big formal ball. I took a girl who was about thirty years old, Sergeant First Class Baker, a band member. I think we each paid $30. She wore an Army dress blue jacket and skirt, and I wore my whites. Only one other major wore whites, all the others wore blues.

***

The company sent word that as soon as we got back that we'd do EIB testing (Expert Infantryman Badge). The morning after we returned we gave the troops First Aid and map-reading classes. They went to qualify at the rifle range and did day land navigation and then after supper did night land navigation.

Around 0300 hours, the company was awakened for a twelve-mile march, complete with helmets, backpacks and weapons. We marched in two columns from the back of Camp Casey down to the end of the golf course, hung a right past the hospital. A SPC-4 who was carrying the M60 machine gun was about to fall out but I switched him my eight-pound rifle for his twenty-five-pound M60. We continued up and over the ridge into Clap Gap where my barracks were back in 1965. We marched down the road, out the gate, hung a left to the main gate, a left through the gate up the main road and back to the company area, through the motor pool and another mile. Then the company turned around and did it all in reverse to complete the twelve miles.

On the way back, when I got to the middle of the bus turnaround circle near our company barracks, I placed the M60 on the ground, took off my helmet and removed my backpack. I lay down and lit up a cigarette. Sergeant First Class Anderson, the first platoon sergeant, came marching up and sneered, "What's wrong? Too old? Can't take it?"

I looked up at him and said, "I have my EIB (Expert Infantryman Badge) and my CIB (Combat Infantryman Badge), unlike some jerk wad who doesn't."

He stomped off to finish the road march. He didn't get his EIB.

***

Not too long after we joined the company, some of us were sent to one- or two-week courses and assigned additional duties: NBC (Nuclear, Biological and Chemical) NCO and Drug and Alcohol NCO.

As in a lot of businesses, the employees are tested every so often for drug abuse. As one of the largest businesses in the world, Uncle Sam has to test a certain percentage of employees every month. People were picked if the last four numbers of their ID were 6911 or first three numbers were 543. One early morning a month we'd set up for testing in the day room. We marked off the soldiers' names on the company roster as they took plastic bottles into the bathroom and made samples. We'd fill out a label with their name and rank, give them the bottle. When they'd bring the bottle back, we'd make sure the lid was tight and taped a red strip over the top, and placed it in a box. When the box was full, it was sealed and shipped to Division for testing.

***

When there was a perceived threat of strike from short-range rockets from North Korea, Division ordered us to cover up the company signs around base up so the North Koreans couldn't figure out what unit was there. We did it, but it was dumb. Camp Casey had occupied the same land for forty years and the buildings hadn't moved more than a hundred yards in any direction, and every one of them had probably been zeroed in for thirty years.

***

My next and last special duty was collecting coins from the slot machines in the officers', NCOs' and enlisted soldiers' clubs. An SPC-4, a Korean and I would go twice a week to empty the slot machines. We had a coin counter to make the tally easy.

We'd open a slot machine and bag the money. We'd separate the coins. For one club, we might collect four bags of nickels ($1,000 dollars), four bags of dimes ($2,000), two bags of quarters $4,000) and one bag of half-dollars ($8,000) for a total of $15,000. We'd take a copy of the receipt and leave a copy, and the club manager would fill out a deposit slip. Then we'd hit the next club.

Prior to me taking that detail, a couple of real brains stole $ 20,000 in bags of coins. They were in a foreign country; they couldn't go to the airport with thirty suitcases and fly off into the sunset. And they couldn't go to the bank and say, "I'd like to make a small deposit." They were caught pretty quickly.

Chapter Twenty-Three

101st Airborne Division, 3rd Battalion, 187th Infantry Regiment Fort Campbell, Kentucky - 1993-97

Back in America, my wife Sylvia was still driving a school bus, and I'd made sure she received $200 allotments out of my paychecks.

Toward the end of 1992, my oldest daughter Nora, who was also in the Army, shipped to Mogadishu, the capital of Somalia. She was there around the time of the events portrayed in the book and movie "Black Hawk Down."

Nora's husband Jeff, Sylvia, Sylvia's niece and some other people started going out partying regularly. Nora's mom and Jeff stopped writing her. Nora wrote me a letter cussing me because Jeff doesn't write. I told her I was in Korea not Junction City.

Nora told her commander that her mother and husband weren't writing her so she was going to kill herself, be cremated and have her ashes spread over the ocean. The commander had her see a shrink. When she wrote me about that, I had a big laugh. She did end up divorcing Jeff.

***

The last two weeks of September twenty of us started clearing Camp Casey. We contacted transportation for our whole baggage, turned in TA-50, cleared Personnel, Medical, 201 file, went to finance to draw two months advanced pay and advanced travel pay, and bought plane tickets from Kimpo Air Base to Japan, from Japan to Travis Air Force Base in California, and from Travis to Manhattan, Kansas.

We were at the replacement company waiting to be taken to Kimpo when I ran across my old squad leader Staff Sergeant Jones. He saw I'd made staff sergeant. He didn't have anything to say about that.

Going home, we didn't have to travel in uniforms. We were sitting on the bus waiting on the driver put our suitcases in the undercarriage. I was dressed in civilian blue jeans, my winter coat, ball cap, sunglasses. I combed my hair back so it hung down below my shoulders. I had all my paper work in my old Samsonite briefcase.

The trip home was around 6,500 miles.

After a ninety-minute ride we arrived at Kimpo, grabbed our suitcases, went inside to check in, put our luggage on the conveyer belt, got our boarding passes, found our gate, went through security and boarded the plane.

The flight to Japan was three hours. Then things got messy when we had to transfer planes.

We deplaned and had to get our bags and run to the other side of the airport and get boarded in thirty minutes. If we missed the change, we didn't know how long we'd be in Japan.

After a mad dash across the terminal, we pushed our way to the airplane counter and got our boarding passes. Then we sat back and relaxed for fifteen hours.

***

Two weeks before I got home to Kansas, there'd been a major rain storm.

The water in Milford Lake, outside Junction City, got so high it washed away the top of the dam. The trailer park on Grant Street where my family lived was under water, and the street was impassable to reach Fort Riley.

My ex-son-in-law Jeff and wife Sylvia rescued some things from the trailer before it was under water. They packed the dishes, the kitchen table, sofa, love seat, chair and ottoman, my trunk of Mack Bolan books, the bedding and dresser. The waterbed was too big to move and became an underwater bed.

A storage company we knew let Jeff put our things in storage for free. When I got to Fort Riley, I went to Transportation to present my orders assigning me to Fort Campbell. Transportation shipped my furniture to Fort Campbell. I thanked the storage owner for not charging me for my furniture.

It was October 1993 when we moved to Fort Campbell.

Sylvia's oldest daughter was in Colorado Springs staying with Sylvia's niece and was pregnant. The youngest daughter was in Salt Lake Utah with her dad.

Sylvia and I remained three weeks in Junction City after I got back then we hit the road. Driving our Chrysler New Yorker through Kansas City, we could see the Missouri River along Interstate 70 was over the river banks. In St. Louis the Mississippi River was high too.

At Fort Campbell, I rented a room at the guest house on post and started in-processing. Personnel assigned me to the 3rd Brigade 3rd Battalion 187th Infantry Regiment, known as the Rakkasans.

I went to talk to the NCOs about the unit. I looked over to see the chain of command, the brigade commander, was Colonel Dees, whom I knew in Fort Carson. The next morning I saw Colonel Dees and told him I wanted to go to PLDC as an instructor. Colonel Dees had the sergeant major call the school and I went over and gave a class and was accepted.

In finishing processing, I requested on-post housing, but a month later I signed for a four-bedroom house. It was next door to Staff Sergeant Cruz, with whom I served in Korea.

***

At the school, we'd get a group of students for thirty days and they were quartered at the school.

All the buildings at the school were WWII wooden barracks. The orderly and supply/ arms room and mess hall were single story. The troop barracks were two stories high with two rows of five bunks doubled, twenty people, per floor. The wall lockers were lined against the back walls with the foot lockers back-to-back down the center aisle.

We'd wake the students at 0600. By 0630 they were in PT suits doing warmup exercises, pushups, sit-ups then a two-mile run. After a week we gave them a PT test. If they didn't pass it, they'd retest a week later. Failed students were sent back to their unit. If the students failed either rifle qualifying or day and night land navigation, they failed the school.

The students also spent a week in the field running patrols and ambushes.

***

Just after Thanksgiving, Sylvia's daughter Ellen called to say that the niece who moved to Fort Carson was murdered.

I took a week's leave and we drove to Colorado Springs.

The husband, who was military, said he met his wife at Red Lobster one night, they argued, she left with $900 cash and that was the last he saw of her.

When we left we took Ellen back with us. She called an ex-boyfriend and found out he was in Columbus, Georgia, so she left us for Columbus.

In mid-December, Sylvia told me her sister in Junction City was sick and she was going to see her. While there, Sylvia got a job driving a bus again for a couple months. She then spent time in Hawaii visiting her son.

By April, the Army had built a murder case against Sylvia's niece's husband, and was going to court martial him.

The military flew Sylvia to Fort Carson as a witness. They also flew in a female military member who'd been having an affair with the husband. I drove out for the trial, which lasted a week.

The Army showed that the nephew killed his wife, cutting off her head, hands and feet, burying them along the highway nearby. He didn't bury the head very deep and a boy's dog dug up the head and carried it to a house.

The few bones left were turned over to family, and shipped to Salt Lake City for burial.

I left Sylvia the car, and I flew back to Fort Campbell. I told her to bring the car and the kids to Kentucky when school was out.

I started thinking that during that first year at Fort Campbell, Sylvia and I had only spent one month together there, plus the week at Fort Carson for the murder trial. She was always traveling to see “relatives.”

When Sylvia took her daughter to Fort Benning, Georgia, without seeing me, I filed for divorce. She drove up to Fort Campbell and said, “I'm home to stay!”

I looked at her and said, “No, you’re not.” We'd been married a little over five years and she didn't have any furniture in our apartment. “You only have one suitcase of clothes, which means in a month or two you'll have to go to Kansas to see your sick sister or someplace else. No, there’s the door. Don't let it hit you in the butt on the way out.”

She screamed, “I'll get half of your retirement!”

“No, you won’t. We've only been married five years. Ten’s required to get a man’s retirement.”

***

In December a bad ice storm shut down everything at Fort Campbell for three days, the governors of Kentucky and Tennessee sent National Guard units to check on people in the country.

In January I went to the hospital for my annual physical. I was fifty-two years old, smoked a pack of cigarettes a day and had high cholesterol. The doctor placed me on 120-day temporary profile until I took a treadmill test showing improved health. I couldn't carry anything over ten pounds or run PT.

I ignored that.

One day we were marching six miles in to the school barracks. A 180-pound stocky student sat down. I stopped to see what was up.

“I can't carry my seventy-five pound ruck any farther,” he said. “Can you have somebody carry it for me?”

I drop-kicked him in the ass and pointed at some female soldiers. “If these 105-pound girls can carry their rucks, you can too,” I said.

Back at the school, I started putting up my TA-50 when my group leader caught me.

“You’re under temporary profile,” he said.

“Bull hockey,” I said, “and cows don't brag about it.”

Two hours later the first sergeant handed me my orders for temporary profile.

***

Being on temporary profile for my health limited the duties I could perform. I started to work but Sergeant Counts stopped me. The post museum was looking for an NCO. It was light work, and Counts said I could work at the museum and still be in the battalion.

I initially told him no, but museum manager Rex Boggs accepted me so I took the job. Orders at first allowed me six months special duty, but they were renewed regularly to allow me to stay at the museum, officially named the Don F. Pratt Museum of the 101st Airborne Division.

I came to find museum work to be fulfilling for myself and for the unit.

The preservation of a unit’s achievements, artifacts and stories are a contribution to our military’s overall history. I helped care for those elements and also share them with museum visitors, which included current and former soldiers, their families, researchers, military enthusiasts, and sometimes dignitaries.

At this time, Fort Campbell was starting to modernize its buildings, replacing some WWII wooden barracks for new brick barracks. To keep a piece of that history, manager Rex Boggs and a couple guys went out and cut the bottom corner room off of a barrack and moved it to the museum. We placed eight heavy-duty wheels under it. Our obstacles were a wall between the main floor and the front of the museum and a WWII tank sitting at an angle. We got around the wall but couldn't get the cut-out room around the tank. I removed a tool box from the back of the tank and started its engines. It had two V8 Chrysler motors that still ran. I backed up the tank and we get the room around it. I moved the tank to its original position and replaced the tool box. The engines were so quiet and smooth I told Rex I wouldn't mind putting one in my Honda.

We set up that cut-out room just like it would've been when soldiers bunked there during WWII.

We put in a five-foot-by-seven-foot plastic window, an old metal bunk with wool blankets, the TA-50 out for inspection, the shelter half folded, steel helmet and liner, pistol belt with ammo pouches, foot locker open, top left drawer with white towel, bar of soap, razor, tooth brush on top, right side with shoe polish, shoe brush and rolled socks. On a wood shelf and the wooden bar under with a Class A service cap, WWII Ike-style Class A jacket, shirts. We even moved in a mannequin from the desk in the lobby. People would ask him questions but he wouldn't answer.

In the museum, each artifact had its own folder and artifact number, and was backed up by computer files on CD.

Among the displays were some scrapbooks that belonged to Adolf Hitler; papers from General William Westmoreland, the commander of U.S. forces in Vietnam; and artifacts from the 101st Airborne Division's work in World War II and Vietnam.

A hand-carved teak wood desk was donated by a former Vietnam officer. It was four feet wide by six feet long and three feet high and weighed 200 pounds. It was placed on a stage and we always had to move it on and off for other exhibits and functions – it was like a regular PT session.

We had a WWII glider plane inside the museum and a taxidermy Civil War-era eagle named Old Abe.

The story was that, when alive, Abe had been adopted during the Civil War by the 8th Wisconsin National Guard while marching to battle. After the war, he lived in a cage at the Wisconsin governor's mansion. He died and was stuffed, and eventually was given to Fort Campbell.

Mounted in a large display case with his beak open, wings out and talons ready to strike, he became the 101st Airborne's mascot and the reason Division members are called Screaming Eagles.

I began giving all the tours, and everyone who came in had to go through the museum tour. During the summer I worked Friday, Saturday, Sunday and Monday and was off Tuesday, Wednesday and Thursday. The only times I trained with the company were annual physical exam and weapons test. If the CO or first sergeant came in to say, "You need to do PT with the company," I said, "Are you crazy? Those are my days off."

***

My guided tour went something like this:

HI, I'm Staff Sergeant Babcock. I'll guide you through the tour.

On your left, if you're an NCO, this is what your room looked like. Next, we have a WWII tank. In the case on your right, the clicker the 101st used at night patrol.

Here is the village of Carentan, France, located twenty miles behind the beaches of Normandy. The 101st liberated it from the Nazis. Next, the Hell's Highway was a sixty-mile piece of road from Belgium into the Netherlands defended against the Germans by the 82nd, the 101st and a British airborne division.

Next, the 101st was surrounded by the German army at Bastogne, Belgium. The Germans told the 101st to surrender, but General McAuliffe told the Germans, "Nuts," held under siege. General George Patton drove his armored division 200 miles in under twenty-four hours to help the 101st.

The wooden bowl here came from Hitler's "Eagle's Nest." If you were a German officer, you would place your calling card in the bowl then Adolf Hitler's aide would present the card and announce you.

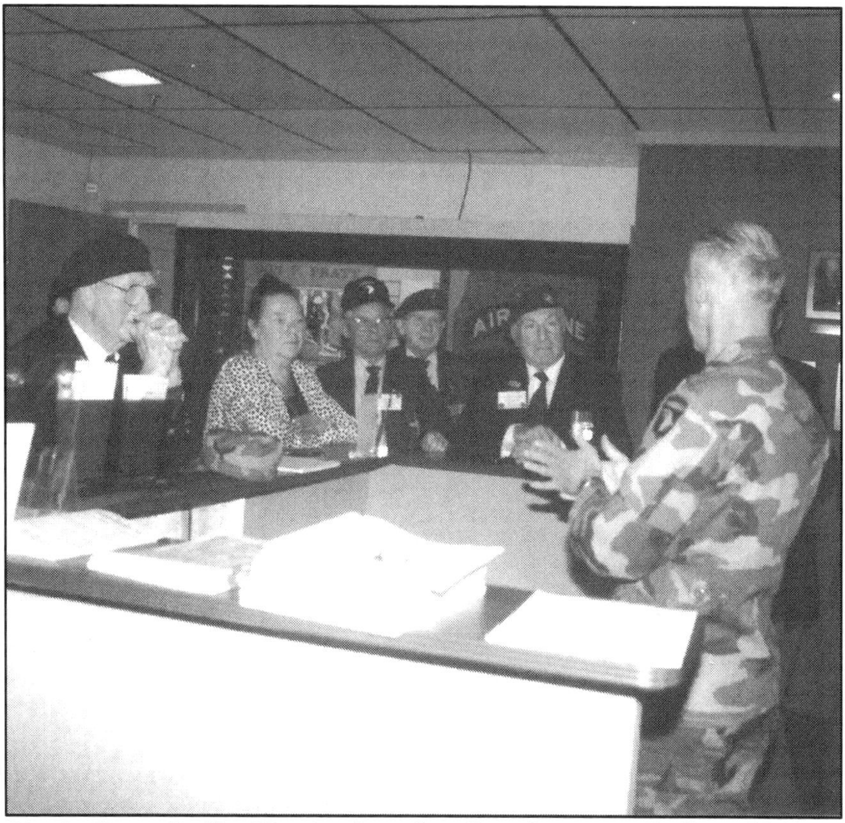

Fort Campbell, Kentucky, is the home of the 101st Airborne Division. At the base's Don F. Pratt Museum, I led many tours, including this one for British veterans of the WWII Hell's Highway, where they worked with the 101st to hold back German forces.

The glider here would've been loaded with troops. A propeller plane would hook to the glider and pull the glider till arriving four or five miles from target then release the glider to come swooping in on the enemy. The museum's namesake, General Don F. Pratt, assistant division commander, and his pilot were killed when their glider crashed in WWII.

Go through the glider, you notice the jeep.

In Vietnam over here, you see Charles in his natural surroundings. He was poorly trained and equipped, but give him a shovel and he'd dig you miles of tunnels or booby trap anything.

On the wall you see the quilt of green berets. JFK said, "Ask not what your country can do for you but what you can do for your country." This quilt along with this globe and the tail of a plane salutes the 248 soldiers from the 101st killed in a 1985 plane crash coming home from overseas. (Eight crew members also died.) They crashed on takeoff from Gander, Newfoundland. Outside the museum are 256 trees, one planted for each victim.

Finally, here you see General J.H. Peay receiving a briefing during Desert Storm, in which he commanded the 101st.

Any questions?

***

The museum had several cannons, vehicles and aircraft that were stored outside. We checked and maintained all of them. These included the cannon that the division fired every morning and evening, a Douglas C-47 and a Douglas C-118 transport planes, and an A-10 Warthog fighter jet.

I was around when the C-118 and Warthog were brought in from the airport. It was on a Saturday. Instead of coming up the four-lane street, they drove the planes through the edge of a housing area and the road had turns. The up-right tail and wings of the DC 118 were off, and there were two people riding on top of the plane with poles to lift up the electrical stop lights. The Warthog's wings couldn't be removed so someone walked in front of it to remove street signs and speed-limit signs. Once the planes passed, the signs were put back up. The move took all day. At one place along the route, the Warthog nearly got stuck between two telephone poles.

Every year, the base hosted a spring gathering for former and current members of the division called Week of the Eagles. One year, a couple of months in advance of the gathering, the museum made arrangements to repaint seven cannons, an anti-aircraft gun, armored personnel carrier (APC) truck, and planes.

Battalion sent me a second lieutenant, twelve men, six Desert Storm SUVs and six pickups to move some things to the paint shop.

We hooked a small cannon to an SUV with no problem, but when we went to hook a 155mm towed cannon to a Hummer, we noticed the cannon had a flat tire and its brakes didn't work. We rolled it out of the museum to hook it to the SUV, and I tied a tire between the SUV and the cannon as a precautionary cushion. I told the SUV driver to go slow and I'd use the emergency hand brake.

The paint shop painted the 155mm, replaced the tire and put a new canvas seat on it. They used a wrecker to return it and the small cannon.

While the cannons and vehicles were gone, I had post engineers lay cement pads in front of the museum for the 155mm, two 105mm cannons, and the landing gear of the planes.

The pilot who originally flew in the A-10 Warthog didn't know how to land it. Instead of landing back wheels first, he landed on the nose wheel, breaking the landing gear and cracking the frame. The engine and electric components had been removed. Fast forward to us moving the plane, and the landing gear broke. I had an engineering unit bring a crane to lift the plane. We welded the gear and moved it on the pads.

For the C-47, the museum hired an alleged painter and his crew of four helpers to repaint it on location. We furnished the olive drab green paint. The painter wanted me to go to the motor pool every couple of days for gas to run his air compressors. I told him, "They're paying you $30,000. Buy your own gas." For the paint crew to reach the plane, I signed out a platform lift from the airfield and also built a wood platform on a front-end loader. The painter claimed the gas generator he had wasn't powerful enough for his spray guns so I signed out a five-kilowatt generator. It took that inept group a month and a half to paint the plane.

While that was going on, I took a six-man detail and a small forklift to the warehouse next door to move wall lockers into the museum to store artifacts not on display. Even though we took them in the back part of the museum, it took some work to maneuver those lockers to the upstairs storage area. We ended up with five rows of lockers back to back.

With that done, we had to number the lockers and their shelves, place the artifacts and then notate the artifacts' positions in their file folders.

***

April 1994 marked the time of my last four-year enlistment.

Because I respected him so much, I asked Colonel Dees to swear me in. Shortly after, Colonel Dees left for war college in London, England.

After war college he returned to Fort Campbell with his first star as a general and became assistant commander of the division. A year after that he made his second star and went to Korea to take command of the 2nd Infantry Division.

***

In four years at Pratt Museum at Fort Campbell, I met a lot of people.

These included Korean War Medal of Honor recipient Rodolfo Hernandez, three Vietnam War Medal of Honor recipients, U.S. Senator Bill Frist of Tennessee, officers from South America, Hungary and Russia.

Toward the end of my enlistment, I met some British survivors of the WWII effort to defend a road through Belgium called Hell's Highway from Hitler's Germans. They'd been part of a British airborne division that joined the 101st and 82nd Airborne Divisions in that operation.

On another museum tour, a sergeant major by the name Fitzpatrick came through. He was second battalion sergeant major of the 503rd when I was in the 503rd in Korea. He'd become the second brigade sergeant major of the 506th

Infantry at Fort Campbell and proceeded to become a pain in my butt. He'd send his troops to the museum to ask me dumb questions about the 506th.

One day a soldier came in to the museum and asked me to sign his in-processing papers. All new soldiers to base had to take the museum tour, and I signed to verify it. This guy wanted me to sign without taking the tour. I pointed to the picture on the wall of Lieutenant General Jack Keane, the 101st Airborne Division commander at the time. "Go ask Jack," I said. "If he says yes, I'll sign them. If he doesn't say OK, I'll sign when you take the tour."

After the soldier left, my co-worker Rosie Quintero said, "Do you know who that was?"

"No," I said.

"That was Michael Durant."

Durant was a pilot whose Blackhawk helicopter crash, capture and rescue during the 1993 Battle of Mogadishu in Somalia were front-page news. Several years later his experience formed the basis for the book and movie *Blackhawk Down.*

Following his rescue and recuperation, he returned to Fort Campbell, where he'd been previously stationed. CNN TV host Larry King brought his show to base to interview him. A couple of months after his return, he left the Army to recover, but after about fourteen months he reenlisted to return to the 160th Special Operations Aviation Regiment helicopter unit.

If you go to the Pratt Museum and ask Rosie for the Larry King video, she knows what drawer it's in.

***

I want to say a few words about my museum coworker Rosie Quintero.

I met her when I started as museum NCO in 1994. She'd started volunteering in the gift shop because her husband was stationed at Fort Campbell as command sergeant major of the 801st Maintenance Battalion. After he retired, he went to work for the Fort Campbell post office, and she stayed at the museum.

In addition to the gift shop, Rosie helped out on other museum projects. If we were grading artifacts, she would be there with her cotton gloves on. When the museum held Christmas parties, Rosie was there setting up tables.

As far as I'm concerned, she's a national treasure.

I'll always remember when in 1997 the Department of the Army's historical department in Washington, D.C., requested our commanding officer logs and records. That meant records going back decades.

That day, Rosie and I joined museum curator Rex Boggs, assistant curator Maggie Arrant, and division historian Captain Schroeder to go to a warehouse to find the materials. We took a forklift and started reaching up on the top shelves. We lowered a pallet of old boxes, brushed an inch of dust off, opened the box and started reading the papers. We saw it was an old CQ log, which tracks movements in and out of the barracks.

Excerpt follows:

C Company 2nd BN 187th Inf. 101st Airborne camp FEU-BI Vietnam, January 7, 1970. Staff Sergeant Ron Franks QC and runner SPC-4 Dave Hicks assumed duties at 1930 hrs.

1. 1st Sgt. states 3rd plat has a squad out on patrol, all quiet.

2. 1830 hrs. I checked the company area by 1st plat door, pick up trash, all quiet.

3. 1900 hrs. sent the runner to get the three people on extra duty, put them to cleaning CO/S and top's offices, empty, trash cans, dust, sweep and mop floors.

4. 1830 hrs. received CID-REPT radio report, all quiet.

5. 2345 hrs. received CID-REPT sprung ambush, killed two VC. Returning to base,

6. 0200 hrs. made check of company area, all quiet.

7. 0430 hrs. had runner wake KPs

8. O5OO hrs. wake company

9. O5OO hrs. relieved by first sergeant.

Rex rented eight copy machines. Whatever unit had division duties on a given day sent ten people to the museum for two months while we copied, boxed and shipped the records to D.C. Going through these records, we discovered that a Colonel Jones, a WWII airborne platoon leader had received the DSM (Distinguished Service Medal), the second highest medal awarded by the Army.

The process never seemed to end, but Rosie kept all our spirits high with her great attitude and work ethic.

As of this writing, I believe Rosie still works in the Pratt Museum at Fort Campbell. Make sure to tell her hello if you see her.

***

Jack Keane commanded the 101st Airborne Division from July 1993 to February 1996.

The first time I met Jack Keane, I was in the lobby talking to the guard. When Jack walked in I realized he was a general by the two shining stars on his cap, along with the two stars on each collar, plus the two stars on his belt.

He wanted a tour. I expected a challenge, but I gave tours every day so I thought I got off easy.

I started by showing him the barrack room, tank, the hall going to the restrooms, Hell's Highway, Bastogne, Vietnam, the stage with display cases and the heavy teak desk. Off the stage, we stopped at the jeep that was painted red, white and blue with 101st patches on it. I showed him the workshop where two displays were being worked on. Behind the stage were wall lockers with artifacts and thirty mannequins.

I thought we were done, but then the general said he wanted to see the historian's office.

We went back to the lobby and I showed him the room on the left with two five-shelf bookcases, a computer and two filing cabinets, and then across the lobby into the clerk's office. Then he wanted to see the arms room. I got keys from the key box and led the way upstairs. I had weapons in racks in the wall lockers. We went back downstairs to the area were we show the short documentary about the 101st, and display pictures of President George H.W. Bush and the WWII, Korean War, Vietnam War and Desert Storm Medal of Honor recipients. There too was the five-feet-by-five-feet plastic display case with Old Abe the Civil War eagle, wings extended, claws up.

Still, we weren't done. We went to the office above the projection room to see filing cabinets and a few more lockers for artifacts. Some artifacts were kept out because we didn't have any more lockers to put them in.

Finally, General Keane felt he'd seen everything, and he left.

Before General Keane received his third star to become a major general and assume another post, he and I bumped heads a few times.

Back while the museum's vehicles and cannons were being painted and I had cement pads poured for when they returned, General Keane tried micromanaging me. The cannons had just been brought back from the paint shop and were sitting next to their pads. We may have even been waiting for the cement to finish curing before putting on the equipment.

By happenstance, Jack had been in a plane over the base and looked at the museum. On landing, he calls me to say, "Get the cannons on the slabs."

I enlisted a tour group to help. We rolled the cannons on the cement, opened the rear trail legs, placed blocks under the wheels and chained the guns to the cement.

Another time Jack got my goat was few days before Christmas one year, he sent word that Division Headquarters Company would hold its Christmas party at the museum. It was short notice, but it was ordered so there was no way out of it.

The first sergeant sent me an eight-man detail to set up accommodations. From under the stage we pulled out forty five-foot-by-twelve-foot tables and put them where there was space. We set twenty in the movie room, ten in front of the stage, and ten in the cracks. The company used bed sheets for table cloths. We got everything set in the nick of time.

We opened the double doors, and the mess sergeant and cooks carried in two tables loaded down with turkey, dressing, potatoes and pies. Everybody went through the line, the chaplain said grace, and everybody ate well. Afterward were some games for the kids. When everything was over, the detail returned and put the tables and chairs back under the stage.

When Jack got his third star, he went to Fort Bragg, North Carolina, to take over the XVIII Airborne Corp. Even though the 101st was under the command of XVIII Corp, he stayed in Bragg harassing the 82nd Airborne Division troopers instead of me. He later earned a fourth star, was appointed vice chief of staff of the Army, retired, and became a defense analyst.

One year Fort Campbell hosted a reunion of the Rakkasans, the members of the 187th Infantry Regiment.

They earned their name when stationed in Japan after WWII. After the unit parachuted onto Japanese soil in 1945, they were called "rakkasans" by the locals, which loosely translated to "parachute men." (The literal translation means "falling down umbrella men.")

The reunion lasted a week. For the Monday morning opening ceremony, a company of current 187th troops dressed in fatigues formed up in the pavilion beside the 187th monument. The honor guard carried a U.S. flag with gold trim, U.S. Army flag with gold trim, and the 187th regimental flag with battle streamers for WWII, Korea and Desert Storm. I mounted two red regiment flags with gold trim on flag staffs and added two more honor guards to carry them; I made them wear white cotton gloves because these flags were artifacts

After opening ceremonies, the chaplain said a prayer and everybody came into the museum for coffee, Kool-Aid, cookies and doughnuts, and to walk through the looking at the displays. In our theater, I ran movies of the 187th in the Pacific, Korea, Vietnam, and Desert Storm.

Every day offered an event. Alumni could watch the young guys repel and parachute from helicopters, stuff like that. Groups within the 187th attended their on gatherings, too. That Thursday evening I took the regimental flags to a banquet hall in the nearby town of Hopkinsville for a reunion of survivors of the return to Bataan, when the U.S. recaptured the Philippines at the end of WWII.

Saturday evening finished the week with a banquet. General Keane, brigade commander Colonel Dees and Mrs. Dees, and other VIPs sat at a table on a stage. Most of the personnel dressed in their Class A greens. I flipped a coin to decide whether I'd wear my whites or blues; I wore the whites.

The meal was a dependable selection of beef-steak, potato, corn on the cob, and apple pie. The wine glasses had "187th RAKKASANS" engraved on them. After dinner was some dancing and talking with old-timers.

We museum staff spent the next day taking down the displays and artifacts in the banquet hall, and returned them to the museum. I spent Monday putting everything back in the storage lockers.

***

Another annual function for which the museum provided materials was a weeklong conference the division commander held with his commanders, including three infantry brigade commanders and the commander of the 160th Special Operations Regiment, which has all the Apache gunships, Blackhawk helicopters, CH-47 chinook helicopters, etc.

The conference was usually held in Paducah, Kentucky, around ninety miles west of Fort Campbell.

We'd spend Sunday setting up pictures, mannequins, and other items for five or six displays, and remove them on Friday.

Did anything we provided actually make a difference in those conferences? Probably not, but maybe things looked less bare.

***

I met my fourth and last wife, Leticia M. Etchison, when she came through the museum in a tour group. She was stationed at Fort Campbell and came back to the museum on a Saturday afternoon, and I gave her a personal tour. She was young and pretty and put pep in my step.

She became a clerk in Division Personnel. We got married in November 1995. I was fifty-six and she was thirty-one. A few years later when Michael Douglas married Catherine Zeta-Jones, I thought it was funny they were the same ages that Tish and I had been.

The next May, I took a week of leave and we drove out to Junction City to meet my family. The trip was uneventful except Tish came down with what looked like heat rash.

She scratched and scratched. I bought her a bottle of calamine lotion and cotton balls. When we got back to Fort Campbell, she went on sick call and they gave her more calamine lotion.

I took her to the emergency room on post. They didn't take a blood sample, just treated her for heat rash and offered more calamine and cotton balls. I took her to the emergency room in downtown Clarksville, where we waited for three hours. Finally, we saw a doctor, who also offered more calamine. A nurse told Tish that in addition to the calamine, take four or five baths a day using Epsom salt and water as cool as she could stand.

The rash remained about six months, and I don't know how Tish didn't scratch all her skin off. Tired of it, she went to a dermatologist who took a blood sample and concluded her thyroid was over producing. For a second opinion, she went to Blanchfield Army Hospital at Fort Campbell, and they took a blood sample and verified her thyroid was over producing. The treatment was a radioactive iodine pill. The only place she could receive the pill was at Vanderbilt University Medical Center in Nashville. An appointment was set, and at Vanderbilt the doctor gave her the pill. A month later we returned to Vanderbilt for a test and another radioactive iodine pill. The treatment cured the rash, and Tish started taking a daily hormone pill for her thyroid.

The ordeal certainly wasn't a fun way to start a marriage, and in some ways it was downhill from there.

At one point due to health issues, she refused to go to the field on an order from her commander. She received a court martial and general discharge from the Army. I hired a lawyer to file for her disability, and it took eleven months for her to receive it.

***

After General Keane left, the 101st Airborne commander was General William Kernan.

There was a visit to the base of the survivors of the British airborne veterans who'd helped the 101st defend Hell's Highway in WWII. General Kernan brought them to the museum.

I left momentarily to get Tish to bring her to meet the British. I also wanted to show her off to Sergeant Major Rodriguez who was with the tour group. The sergeant major's wife was pleasantly plump and on the low side of plain, and I wanted to jibe him a bit. I introduced Tish to Rodriguez, and his jaw dropped to the floor.

It was an honor to meet the British veterans. I'd mentioned them to every tour group I led in the museum. It was interesting to meet polite, grey-haired old men and realize that in their youth they'd survived fighting tooth and nail against Nazis in bitter cold.

Now, years after meeting them, I've heard people say similar things about me. "You did what in Vietnam?" they say with surprise.

***

The company commander came to the museum and told me the company was going on a live-fire exercise.

"Sir," I said, "I'm on permanent profile and I can't lift over ten pounds or march over a mile."

"We won't be doing any of that," he said. That was false.

I showed up at the company with my duffle bag, sleeping bag, helmet, pack. We drew our rifles from the arms room. We loaded on trucks and went to the training area. There were four medium-size tents set up and we picked our bunks.

A couple hours later the first sergeant passed out ten-pound flak jackets. "Mount up, we're going on a road march," he said.

We got our rifles off the racks, put our helmets on, and got our ruck sacks. Usually they weigh sixty pounds, but since I couldn't carry that much, I filled mine with Styrofoam packing chips. We formed up and marched a mile down the road and back. We atc chow around 10 and I went to bed.

Sam, the first sergeant, woke everybody up and had us get in full field gear: helmet, flak-jacket, pack, weapon. We ate breakfast and milled around like a herd of cows, waiting for the range to open. By 0700 I could hardly move. I checked with the medic, and he had me bring my duffle bag and wait for an ambulance to take me to the aid station. Two hours later, 0900, there was still no ambulance so the first sergeant had his Hummer driver take back to the company area. At the company area, the driver put my duffle and ruck in the trunk of my car and I turned in my rifle and got a sick-slip. I hobbled into the aid station, where the doctor gave me two shots in the shoulder joints, an order for three-day bed rest, and a prescription for Tylenol 3,

I had to pick up the prescription at the hospital pharmacy. I parked in a handicap space as close to the doors as possible. I walked in so bent over and slow that people asked me if I wanted a wheelchair. It took about an hour a half to get to the pharmacy, get the prescription filled, and back on the main floor headed to the car. If a snail wanted to race me, he'd have won.

***

In spring 1997, the WWII, Korean War and Vietnam War 187th Infantry survivors held their Rakkasans reunion at Colorado Springs.

Museum assistant curator Maggie Arrant, her husband, my wife Tish and I took some artifacts out there at the request of the reunion organizers.

Maggie and I went to personnel to request ten-day temporary duty at Colorado then we went to Finance to draw advance travel pay. Maggie called around for a van rental to haul the displays. She settled on a company that rented a van for $800 for ten days and didn't charge for mileage. If I'd had to pay mileage of 85 cents a mile on a 2,000-mile round trip, it would have cost me $1700.

We loaded the regimental flags, a few foam mannequins, and a real-looking mannequin that we'd dress with steel pot, backpack, parachute, jump suit and jump boots.

At 0400 hours on a Friday morning, Maggie and her husband and Tish and I met at the museum. I locked my car in the holding lot, and we all loaded into the van. Tish wasn't a morning person. She usually didn't like to get up before 0900 so when we left through the main gate, we stopped at a truck stop to eat before getting on Interstate 24 West. We went through Paducah, over the river into Illinois, around thirty miles to Interstate 57 North to Mt. Vernon, then a left on I-64 to St. Louis and catching I-70 looping across the Missouri prairie into Kansas City, and skipping across the river into Kansas.

Continuing on I-70, we went through the edge of Lawrence, hung a hard right at Topeka, and stopped in Junction City at around 1800 hours. We took a couple rooms at a hotel with both outside and inside pools. As fancy as that sounds, across the parking lot was a Denny's, and that's where we ate.

After dinner, Tish and I went out to see my daughter Nora for an hour. On the way back to the hotel, rain started falling and there was lightning without thunder. Using the inside pool, Tish and I swam a little then sat in the sauna.

We were back on the road at about 0400 hours, after eating again at Denny's. I-70 West would take us all the way to Colorado, but it was still eight hours of driving. When we got to Limon, we turned southwest on a state highway that took us into Colorado Springs. We called the Rakkasans to find their hotel. It turned out to be a Hilton, so our room was $90 a night. Eight nights made the bill $720. It would've been nice to know about that ahead of time.

The Rakkasans held their get-together in a couple of conference rooms. We set up the life-like mannequin, old steel pot helmet, light-tan jump suit, field pack, brown jump boots, main parachute on back, reserve parachute in front. We stood him just inside the door, hand up saluting the Rakkasans as they walked in. The regimental flags were in stands behind the front table, and we placed vintage pictures in both rooms.

They held meetings about their experiences and offered a lot of activities. Some rode the train up Pike's Peak, went hang-gliding or rode hot air balloons. I took Tish to the Royal Gorge and white-water rafting. The rapids were pretty tame that day, disappointing Tish, who wanted a real ride. The guide took us in a rubber raft, and put on our helmets and life jackets. At one curve a photographer took our picture. By the time we finished we were soaked to the skin, and I turned the van's heater on to dry us out.

One evening we could ride out to a dude ranch for BBQ, but we didn't go. I took Tish up the side of Pike's Peak where they have auto races every spring. We went through part of the Garden of the Gods (an area of amazing rock formations) and climbed up the Seven Falls.

On Friday Tish and I went to Cripple Creek, Colorado to gamble. In the 1890s Cripple Creek was producing millions of dollars in gold and silver. Today it's a tourist trap and you can get permits to pan for gold and silver in the river. While there, I gave Tish $100 to buy a nice dress to wear for the concluding Saturday banquet at the hotel.

As it turned out, for the Saturday night banquet, the Rakkasans placed the museum's assistant curator and me at the head table to thank us for our contribution to the reunion.

Tish wore her new light blue dress and had her hair cut and permed. We felt so good, we had our picture taken by the fancy event photographer and I shelled out $20 for a photo packet. Some other nice keepsakes were the wine glasses engraved with "Rakkasans, Colorado, 1997. "

Sunday afternoon we loaded all the artifacts and mannequins back in the van, and hit the road. When we stopped at Junction City, Tish and I were so pooped out, we didn't bother seeing my family. We just sloshed around the pool and sauna. Back at Fort Campbell, Maggie and I turned in our TDY papers, and I had to draw another $200 to cover expenses.

***

Inconvenience struck the Don Pratt Museum around this time: Asbestos was found under the carpet in the front lobby, and we had to remove it.

To do that, we had to move the helicopter from the front of the museum. Curator Rex Boggs and I took a medium-sized forklift and positioned it to support the chopper when we unbolted its two-inch cable from the rafter above. With the helicopter on the forklift, we slowly back down an aisle, making sure to keep the propeller blades below the lights but about two feet above the glider. Rex found a beam strong enough to hold the helicopter above the ramp going onto the stage, and had bolted the cable around the rafter. Fortunately, there was enough room between the glider wing and the ceiling to lift the helicopter above the glider wing.

The chopper's mannequin pilot and co-pilot did a great job of "flying" it from the front to the back.

Once the front area was clear, the asbestos removal team built a frame so they could hang plastic across the top and down the sides to seal the area from asbestos exposure. A lot of area was covered with plastic, but it was set up so we could get to the offices. At night when we left the museum, we would set the alarm in the office then had three minutes to run eighty feet to the door, going through the repair shop and out the back door, and slam and lock the door before the timer tripped. In the morning, we did it all in reverse. Once we unlocked and opened the outside door, we raced through the repair shop, through the museum, through the plastic tunnel to the office and punch in the code to clear the alarm.

The asbestos removal took a month and the museum remained open the whole time. We did close for a week shortly thereafter when General Kernan decided we needed to replace the museum's carpet with tile.

The tiling started in the museum theater. We wheeled out Old Abe the eagle and workers removed the carpet and laid the tile. Basically, if the workers were on one side of the museum, all the displays and artifacts needed to be shifted to the other side. Two crews worked twenty-four hours a day. I worked the night shift. The crews pulled up the carpet then laid the tile over to the glider. We jacked up the glider to remove carpet underneath then laid tile and let the tile set for twelve hours before setting the glider back down. Once we got to the glider we moved all the display cases back to the other side.

There was a tank inside the museum, and I drove it near a wall while workers laid tile over its usual spot. When I backed the tank into final position, we put in a rail around it. When the tiling was complete we returned all the display cases like they were, and wheeled Old Abe back from the projection room.

***

In early 1998, my last stint in the Army was winding down and at the same time General Kernan made his third star and would be going to Fort Bragg, North Carolina, to replace General Keane as commander of XVIII Corps. It's worth noting that Fort Bragg was the largest Army base in the country.

I went to the major who was the highest aide for General Kernan, and I told him – I didn't ask – "You will get me one of General Kernan's challenge coins." A challenge coin is a commemorative coin that is often given to members of a military unit. In this case, the coin marked the change of command. I respected the general, and his departure from the base coincided with mine so I felt connection with the event.

The change of command ceremony in February was at the Division parade field. Rain started to fall so the reception party came to the museum. General Kernan himself handed me a coin. I appreciated the gesture. It wasn't engraved, but his aide told me he'd have it done for me.

A few days later, the officers' wives gave Mrs. Kernan a going-away party. The young second lieutenant's wife didn't send a detail to set up, so the Kernans' cook brought some food in and Mrs. Kernan and three of us sat up the tables ourselves. The rest of the party went smoothly, and a detail did show up later to clean up.

My own farewell to Fort Campbell was pending.

Three months before I retired, museum curator Rex Boggs typed a request for me to receive the Legion of Merit, which was a great honor.

General Kernan signed it and had Personnel prepare the certificate and medal for my retirement ceremony.

Three weeks before retirement, I started the process for clearing the post. I turned in my TA-50, cleared company by turning in my rifle, picked up my medical and finance records and 201 files. I took all my records to the museum to make copies of everything – that way I wouldn't have to go to St. Louis to look at my records.

I asked Personnel when they were going to change my rank from staff sergeant to sergeant first class, the highest rank I held.

"You don't have thirty years of federal service so you'll have to wait ten years," they said.

"Show me that regulation," I said.

They couldn't, so I wrote Secretary of the Army Togo West. His office sent me a copy of the regulation. I'd have to wait ten years after retiring to start receiving the sergeant first class pay rate. At Personnel, a lady typed up the DD214. I signed it and received five copies.

Museum curator Rex took a flag hanging in a conference room, had it cleaned, folded and placed in a shadow box with black cloth background, with eagle patch, blue cloth, and foam mounts with my miniature medals. It was a great gift, but I spent over a hundred dollars replacing my mini medals.

Rex gave me a retirement dinner. Guests included Colonel Jones, Colonel Davis, Colonel Croshner, Sergeant Major Counts, and others. They presented me with two different letters of appreciation plaques, and a 101st Airborne Division lifetime membership certificate from the new commander plus his challenge coin.

I also received a letter of appreciation signed by President William Jefferson Clinton, the famous draft dodger.

I had post transportation put my household goods in storage until I figured out where I was going to live.

Tish and I drove to Nashville, staying two weeks in a Red Roof Inn before finding an apartment in Burning Tree Apartments in a suburb east of the city, but just off I-40. It was a two-bedroom apartment for $650 a month. The complex was on a hill, and some of the apartments had good views.

I drove back to Fort Campbell to give Transportation the directions for how to get to the apartment and how to deliver our furniture. They said it would be delivered the next Wednesday, and they did, arriving around 0900 hours – but since I was no longer in the military, it was 9 a.m. for me.

I'd thought I'd have to go to the VA hospital to take a test to receive disability payments, but I received a letter when I was out-processing saying that Personnel already sent a copy of my medical records to the VA. The letter said I'd be receiving thirty percent disability: ten percent for each shoulder and ten percent for my chest wound. Payments would start June 1.

My military service had ended.

In thinking about it, I'd say my first stint in Vietnam was spent fighting for my country and my second stint twenty years later at the Don Pratt Museum at Fort Campbell was spent preserving the legacies of soldiers just like me so future generations of Americans will know the cost of freedom.

CERTIFICATE OF APPRECIATION

FOR SERVICE IN THE ARMED FORCES OF THE UNITED STATES

RUSSELL A. BABCOCK STAFF SERGEANT

I extend to you my personal thanks and the sincere appreciation of our nation for your honorable service. You helped to maintain the security of the United States of America with a devotion to duty that is in keeping with the proud tradition of our Armed Forces.

I honor your service and respect the commitment and loyalty you displayed over the years.

My best wishes to you for happiness and success in the future.

Bill Clinton

Commander in Chief

SEAL OF THE PRESIDENT OF THE UNITED STATES

When I left the Army in 1973, President Nixon sent a certificate of appreciation. When I retired in 1997, the certificate of appreciation came from President Clinton, America's most famous draft dodger.

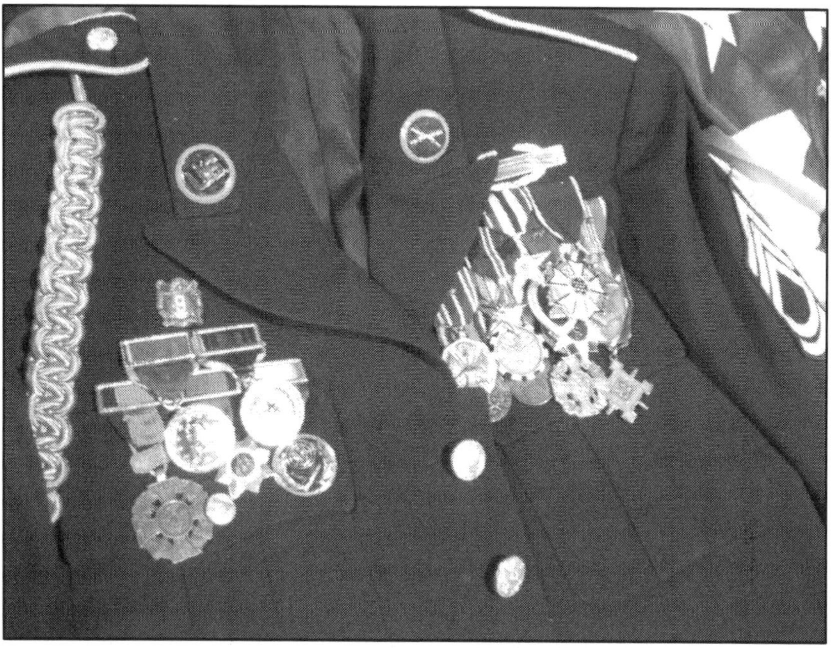

My dress green jacket with my medals.

Chapter Twenty-Four

Nashville is My Beat

After eight years, I was a civilian again. That meant looking for a civilian job.

In reading the newspaper want ads, I saw that the security company Wackenhut was looking for guards. I went to their office at Airport Road and Murfreesboro Road, and there were ten or eleven people there. Men and women were filling out applications: name, last three places of employment, references.

The secretary explained that if hired we'd have to get Tennessee state security licenses ($95) and take the unarmed or armed course ($60), and the company would pay the costs up front then deduct it from our paycheck in two payments.

The secretary gathered the applications and told us to take a break. I and a few others got Cokes and went outside to smoke. After twenty minutes the secretary had us sit then said, "If I don't call your name, you can leave. Anderson, Babcock, Dole." She called about six names, and the others left.

Major Hollenbeck came in and told us about the company. "Wackenhut was started by two brothers, who built the business into a worldwide company," he said. "The headquarters is in Miami, Florida. Besides doing security work, in some states Wackenhut operates state penitentiaries, and in some big cities the police stop and arrest people then call Wackenhut. Guards are sent to the police officer's location and take the suspect to the closest police station and start the booking process, which allows the police to stay on patrol instead of being at the police station two or three hours. In Alaska Wackenhut also handles drug testing."

Major Hollenbeck brought us into his office one at time for interviews and to assign the type of security post we'd be on.

He asked me, “Why’d you only list one job?”

I showed him my DD214. “For the last eight years, I’ve been in the Army,” I said.

Showing the last three jobs gave the major an idea of a guy’s work habits, and the personal talk exhibits your appearance. If you list all three previous jobs in a year and a half, it usually indicates bad work habits and undependability.

Wackenhut furnished all equipment: two light blue long-sleeve and two light blue short-sleeve shirts, two pairs dark blue pants, pistol belt, blue baseball cap. Guards were responsible for buying their own black shoes.

The majority of the security posts were dull. Nothing happens.

One post was a construction site three miles out in the country. There was only one road to the site, no 7-Eleven to go for coffee at 4 a.m., nobody to talk to, and the last activity was two hours previous when three rabbits sat in the middle of the road talking. Usually, one of two things would happen: 1) you fall asleep or 2) you don't come to work.

The company said no books or cellphone games at work, but the supervisors would prefer to see you sitting there reading a book or playing a game than being asleep. If you weren’t coming to work, the company's policy was to give them eight hours’ notice so they could get somebody else to work. There’s nothing that made a supervisor madder than finding an empty post. This meant he’d have to stop his patrol checking on the posts and had to start calling his roving guards to get one of them to come and finish the shift. He had to stay at the empty post until a replacement showed up. A supervisor preferred catching you reading a book or playing cellphone games because at least you’re awake and watching the equipment.

Hollenbeck asked me if I’d be a roving guard. I’d be on call twenty-four hours a day, seven days a week, I'd get paid $8 an hour even if that post didn't pay the regular guard that much.

I told him yes.

It wasn't about the hourly pay. The main reason I accepted being a roving guard was that it meant I wouldn't be on a dull post at the same time at the same place every day. As a roving guard, I was also issued two white long-sleeve and two short-sleeve shirts and two pairs light blue pants.

The next day being Friday, the major told me and three others to be at APPS, the Academy of Personal Protection and Security School, at 8 a.m.

The name of the instructor was Buford. I was an unarmed guard, so I only attended one day of training. "You can only use enough force to subdue and restrain the person," Buford said. "As security guards, we can't arrest the person. Only police can arrest the person. Some young gung-ho people get into trouble over the wording 'AS SECURITY OFFICERS, YOU CAN'T ARREST.' Make sure you remember that."

Training for armed guards took three days. The second day gave some examples of when you may fire at a person and when you can't. If a group of people comes toward you with bats and pipes and you're afraid of being hurt or killed, you can shoot a warning round. But if the person has turned around walking away, you can't shoot him in the back and claim self-defense.

Friday afternoon after Buford finished giving his classes, we turned in security application forms for licenses with our names and information. Buford sent a copy of that, a certificate of completion and a check to the Tennessee Department of Commerce and Insurance. In between thirty and sixty days, you'd get your license. We'd get a five-by-seven certificate to frame and a wallet-size card. All guards had to keep this card while on post. If a policeman or a commerce and insurance inspector asked to see the card and a guard didn't have it, he'd be fined up to a $1,000.

While waiting for a license, a guard could work while carrying a copy of the application.

Just before I started to work for Wackenhut, there'd been a lot of tornado damage around Nashville, and money was passing through local insurance agencies. Hollenbeck sent me to guard a State Farm insurance agency. I took out a time sheet form and a post log form from my Samsonite briefcase. On the time sheet I marked that I arrived at 0200 hours. Then I marked my post log:

1) Arrived at 0200 hours and made a security check of the property, all doors locked, nobody around.

2) Performed security check of property doors locked all secure

3) 0330 made walk around check of property nobody around

4) 1000 relieved by agency personnel.

I marked my time sheet 10 a.m. and went home to bed. I had the same post that night. Monday morning I went to the office to turn in my logs and time sheet to the secretary, Thelma. On the way home, I stopped by Radio Shack to buy a cellphone and a pager. I went back to the office and gave Thelma the phone and pager numbers.

On Monday the major and another supervisor took all the time sheets, filled out how many hours each guard worked that week, what post the person worked and how much the person got paid an hour. The major faxed this information to headquarters in Florida so the checks can be made.

The company pay schedule lag time was three weeks. When I finally received my first check, there two errors: 1) I didn't get paid $8 an hour and 2) I was shorted eight hours. I turned in a correction time sheet, and I still didn't get paid for that eight hours.

On a small legal tablet, I started writing down what post, what time and what day to keep my own ledger.

I asked the major, “When am I going to get $8 an hour?”

“You’ll get it,” he said.

After two months I still hadn't started receiving $8 an hour.

Thelma the secretary guarded the major's and the operations manager's doors like a mother bear. When Thelma left her desk for a moment, I slipped in to talk to the manager. I told him that

"As a roving guard, I was told I'd be paid $8 an hour and I haven't been, and the major hasn't put in the code," I said. "My light bill is $200. If I don't pay by the 15th of the month, the light company will turn my lights off then I'll have to pay the light bill plus another $150 light deposit."

We went to the major's office. The manager asked, "Why haven't you put the code in?"

The major was surprised and came up with a poor excuse. The manager told the major, "Do it now."

After six months, Major Hollenbeck wanted me to become an armed guard. For armed guards, the Tennessee Bureau of investigation runs a background check to see if there are any felony charges on their records. Wackenhut furnished the guns, .38's. Another $60 was paid to APPS and $120 to Tennessee Commerce and Insurance.

The next morning was a Friday, and the company issued me a pistol and holster. Then I pulled guard duty at the farmers' market at Eighth and Jefferson from 4 p.m. till midnight.

There was a Friday and Saturday when I sat through another class of Buford's on dos and don'ts of guarding. Buford gave examples of when you can draw and fire your pistol and we took a test with Buford reading questions like, can you shoot a man if he's walking away? That Sunday we met Buford at the Tennessee Air National Guard airfield at Smyrna for a shooting test. The price of the class included a box of fifty .38 rounds. To pass you had to put thirty-five bullet holes inside a man-shaped target. We were lined up on the firing line, pistols in holsters, ten feet in front of the targets.

"On command, draw and fire five rounds," Buford said.

Bang, bang, bang, bang, bang. My revolver only held five rounds, and I made five holes. I used a speed loader and reloaded my pistol and re-holstered.

"Cease fire," Buford called.

We walked to the targets and marked our hits then returned to the firing line. "On command, fire five rounds," Buford said.

Bang, bang, bang, bang, bang. We marked the targets and returned to the line. We repeated until we'd fired up half the box of bullets then we moved back to twenty feet.

"On command, fire all remaining rounds," Buford said.

When out of bullets, we took down the targets and collected the brass bullet casings. We turned in our targets to Buford and he counted the bullet holes. Thirty-one, thirty-two, thirty-three, thirty-four, thirty-five – he stopped counting and marked my score on the application. He sent in the paperwork and the Tennessee State Department of Commerce and Insurance issued me an armed guard license.

The Nashville chief of police had a great racket going: before a guard could carry a gun on a post in Nashville, the police had to be paid $15 for a local gun permit. Before I could get my gun permit from the chief of police, I had to explain to the Nashville city attorney about my two felony charges: obscene literature in 1962 and a bad check in 1975. They issued me the gun permit.

Major Hollenbeck wanted me to become another class of officer, a customs officer in brown uniform. The pay was variable depending on the client, but the most the job paid was $10 an hour. One bank paid the customs officer $10 an hour. Nations Bank now Bank of America wanted regular armed guards for $8.50 an hour.

Now I really had to keep my times and dates and places written down if I wanted to keep my boss honest.

I was posted at the Bosch brake plant in Gallatin, fifteen miles north of Nashville from 7 a.m. to 3 p.m. Monday through Wednesday and Friday for $8 an hour. One of the permanent guards came in at 2 p.m., an hour early. I asked him to clock in to relieve me so I could answer a page my supervisor sent me. I headed to the office a mile away, and received instructions sending me to Avis car rental return at the airport from 3 p.m. to 11 p.m. A half-hour before my shift ended at

Avis, Captain Roberts called to send me to Columba, 70 miles away, to watch a warehouse till 7 a.m. So, I'd be working a full twenty-four hours.

I decided to drive by home for food en route to the warehouse. At the foot of a hill near the apartment, my Chevy's alternator died. I locked up the car and walked to the apartment and took my wife's Mazda.

It was 1 a.m. by the time I arrived in Columba. The post commander started harping, and I said, "Listen, I've already worked fourteen hours. If you don't want to sit on post holding a new guard's hand, then shut up."

The next morning when I got home, I turned off my home phone, cellphone and pager, and slept most of two days. Then I turned everything back on, and told them I was ready.

One post I worked as an armed guard was the farmers market, 5 a.m. to 4 p.m. at $9 an hour, 4 p.m. to midnight or from midnight to 5 a.m. at $8. Unarmed made $6 an hour. The one guard who worked it five nights a week always took Tuesday and Thursday off and the supervisor couldn't schedule one person on Tuesday another on Thursday so I did it both days.

When we picked up a new account that was larger than most of our others, Captain Roberts was caught in the middle. Technically, he was in charge of people working for the new company, like making schedules, but the client's head of security used him as a gopher instead.

The name of this company was Dell Computers.

They put up a prefab plant at Interstate 40 exit 231. The people working for them had to wear a brown uniform like the customs uniform but with a Dell patch. The plant was inside a wire fence, a guard shield at the main entrance. There were four doors side by side. Just inside the door on the right was a room where the shift commander sat monitoring the cameras throughout the building. Beside the supervisor's door were five metal detector machines. You'd walk through to go in the main plant. There were five guards with wands to check for metal.

Right in the middle of the plant was a wire fence ten feet high. At one gate the guard sat inside the fence. If he wanted to go on break or go to the restroom he called the shift supervisor to relieve him. There were five loading docks on each side of the plant, with a guard at each door. A truck driver would back his trailer to the dock and the guard would open the trailer doors and escort the driver to a break room with vending machines, restrooms, TV. The driver was locked in to prevent theft. The guard returned to the dock to supervise loading and unloading and check the invoices. In other words, he also served as a shipping and receiving clerk.

The company loaded some trailers and locked and sealed the doors, moved it a half-mile down the road to another fenced lot where another Wackenhut guard made sure the doors were locked and sealed. He'd note the seal number in his log. When a driver came in for his trailer, he stopped at the plant for the shipping papers and came to the storage lot. He hooked up to the trailer, turned in a copy of the invoice, and he'd be off and running.

The plant was ten miles north of town, and Dell also took the bottom floor of a building twelve miles east of town. There were four rooms inside two doors with keypads. All new employees trained there for a week before going to work at the plant. There was another building down the road a mile from the warehouse with three or four rooms and four Wackenhut guards and a bunch of people on computers. I worked all these places.

Dell also bought a two-year-old Mercury Grand Marquis highway patrol car with a big V-8 engine and interceptor transmission, and two Wackenhut guards would fly it two twelve-hour shifts seven days a week.

As for banks, Wackenhut guarded several that I dealt with.

The SunTrust Bank's main local bank at Fourth Avenue and Central had two towers twelve floors high. Pinkerton guarded both east and west ground floors. Wackenhut had the second floor west with two guards nights and weekends. They monitored the TV screens showing the vault building server room, and we'd go check the temperature, and hourly checks riding the elevator to the fifth floor, walk across to check the records door was locked, go to the seventh floor, walk back across, go to the tenth floor to check the banquet room and outdoor pool, return to the second floor. On Fridays I'd go to the SunTrust on Dickerson Road. I'd sit in the car and once an hour walk around the bank to keep the working girls from going up to cars in the drive-through lanes asking for money. Then I'd go inside to sign the log.

I worked the SunTrust vault for $10 an hour, and the same for the Nations Bank (now Bank of America) vault at Fourth Avenue and Central. I worked the Nations Bank branches at Antioch, Hermitage and Madison for $8.50 an hour.

As the year 1999 closed in on 2000, or Y2K as the media called it, the banks worried that the computers would hiccup.

If the vault computers failed, the banks wanted us to be able to move the money to a safe location. Another supervisor, Donna, and I had to go to the main office and have photo IDs made then we made a trial run from our office to Fourth Avenue and the vault to simulate signing for different-sized bags of money then back to the office for an hour of work. We received $40 each.

The Friday before New Year's, I was at the Regions Bank in Antioch when the supervisor brought in another guard. I was told to pick up a guard at Nations' main office then go to the vault and sign for a bag of money and transport it to Springfield, Tennessee. I left the bank, hopped on I-24 West, raced to Fourth Avenue, turned right, went two blocks, and there the guard was waiting. I made a U-turn and went back up Fourth Avenue to Central, down to the vault, talked to the clerk, signed for a bag of money: $250,000.

I lock it in the trunk of my car, and we went back down Fourth Avenue onto 1-24 West to Exit 24, turned right, and drove about fifteen miles to Springfield. I took the money into the bank and had the clerk sign for it. On the way back, the supervisor wanted to know how long before I got back. I said an hour. Another bank wanted some money, so he sent somebody else to that bank. They wanted $20,000 but $5,000 of that was in coins. I think I got paid $100 for that run.

During holidays, a lot of the posts paid time and a half if you worked Thanksgiving or Christmas. From midnight to 5 a.m., I played supervisor driving around in a company car checking the posts. When I played supervisor, I was supposed to get fifty cents more an hour but normally didn't. Wackenhut didn't pay supervisors time and a half for working holidays. At 6 a.m. I went back to the office, left the patrol car for the next supervisor, signed out as a supervisor and I took my car to be a regular guard at Conway Trucking from 7 a.m. to 3 p.m. at double pay, $16.

Wackenhut had one patrol route with seven or eight properties. You'd leave the office south on Murfreesboro. First stop was Aramark at Spruce and Elm Hill. Second stop was an Elm Hill dance club where they taught ballroom and fancy dancing. Another was Woodlawn Apartments off Harding Place.

Jared Jewelry built a store in Antioch. I worked there twenty-one days straight during construction. The last couple days I started contributing to the finishing touches: installing glass display cases, metal blinds over windows. One of the shopping malls wanted to come look around, but no.

Two days before the store opened, Brinks arrived with two armored trucks loaded with jewelry. The trucks backed up to the door, put the ramp down and started unloading carts of jewelry. When the drivers were done, the manager signed for all the trinkets. I locked the outer glass door, rolled down the metal door, locked the inner door, and lowered the metal window blinds. The sales people started placing rings, necklaces, and watches in the different display cases. We were there from 9 a.m. to 10 p.m. At 9:30 the sales people put the most valuable jewelry on carts and rolled them into the vault, and we went home.

The next morning was the grand opening. I was out front at 5 a.m. The manager and sales people arrive at 8:30. The manager handed me the keys and I unlocked the first glass doors. The manager and I entered, I locked the doors then turned the key for the metal door and it began rolling up. We entered. I rolled the door down, unlocked the inner door. The manager waited as I locked that door and walked through the building turning on lights and checking to make sure nobody was in the store. I returned to the front to let in the manger, rolled up the metal door, and unlocked the outer door to let in the sales people. I locked the outer doors, rolled down the metal door, unlocked the inner door, we entered, I locked the door, went around the windows lowering the metal blinds, and they brought in jewelry from the safe and put it in display cases. The high sign was given at 9:55 that we were ready to open so I raised the window blinds, unlocked the inner doors, rolled up the metal door and unlocked the outer doors.

Was that enough unlocking, locking, rolling and unrolling?

About once a month Jared would try to get a celebrity to come in to meet and greet. I can't remember the first one's name but he was demanding to be paid $10,000 cash with a $20,000 line of credit toward jewelry, and two armed guards.

He got the guards but didn't get all the rest of it. He was a local racecar driver and owned a car dealership. He didn't even display his racecar. He was a dud. The janitor and I picked up all the trash. All the paper cups and anything paper went in one container and anything glass or metal went in other containers. Everything, all the bags, had to be checked with a metal wand to make sure no jewelry was inside. After all that, the bag in the vacuum cleaner had to rip open.

One morning while placing the jewelry in the cases, someone dropped a $5,000 ring fell on the floor. Nobody noticed and the janitor vacuumed it up. The manager had to call and report the ring missing. Headquarters sent a person down. I went and opened the vacuum bag and found the ring.

For one two-week pay period I lacked $20 of clearing $2,000.

The fun and games at Jared and the banks would be coming to an end.

I'd been resisting going to classes for baton and pepper spray but finally had to. I was working at a Pilot truck stop off I-24. A man came in and stole a $3 pack of lunch meat. When he went out the door, the alarm went off. I went after him and told him to stop. He went across the road. I couldn't legally shoot him for stealing $3 lunchmeat.

So, I went to Buford's classes on baton and pepper spray. There were a couple of methods for teaching about pepper spray. Some places spray a little of it on a Q-Tip and rub it under your eyes. Buford would stand eight feet away and spray you in the face. You'd stand facing the wind to let the wind clear out your eyes, then go inside and wash the remains off your face with Buford's no-tear baby shampoo and a towel.

I went back to the Pilot truck stop, and a trucker came in and said there was a woman knocking on doors propositioning drivers.

I walked out to the lot and saw her. I told her to stop and leave the lot. She said she was going to continue, and started to walk away. I swept her feet out from under her. She hit the ground and I started to cuff her. I got one arm cuffed and a trucker helped me cuff the other arm. She weighed around 250 pounds. I took her inside, took her photo, filled out a report, and called Metro to arrest and take her to jail.

There was a night when I was working night court from 4 p.m. to midnight. I was on smoke break when one of the judges came out for a smoke too. The judge pointed to a blonde woman nearby and said, "She's a prostitute and she runs a tab with about half of the police. If she's ever arrested, she doesn't spend too long in jail.

Another night, a Nashville DEA squad bade a big drug bust and arrested six or seven people. One of the men owned the house where the drugs originated, and he told the judge that for payment of a little pot, he let these men sell drugs out of his house. The judge told the man that the under the new drug laws, the DEA just took owner-ship of his house. For the other men, the judge set the bail at $40,000 apiece. They faced the wrong judge. He was hard on drugs. That same night, the judge presided over a drunken man who'd pulled out a .45 pistol at a bar; the judge set his bond at a hundred dollars.

With the use of closed-circuit TV, the outlying police stations had people see the judge and have their bonds set and some court dates set without leaving the police station. A young couple who was stopped in Hermitage for half a joint of pot had their bond set at $1,000 by the hanging judge.

At night court, the police took people into the back to holding cells, to booking, from booking through a tunnel to a glassed-in room. The judge sat in his own bullet-proof glass room. The gallery was where the guards and witnesses, lawyers, and other court cases or general public sat.

Two police officers brought in a little old lady some standing around four feet tall. Soaking wet with rocks in her pockets, she might've weighed ninety pounds. She was in handcuffs. The plaintiffs were her son – standing six-foot-two and weighing around 210 pounds – and his petite girlfriend. The old lady had scared the two of them via assault with a knife.

Around 7 a.m. my supervisor called to send me to general session court at Second Street and Fourth Avenue, across the street to the east from the night court and jail. Across Fourth Avenue was the county court. I went in the county court parking lot, but it was full. I went to the underground parking lot and was successful. I went upstairs and reported to the post commander. There were supposed to be six people at the post, including four at the X-ray machines.

I took up my station at the X-rays. The people came in and put their briefcases on a conveyor belt that went through the machine. You empty your pockets, phones, watches, lighters, change, billfold and purses in plastic buckets and these buckets go through the machine. The guard sees the contents of the keys, combs, lipstick, change. Then you walk through the metal detector; if you buzz, you go back through, if you buzz again, you stand in front of an officer who runs a wand across your body then lets you retrieve your things. Some items weren't allowed in the courthouse: handcuff keys, pepper spray, knives, bow and arrows and definitely not guns.

At noon, when I got a thirty-minute break, I looked in my wallet. The previous night when I went to bed, I had $12, but now there was no money.

At 4 p.m. the supervisor called to send me to the Greyhound bus station. I had to borrow $5 from the post commander to get my car out of the parking lot.

I turned right on Fourth Avenue and drove to Eighth Avenue, but I didn't see the bus station. I drove around and around for thirty minutes and still couldn't find the bus station. I drove back down Fourth Avenue to I-24, turned right to I-40 and hit Eighth Avenue, went that way and found the bus station. I was there until midnight.

The next morning I told Tish, "Never take money out of my wallet again. If you need money, ask and I'll give you money."

***

Wackenhut hired an accountant, Miss Dole, an older lady. She took over doing the time sheets on Mondays. Once in a while she'd miss one of my time sheets. I'd show her my yellow pad and which post and time. She'd apologize.

I told her that since she took over the time sheets, there were very few times that she missed a place.

It gave me a headache trying to keep my pay straight. As an unarmed guard on an unarmed post at Dell, I made $8 an hour. As an armed guard at Nations Bank, I made $8.50 unless I was working the vault, then I got $10. As an armed guard at Pilot, I made $10, and Jared $11, and some days I worked posts on each pay. I might work Nations Bank 5 a.m. to 3 p.m. at $8.50 then go to Avis rental at the airport from 4 p.m. to 11 p.m. at $8 then go to Pilot truck stop from midnight to 5 a.m. at $10 an hour.

Sunday nights I got to play supervisor from midnight to 8 a.m. arrive at the office. If the off-going officer was there I talked to him to see what kind of night he had. If he wasn't there I filled in my time and had the time clock stamp it, started my patrol log, listened to the phone messages, then I'd flip a coin to see what I wanted to do first. I'd go out and walk around the patrol car to check for broken lights or windows, dents or paint strips where the other drivers hit a pole or car, tires good, open trunk for the spare tire, jack, lug wrench, jack handle. I'd pop the hood to check water in the radiator, check oil and transmission fluid. I'd check out the engine fluids every time I drove a patrol car because most security companies were small companies and they bought mostly used police cars, highway patrol cars, with over 100,000 miles. So some cars burned a lot of oil. I'd look inside to see that the car was clean.

Then I'd be ready to start my patrol. I turned left on Murfreesboro Road, go to the light, turn right on Donelson Pike, stop and check the guard at the Holiday Inn, pick up time sheets/log sheets, get on Interstate 40 North to Exit 231, and hop off. This put me at Dell, an unarmed post so I can't wear my gun inside. I locked the gun in the trunk, went into the supervisor's office for time sheets/daily logs, returned to the car, opened the trunk for my pistol, got in the car, turned right on I-40 South to Exit 318, left on Bell Road to Antioch, stopped at the Holiday Inn and Red Roof Inn to talk to guards, picked up time sheets/logs. On the other side of I-24, Bell turned into Old Hickory Boulevard. I went to Brentwood to the Super 8 motel, where the guards used a big old-time clock like in the old movies. I used the time key to open the back of the clock to replace the roll of tape for new one. The old roll showed what times the guards made their rounds and if they checked each place they were supposed to.

For payday, checks could be direct-deposited or available to pick up at the office. At 5 a.m. I went to the general session court for time sheets/logs and to give the guards' checks to the supervisor, walked across Fourth Avenue into the county courthouse to pick up logs/time sheets and give the supervisor the checks, hopped on I-24, a left at I-40 to Exit 316, right on Donelson Pike through three stop lights, a ninety-degree left turn onto Murfreesboro Road for one block, a two-wheel ninety-degree right turn, slammed on the brakes with both feet, and slid to a halt in front of the office. All the logs/time sheets fell off the back seat. I pushed them into a pile, put my clipboard on, grabbed the papers, and put the bundle on Major Hollenbeck's desk.

I made my last two entries on the time sheet, "8:30 a.m. off duty," and stamped it with the time clock, logged "8:30 a.m. at office" and turned them in and went off duty. I picked up my check from Thelma and went home.

***

We had nine or ten businesses and apartment complexes. I remember these because it was the beginning of around ten years of patrolling – first for Wackenhut then SecurityWise and later for Hayes Security.

From the office I'd go across Donelson to I-40 South to Exit 213, Massman Drive just before Elm Hill Pike. On the right, there were other businesses in the complex. You drove to the end of the buildings, left at the corner of that building and an open area. The dock doors were on the left side of this lot. We'd get out to check the doors. There'd be seven or eight trucks and we'd check them to make sure everything was OK. Over the years a few were taken. I took a left on Elm Hill Pike to Orr Road, right on Orr. At the end the road split, one road going left, the other right. The Elm Hill complex had spaces for 30 or 40 businesses. Where the road split, those buildings were like a lopsided octagon, a road between these buildings and the other set of building in line. The first business on the front was the dance club teaching ballroom dance.

For the Woodlawn Apartments, you'd go back to Fesslers Lane, turn left, cross over I-40, get on I-40, drive three miles, take I-24 East to Chattanooga, to Harding Place, turn right, drive two miles and you'd come to Woodlawn Apartments. On the right side you'd be coming down a hill and see four entrances to Woodlawn. On the right was Building S, two floors high with four apartments on front and four on the back, then Building R with six apartments on front and back. On the left side of the road was the laundry room, with office on the back side, mechanical shop, and a roadway going into Buildings O, P and Q. I turned right then right and was outside the pool, weight room and a little day room. I'd park. The pool closed at 10 p.m. so if any people were in the pool I'd chase them out, lock the outside pool gate, unlock the weight room, go to the middle door, unlock it, go in the day room to check bathrooms for people. There was a sliding glass door with top and bottom latches to lock. There were three other roads with apartments. Behind Building A was a tennis court. Then you're at the top road and it connected to the one you came in on.

I was home at Burning Tree Apartments, Exit 221 on Old Hickory Pike, about seven miles north of the office. At 3:45 p.m. Captain Roberts called to send me to the farmers market. It was a Thursday and they'd forgotten to schedule somebody on the regular guard's day off. I got dressed, got in the car (a 1996 KIA), got on I-40 South all the way around Nashville and came up on Eighth Avenue from the southwest. It was 4:30 p.m. rush-hour traffic. At the top of the ramp to Eighth Avenue was a stoplight and traffic was backed down onto I-40. A white van was hanging out of the ramp lane onto I-40 and I couldn't stop. Bam! I hit the van. The backdoor of the van had two small windows and one was knocked out, the back bumper was bent and that was all the damage to the van. I bent my front bumper, and the grill and hood of my car had buckled.

I got out of the car to walk up to the van and ask the driver if he was hurt. He said he had whip lash.

I saw he had a phone so I told him to call Metro police. I called Captain Roberts. The firetruck and ambulance showed up and the medic put a neck brace on the van driver and carted him off to the hospital. Metro showed up and called a wrecker, Metro made out the accident report. I was cited for hitting the back of the van so the Tennessee Department of Motor Vehicles deducted four points off my driving record. I had the tow truck driver drop me off at the farmers market and I called Captain Roberts and told him I was at the market.

I called the insurance company about the accident. They said to mail them a copy of the accident report. Around 6 a.m. I called the office and left a message for my supervisor to come and get me from the market and take me home.

The farmers market took up one city block. It was a modern-looking complex with concrete pillars and lots of glass. The area for the booths was under a roof. On the left side was the flea market that's open Friday, Saturday and Sunday. The middle building had three floors, with the top floor housing the market's office, the guard office, and a couple conference rooms. The main floor had three or four food places, booths, hot sauce, and clothing.

One Indian family owned some of the booths in the main building. They had can foods, fresh produce, and fresh fish, trout, lobster. Two years later, a building across the street went up for sale and they bought it and slowly transferred from the farmers market. Their new basement had coolers, freezers and storage area.

On the right side of the farmers market was produce. All the way around the market was a steel fence. The back fence facing Bicentennial Mall had eight walk-through gates. The front and back each had a vehicle gate.

The shift from 5 a.m. to 4 p.m. had an armed guard, from 4 p.m. to midnight an unarmed guard, and from midnight to 5 a.m. an unarmed guard. On the night shifts you'd see homeless people in ones, twos, threes or fours walking up and down Eighth Avenue all night long.

I'd make hourly checks all through the market then return to reading books, usually from Don Pendleton's *Mack Bolan: The Executioner* series about a Vietnam War veteran who seeks vengeance for his family's murder. Those books were a life-saver over the years of security work, and I've collected about 400 of them, even with losing and replacing various copies over years of moving around.

About three weeks after my wreck with the van on the highway, a sheriff's officer knocked on my door. When I opened the door, he handed me a court summons: The van driver and his wife were suing me for $75,000.

Part of the lawsuit was for the driver's past, present and future pain for $50,000. The other part of the suit was on behalf of the wife, who wasn't in the wreck, for $25,000 because her husband would no longer be able to do the dishes, take her out for dinner and a movie, or perform his husband duties. They demanded trial by jury.

I called the insurance company.

"How quickly is a reply expected?" they asked.

"Thirty days," I said.

"Send us the summons and we'll get a Tennessee lawyer for you," they said.

I made a copy of the summons for my records. Nine months later I got a call from the lawyer to meet the next Monday morning for affidavits at the other side's lawyer's office.

The van driver and his wife were there. They were both in their fifties, and had been married thirty years. Given the ridiculousness of the lawsuit, I thought the wife would be so fat and ugly her husband would need four brown paper bags to cover her face. I was half right. She was tall and weighed more than 200 pounds, but her husband probably needed only one bag for her face.

I wore my Wackenhut uniform, white shirt and blue pants. It was actually the first time I'd ever met my lawyer. We went in their lawyer's office, and their secretary took notes for the affidavits. Their lawyer got first crack at me.

"Have you ever been in the military?" their lawyer asked.

"Yes," I said. "Twenty years with two-and-a-half years in Vietnam, plus ten years of active National Guard duty."

"Are you married?"

"Yes."

"Have you been on vacation any time during this last year?"

"No," I said.

That concluded my affidavit. None of it had to do with the accident.

Then my lawyer took his turn to go at them. He talks to the man first. "Have you ever been in the service?"

"Yes," the van driver said. "Navy four years, six months off the coast of Vietnam."

"The weekend of the accident, did you return to the hospital?"

"No."

"When did you return to work?"

"Monday."

"Did you apply for workman's compensation?"

"No."

"Have you been on vacation any time this last year?"

"Yes, we spent thirty days in Cancun."

Then my lawyer talked to her.

After the affidavits were taken, I thought to myself, "Let's give this couple their wish for trial by jury." They'd walk into the courtroom and sit then I'd walk in the courtroom wearing my Army Dress Blue uniform with my eighteen full-size medals and my thirty-five-year-old wife. The jurors would look at them then look at me and those jurors would probably give me the $75,000.

A couple weeks later, my lawyer called to say the van driver and his wife took the $4,500 that the insurance company offered for their vehicle damage. With all their fake claims and time wasting, their lawyer probably got most if not all of that insurance money.

***

I was at a Regions Bank a little before 4 p.m. one day when the young assistant manager showed me a note that a young woman had given her through the drive through: "Open the vault and give me all the money."

The bank called Metro police came, along with the TBI and the FBI. This dumb girl just sat in her car while the police thundered in and arrested her.

Another day I was working in the bank vault and clocked out thirty minutes early to go to another post – under orders of my supervisor. The bank's head of security was unhappy about that and demanded Wackenhut fire me.

Wackenhut fired me. I tried to appeal, but it didn't work.

Chapter Twenty-Five

Changing Times

A few job leads didn't work out.

Months later, I saw a listing in the newspaper for "security officers wanted." I went to the address and filled out an application. The owner and assistant interviewed me.

The owner was retired WWII or Korean veteran. His son was part owner and a helicopter pilot at Fort Campbell. The assistant was a retired Army sergeant major, 1974 to 1994. I took their test, showed them my guard license, baton and pepper spray permits.

They hired me. You paid for your uniforms $20 every paycheck until you'd paid in $100. Because of my military service and experience as a security officer they made me a sergeant. I got $6.75 an hour. The maximum they paid their armed guards was $7 an hour.

The name of the company was Strategic International Security. The name was larger than the company itself.

One of the main accounts they had was the farmers market. The post was armed from 5 a.m. to 4 p.m., and the other two shifts were unarmed, just like with Wackenhut. One of the day officers, security guard Hayward, was armed with a 9mm Glock. He rode the city bus to and from work, and he carried his pistol in its gun case instead of a holster, against the rules at the farmers market. One day when I relieved him, I noticed that one side of his pistol's barrel was pitted with rust. I ask if he ever cleaned his pistol. He didn't even know how to disassemble it. I went and asked a pistol range instructor how to disassemble a Glock, and the next night I went to work thirty minutes early with a cleaning kit. I disassemble his pistol and made him clean it. I took a steel brush to the rust and removed most of it but the pit was too big. I made him assemble the gun.

There was a one whole family that worked for the company. They got their armed guard licenses. The man and wife were armed with a 9mm Smith and Wesson pistol, and their two boys were armed with some brand of .38 pistol. The man and wife had one holster between them, two pistol belts and ammo pouches, so when the man relieved his wife at midnight they exchanged the holster – however, they weren't supposed to be armed at night. One night while they were exchanging the holster, the wife was cleaning the gun and her hand was over the barrel, but her finger was on the trigger and she shot herself in the hand. The husband called the supervisor and said he was taking her to the hospital.

The supervisor had me go in and watch the market the rest of the night. The man had left the keys behind a sign in front of the main door. I opened the gate, drove in, locked the gate, and went into the main building, upstairs to the guard office, logged in. I made my first round and saw where the bullet had hit the cement floor and ricocheted into a cinder block wall. The woman couldn't work for two weeks.

About three months after starting with the company, I got my wife Tish a job there. According to company rules, if you sponsor a person and the person works two months, you receive a $100 bonus. I paid for Tish to get her permits for baton and pepper spray.

Two months passed and Tish held the job, but I hadn't received my bonus. I asked the sergeant major why I hadn't received it. He said it was because she's my wife. The boss's son was there, though, and he told the sergeant major to write me the bonus check.

***

A few of the properties the company guarded were two Red Roof Inns in the suburbs, the farmers market, the old Nashville hospital, an office complex in Metro Center.

I was working at Metro Center. You'd walk from the manager's office down the hall a hundred yards, walk upstairs, walk back toward the manager's office, downstairs, across the courtyard, upstairs to the second floor, walk 200 yards downstairs back along the hall, across the courtyard to the manager's office.

My right knee became weak. I used a knee brace but it got worse. I went to an orthopedic doctor at Summit Hospital. He X-rayed my foot for $200, and set up a specialized test for the nerve endings in my legs. The specialist said the nerve endings were fine, that it was something higher. He suggested an MRI.

I went to my VA doctor, who set up inpatient care to have the MRI. I arrived at the hospital at 11 a.m. and they were getting a room ready for me. The janitor was mopping and waxing the floor. I had to wait in the hall for two hours. If you wanted to smoke, you had to go down to the ground floor and out the back door to the smoking area.

The doctors did the MRI on a Friday morning. I called my supervisor and told him I'd be out that afternoon. He said to go to the old hospital and train for a couple of hours. Around 4.30 p.m. three in-training doctors came in and visited about what was going on. The head neurologist came in and told me to wait a few minutes for the MRI results.

A surgeon came in and told me there was a tumor around my spinal cord between the C-3, C-4 vertebrae. The surgeon said he wanted to operate at 6 a.m. Sunday.

They released me from the hospital for the next day and a half. About 5:30 p.m., instead of driving ten miles home and dressing in uniform then driving ten miles back, I just drove to the old hospital. I called the supervisor to tell him I was at the old hospital. I also told him that on Sunday morning I'd be in the hospital for surgery.

My usual work schedule had twelve-hour shifts Saturday, Sunday and Monday with a six-hour shift Tuesday. Across the street from the hospital was an overnight café that came in handy.

The next day, Saturday, at 5 p.m., I was dressed for work and eating supper and the surgeon called with a reminder to be at the hospital in the morning. I arrived at work to relieve the day guard. Most of the buildings on that route were boarded up, and we had to check to make sure no boards were off and no homeless staying in the buildings, make sure the mortuary doors were locked, drive through parking lot, return to the front gate.

I called the supervisor to tell him to have the day guard be there at 4 a.m. to relieve me because I had to go home and shower and be at the hospital at 5:30 a.m. The guard wasn't there at 4 so I locked the gate and placed the keys behind a brick.

I arrived at home, did my business and woke Tish even though she didn't like to get up early. We arrived at the VA hospital and they took my blood pressure and prepped me. I took out my dentures and gave them to Tish to take home. It wasn't long and I was face-down on the operating table, probably by 6 a.m. I woke up in intensive care around 1:30 in the afternoon with neck brace on. I take my IV cart and walked around. That night, I slept at a forty-five-degree angle.

Around 11 a.m. Monday I was placed in a bay with five other patients. I took my IV cart and a pack of cigarettes down to the ground floor to the smoking area. I didn't have a lighter or matches, and there no other patients outside. Some security officers walked by and I asked them if any of them had a lighter but they were all non-smokers.

I went back upstairs and there was a woman in the ward who had a hip replacement, and she had a lighter but no cigarettes. She was in a wheelchair so I pushed her around the corner and onto the elevator, rode down to the first floor, went outside and we smoked a couple of cigarettes. Now there were other patients smoking, so maybe I should have waited down there in the first place. I pushed the old lady back upstairs.

I was released that Wednesday but couldn't work for two weeks.

***

A couple of months before my surgery, I'd received a letter from the Social Security office stating that if I wanted to take early retirement at age sixty-two, I'd receive $675 a month but that when I reached age sixty-five the amount wouldn't increase.

The letter also showed a summary of what I made each year going back to 1961, my first year in the Army being paid $67 a month before taxes, $804 total.

In 1973 as a sergeant first class with twelve years in the Army, I made $650 base pay plus $200 housing and $50 for rations, so $900 a month and $10,800 total. In 1974, with $90 a week unemployment, I made $4,680.

In 1990 I was back in the Army as a corporal E-4 making $1,070 a month, $12,840 total. In 1997, at retirement as staff sergeant E-6 with twenty years' service, base pay was $2,460 a month.

That pay at retirement was what Social Security based part of its calculation on. Fifty percent of $2,460 a month was $920 plus my thirty percent disability of $270 was $1,190 a month. Also, Uncle Sam can only tax seventy percent of my retirement.

In 1998, with my Army retirement of $9,520 and Wackenhut income of about $36,000 dollars before tax, my total income for the year before tax was $ $45,520.

I thought that was pretty good.

Just before I retired at Fort Campbell, we were living in a trailer park. Somebody moved out leaving a female black-and-grey tabby cat. Tish was a cat lover and started feeding the cat and it started coming in the house. The last week there we stayed in the brand new guest house on post. No pets were allowed in the guest house so during the day we had Kitty locked in the trailer and around 11 p.m. I'd go to the trailer to put kitty in a carrier and bring her to the room. Around 6 a.m. I'd return kitty to the trailer.

When we moved into Burning Tree Apartments, I think we paid a $200 pet deposit for the tabby. A little after we moved in to Burning Tree, we bought a black-and-white male kitten, Romeo. When we sat down to eat we had to put Romeo in one of the bedrooms or he'd try to eat all our food. When we fed the cats we put them in different rooms, or Romeo would eat all the food. When we moved into a three-bedroom house, Romeo would jump on the counter then on top of the refrigerator. If there was anything up there he'd knock it off and lay down.

At night, I'd take a drink of water before going to bed. Romeo would jump on the counter and demand his drink of water. We let the cats out three or four times a day. A skunk, another cat or something else bit Romeo on the tail and it got infected. We took him to the vet. The Vet gave him an antibiotic shot. It was time for annual shots anyway so the vet gave him all his shots. I didn't notice that soon after he stopped eating. He died and we had him cremated.

***

The woman who lived next door had a son with a bulldog. They kept the dog in a fifteen-by-fifteen wire cage in the yard. The woman had a lazy drunk munchkin living with her too. Every time he got in the car to go get beer he'd have his right arm in a temporary cloth sling like he was disabled.

One day the man let the dog out and it ran over to my front porch and caught our tabby, biting her several times. One of the bites broke a back leg in four places. If the vet put braces and rods in her leg it'd cost between $1,200 and $1,500. To have the leg amputated was $670.

I took the woman to court and sued for the cost of amputation. The court ordered her to pay them $25 every two weeks until the bill was paid. So, I had to go to the court every two weeks to get my check.

***

After I was released from the hospital for my tumor operation, I couldn't work for two weeks. I took my medical records to Social Security to see if I could receive disability pay.

I'd been working forty hours a week. The maximum amount a person could make a month and draw disability was $750 a month. I was making $900 so I didn't qualify.

I called the lawyer Tish used for her disability case. He'd charge me $1,000 to run the papers through Social Security.

After the two weeks off, I went to work for three twelve-hour shifts plus a six-hour shift. By the time I completed my first week I could barely move, and by the end of the three days off I recovered to about where I was.

At the end of the work week, I went into the office and told them that until I recovered from my surgery I'd only work twenty-four hours a week.

I worked two weeks and my check stub showed twenty-four-hour work weeks so I returned to Social Security with the pay stub. I gave them my copy of the VA operation papers. Social Security said that since I only worked twenty-four hours a week I qualified for disability.

There was a five-month waiting period. Six months later I received my first check, $900.

Until you reach sixty-five years old you can work a certain amount of time and make a certain amount of money. If you go over, the IRS will take $3 for every dollar you make over the limit.

***

During the two weeks I was waiting to go to work, the doctor told me not to drive. I'd wake up around 3 a.m. and walk to the bottom of the hill near Burning Tree Apartments. At the corner of Central and Old Hickory was a Mapco that stayed open twenty-two hours. Some mornings they'd be closed for restocking so I started going to a big Exxon station to get my coffee. I'd hang around for an hour drinking my coffee and talking. I went in there often enough they quit charging me for coffee, and I'd hang around a couple of hours flapping my gums.

The sergeant at Strategic International was a Vietnam vet who was jealous of my accomplishments, and gave me trouble, imposing rules on me that didn't apply to other employees. He told me I couldn't go around to any of the posts unless I was working. One day I went and talked to the female guard at the old hospital. Someone saw me and told the sergeant major, and he called me and said I was suspended for three days.

The armed guard at the farmers market, Herb, had been promoted to supervisor, and the sergeant major had Herb write a false sexual harassment charge against me that was supposed to look like the female guard wrote it.

Five days after my suspension, the sergeant called me and said I could come back to work but I had to sign a reprimand form.

For some reason I'd bagged my uniforms. I'd put the metal pocket badge and collar brass in a plastic bag but didn't put them with the uniforms.

At the office, the sergeant major told me there was a sexual harassment charge against me and until it was cleared he was suspending everyone involved, and the only one was me.

"I want to see the report," I told him.

"I don't have to let you see it," he said.

"You'd better," I said.

By this time we were talking loudly, and the owner came out and told us to stop. The sergeant major told the owner that he'd turned in the papers to OSHA.

"I'll be right back," I said. I went home, grabbed the bag of my uniforms, and hauled it into the office. "Here. We're done."

Normally, the guards turning in their uniforms had to wait two weeks to get their reimbursement checks. The sergeant wrote my check right there.

I said to the owner, "As long as you have that liar working here, you're going to have trouble."

The female guard told me she didn't file that complaint, and I testified on her behalf at trial when she was accused of pepper spraying a woman. Police arrested her on the job, saying she'd left her post to drive ninety miles to attack this woman and driven back to finish the shift. I testified that it wasn't possible for her to leave that for long without being noticed by a supervisor. She was found not guilty. At work, when that sergeant major asked her why she'd been arrested, she told him it was none of his business.

I went to both the state and federal OSHA offices to turn in complaints against the company. The federal office looked at my papers and told me I had a complaint but I needed to talk to the state OSHA. State OSHA tried to get the sergeant major to come in and he wouldn't. The lady said that Strategic International didn't guard any state property so if she received a complaint, she'd shred it. She was wrong: the company guarded Howard School and it was state property and housed the vehicle tag office and child care services.

Anyhow, around ten months later the federal OSHA sent me a letter saying that Strategic International had gone out of business, but I could sue the sergeant major and Herb for the false report if I wanted.

Well, Herb didn't have a pot to pour pee out of, and I could take the sergeant major to court and get some money, but hiring a lawyer and paying court costs wasn't worth the hassle.

***

Out of work, every Monday I went to the employment office.

This one Monday I saw a listing for a security company named SecurityWise.

I marked down the name and address at the corner of Elm Hill and Spence Lane. The next morning I drove over to fill out an application. After I filled it out, Captain Mercer called me into his office. He was a retired jarhead.

He hired me and said I'd mostly be on patrol. "Be here at the office Friday," Mercer said. I arrived, they issued me black uniforms for patrol, and I signed for them, filled out a W-2 form.

At 5:30 p.m. the patrol supervisor, Lieutenant Warren, had the drivers check the cars' gas, oil and tires. Then we rolled out. At one apartment complex I couldn't remember the gate code so I called Warren for it. At another complex, I forgot where the gate button was so I had to call Warren again. I ran the last two rounds with no problems and got back to office around 5 a.m. After a week, I trained on another route and we got a female patrol officer named Susan.

The south route I started running went from the office a half mile to Elm Hill Business Park. At the upper level I had to unlock the gate, drive around the back, hit two buttons, come out, lock up, turn right, stop at the lower level, hit a button, go back right on Elm Hill to Massman Road through Aramark, left on Elm Hill to Fesslers, through Elm Hill Business Park, get on I-24 to Shelby Housing, through it back on I-24 to Fourth Avenue before crossing a bridge, right on First

Street to Arrow Business Park, back to I-24, left on I-40 South to Bellevue, through town to Walgreen's, right on Sawyer Brown Road, through six sections of Gen. George Patton subdivision, right on old Harding Place Road, right on Poplar Creek Road to Sheffield Apartments, drive to the pool to lock it, return to the starting point, and hop, skip and jump three more times a night.

You're probably wondering how I remembered all those streets, roads and highways. Well, Google is a big help for an old memory.

SecurityWise had the misfortune of getting a security contract at Fisk University for a year. The director of security there, Miss Hagman, was an ex-FBI agent and a major pain in everybody's butt. Before we could let police or firetruck on the property we had to get her permission.

Before we could start patrolling there, Captain Mercer, Lieutenant Warren, Lieutenant Williams, Sergeant Susan and I had to go to Bicentennial Hospital for Red Cross CPR class.

At Fisk, we guarded three shifts during the week and two shifts on the weekend. Miss Hagman wanted to be kept in the loop but she didn't want us to call her after 10 p.m.

I went to work on the second Saturday we guarded there. Miss Hagman came in the office and started yelling at me, "I told you not to call the police or firemen on campus without my permission!"

"I haven't," I said.

"Yes, you did," she said. "Now write down a hundred times, 'I will not let the police or fire truck on campus without Miss Hagman's permission.'"

I read over the logs. There was a shift leader, assistant, guard on the ground floor, women's dorm, men's dorm, campus radio station. I found the report about the firetruck and ambulance: A student was stabbed by another student, and one of the male faculty members had called the ambulance and police. I think the police arrested the student who did the stabbing.

If Miss Hagman fired you from campus, then you'd call the company to send someone else. But before a person could work there, they had to train. Every shift had six guards and three or four trainees on the day shift. After 10 p.m. a male guard had to be escorted above any of the dorms' first floor. For example, in the women's dorm, a college student would be with the officer at the desk for two hours then another student would work two hours.

I lasted around three months before getting on the dragon lady's hit list.

We had five patrol routes, and I was training a man named Alford, in one of the north routes. I'd turned off Gallatin Road into the West End Mall when Metro police stopped me for having the wrong tag on our patrol car.

The patrol cars included an older white Ford Crown Victoria, two other not-so-old white Crown Victorias, two white Chevrolet Impalas, and a white-and-black Pontiac Firebird, which was what I drove the most. All the cars were marked with decals SecurityWise and equipped with two-way radios. The drivers also carried cellphones. Every year, the company renewed the tags and sometimes this was hard. In Tennessee, any car newer than 1985 had to go through emissions testing for carbon dioxide. If the car didn't pass, you had thirty days to fix it.

This one evening I was to go to mechanic's shop and pick up one of the Impalas. I sent the other drivers on their routes, and I took this young driver with me. We were in the old-old Crown Victoria and the battery light came on. I checked that the cables were tight, but the light stayed on. It was about fifteen miles to go to the shop. We went Briley Pike to I-24 East.

The only thing furnishing electric power to keep the car running was the battery and I have the headlights on, so it was probably draining fast.

We had four exits to get to the mechanic. We got off the Haywood Exit, turned left on Haywood, got to the stop light, turned right just before the bridge and then the car kicked up its feet, rolled over and died. A Metro cop pulled up, and I told him the battery was dead. We had two blocks to go to the mechanic. We phoned another car to jump us. Finally, we got the car to the mechanic. The other guard, a young guy, took me to the office in the Impala. I got in the Firebird and started my route. He went along on his.

Three or four hours later the young guard called me, saying one of the motor mounts on the Impala was broken.

He was at the Lebanon Mall. I had him picked up by the driver of the route next to him. A couple days later I found out how the motor mount broke. He'd been in the Lebanon Mall parking lot jumping the cement islands. I told Captain Mercer and he fired the kid.

Around this time, Captain Mercer got married in a church sixty miles down the road in Murfreesboro. He was a retired Marine so got married in his dress blues. He had me wear my dress blues too. Major Pineway, Lieutenant Warren, Lieutenant Williams, Sergeant Alford, Sergeant Susan, and one other patrolman dressed in black patrol uniforms. The chaplain borrowed sabers from a National Guard unit so we held crossed sabers so Captain Mercer and his new wife could walk under them. The reception was at 5 p.m., but Lieutenant Warren, Lieutenant Williams, Susan and Alford left to go on patrol.

Major Pineway was the one who negotiated the work contracts. He also placed the guard buttons on the properties, and he liked to hide them. Security guards push these buttons while doing the patrols to show that they were actually doing the patrols.

One Saturday night we arrived at work to find that someone had sliced one front tire on each of the Crown Victorias. Officer Jackson had a floor jack, so we used it to change the tires. We had enough cars to put to put all the regular tires on a few, and all the spare donut tires on one. We put Officer Jackson in the donut car.

Major Pineway and Capt. Mercer ran a couple of routes in their cars checking on the other drivers. Around 3 a.m. one day they met at the office for the route check and they opened mail drop box and saw car keys and a guard report form. The driver listed his time on the report form as being through at 5 a.m., two hours in the future.

A new policy was instituted: when you got done, you drove to the bottom lot of Elm Hill Business Park and waited until the last driver arrived, and then race the half mile to the office to turn in paperwork and keys and clock out.

We had ten hours to complete routes. Most properties got four hits per night and a few properties paid for six hits at night and one or two in the daytime. Woodlawn Apartments was one of these places.

We got paid every two weeks, on Monday mornings. The boss had two accounts at a bank: one checking and one savings. Instead of having payroll on one account by itself, he'd combine everything and put it in savings to draw interest until payday. Bills, payroll, and maintenance costs all came out of the same pot so he'd never know how much had to be in the bank at Nations Bank. We'd get our checks and race to the bank because if you didn't deposit it quickly, the check would be returned – then you'd have to go to the office and have them rewrite it.

***

When one of the Vanderbilt University sorority houses would have a party, one or two guards would babysit them. Graduation time was reason for a weeklong celebration. The main commons area would have erect ten or fifteen booths to sell different things, and a music stage. One night there was a band, I don't remember the name, but the guys were dressed like an Indian, a policeman, a construction worker, a biker, a cowboy and a sailor.

Other regular posts weren't as enjoyable.

It wasn't uncommon at the apartment complexes to have to kick people out of the swimming pools at night or curb other rowdy business.

I pulled into the Paragon Apartments thinking it'd be an easy stop because their pool was closed for repairs. I stopped to make an entree in my log when a car came speeding around thirty miles an hour through a lot where the posted speed limit is five miles an hour.

They parked. I initially thought they were going to hit my car. I got out and went to the passenger door. They were two drunken Mexicans.

"Slow down," I said. "It's five miles an hour." he says

"We live here, man," the driver said from across the seat. "We don't have to slow down."

"Sir, the speed limit applies to everybody," I said. I took out my pepper spray in case they became more troublesome.

"We don't have to slow down, and you're not going to spray me," the passenger said.

I'd raised the can about a foot from his face and then I sprayed him in the face. The driver parked the car and the two of them jumped out and started toward me. I pulled out my pistol and pointed it at them. "Stop, if you come any closer I will shoot you," I said.

They were about six feet from me, and tears were running down the passenger's face. I told him to go in the house and use baby shampoo to wash up.

"I'm going to call Metro on you," the driver said.

"Call Metro, I don't care. Just don't come any closer or I will shoot you," I said.

The drunks went inside, and I remained in the lot writing in my log. Soon two Metro police cars drove in. One officer talked to the Mexicans and the other officer talked to me.

I told him what happened.

"Who's the supervisor?" the officer asked.

"I am," I said.

The other officer walked up and I asked for the names of the two men. With that, I drove off across the road to mall parking lot to write an incident report and to continue my route.

Everything was quiet at the mall: Pay-Less Shoes, a liquor store, Safe-Way, a tobacco store. I proceeded to the Woodlawn Apartments. There were some people in the pool to chase out so I filled out another incident report. With that I drove back to the route's starting point.

***

Our most imposing officer may have been a guy named Jeremy Holmes. He stood about six-foot-two and weighed around 185 pounds, and was in his late twenties. The first time I met him, he was one of the guards at a condemned building about to be torn down, and was there at night to keep out the homeless. He had an argument with a guy coming out of the club next door, and Metro was called. The police were about to take Holmes to jail, but I talked the officer out of it.

It was an unarmed post, but Holmes had a pistol, and it could've gotten him in trouble. I made him lock the gun in his trunk. As he opened the trunk, I saw he had a semi-automatic twelve-gauge shotgun sitting in there too. I continued on my patrol, but on my last round I dropped by to check that Holmes was awake and hadn't started a gun battle.

A couple of months went by, and I was running one of the Hermitage routes. Holmes called me.

"I've caught an old woman digging up flowers at Pinehurst Apartments," he said. "I'm going to call Metro."

"OK," I said. I figured Metro wouldn't respond in a short time. Their response time varied depending on shift changes. We could wait hours for police to show. Around two hours later I received a phone call from a Metro officer

"I've arrived at Pinehurst," the officer said. "Your man Holmes has this old woman in handcuffs in the back seat of his car."

He made Holmes un-cuff the woman. She'd cut five or six tulips. I told the officer Holmes caught her digging up the flower bed, but we weren't pressing charges. I apologized for wasting his time. I wrote an incident report.

In May 2008, Holmes got himself in some real hot water.

At the corner of Old Hickory Boulevard and Edmondson Pike was a small mall we'd drive through twice a night. Before 2 a.m. we'd go in the bar to hit a security guard button near the counter, after 2 a.m., when the bar closed, we'd drive behind the mall to hit a button by a door.

It was about 3 a.m. when Holmes drove through and saw a bar customer still sitting in his car in the parking lot. Holmes told him to call a cab. There was an argument. I think Holmes was writing down the license plate when the driver started backing out of the space, almost hitting Holmes. Holmes claimed he felt threatened and so drew his pistol and fired through the driver's window. He shot the man in the neck, and the man died.

Holmes went to trial, which ended in a hung jury. Instead of another trial, he accepted a six-year sentence with parole eligibility in two years. He was released in 2016, according to the Tennessee Department of Corrections

***

Along Tennessee State Highway 45, or Old Hickory Pike, was the small town of Old Hickory. It had a four-man police force, and if you sped through over thirty-five miles an hour, you'd get a ticket. They'd hide by a used car lot, next to a tobacco store, or by a company that built wooden storage sheds, which was their favorite hiding place.

We'd have to drive through on one of our routes. From Madison on T45 East through Old Hickory at Shute Lane, you'd turn left about a mile and on the left side of the road was development called Brandywine Pointe.

The houses there ranged from small to large. The roads ran left, right, up, down, around. We'd have to navigate through them to check the tennis court, office building, clubhouse, fenced-in pool, another pool at the safety harbor. This property was patrolled seven nights a week. The officer would drive the old, old Ford Crown Victoria from 11 p.m. to 5 a.m. If I ran it, I'd stop at the Exxon at Lebanon Pike and Andrew Jackson Pike for morning coffee.

In that neighborhood, there wasn't much actual crime, mainly kids' pranks.

Usually the worst the kids would do was either to throw eggs at cars or houses or throw toilet paper over houses and yards. The kids might use a whole twenty-four-roll pack until a house or tree was covered with streamers of toilet paper. It wasn't as mean spirited as my childhood prank of leaving a flaming paper bag of dog poop on someone's doorstep, ringing the bell, and watching them stomp out the fire while dirtying their shoes.

On Brandywine Road was a guardhouse. When we arrived at 11 p.m. we opened the guardhouse, punched our time card in the time clock to show when we arrived. I'd lock the guard shed then start my round, checking the office building door, chasing out anybody in the pool and locking it down, and finally park under a light next to the tennis court and fill out my duty log.

It was almost always a quiet shift, and I'd bring one of my Mack Bolan books. A book of around a 190 pages I'd read by the end of the shift at 5 a.m.; a book of around 320 pages I'd read in two shifts. I'd make a coffee run, return and sit under the light reading, sip, read, sip, sip, read, watch a car enter, stop it to check the parking sticker, sip, read, make a third patrol around 2 a.m., make a second coffee run. If I needed to relieve myself I'd walk behind a tree.

One night I was on another route when about 2:30 a.m. I received a call from police that the guard at Brandywine Pointe had been in an accident

I told the officer I'd be there in about thirty minutes. I was all the way south in Bellevue, forty miles from Brandywine Pointe in the north Hermitage area. I caught the I-40 loop around Nashville to get there. I entered the neighborhood through Andrew Jackson and Lebanon, and saw two power trucks working on overhead light lines (all the power lines in Brandywine Pointe subdivision were underground). I turned in the subdivision to see no lights on Shute Circle. There was a fire truck ahead fighting a ground fire, an ambulance was there treating the driver, and a couple Metro police. It didn't look good. I called Captain Mercer, Major Pineway and the company phone and left messages on all of them.

It looked like the car went over a sidewalk through a man's yard, knocking down a small tree, going through a four-foot-square metal box for light lines going to houses, and through another yard, wiping out bushes. The front end of the car was wedged between two trees. The front bumper had dented the side of a high-power transformer. T

The medic told me that, except for minor cuts and bruises, the driver was OK. I called one of the guards from the north route to take the rest of the shift. He was actually passing nearby on his way north, so it wasn't an inconvenience. I had the replacement guard take the original guard's keys and paperwork and clock him out.

Metro called a wrecker. The driver had to winch the car back up the hill. The front bumper, hood and fenders were bent, rolled and crunched. He got it on his flatbed and chained it down, and followed me to the SecurityWise office to drop the wreck in the lot for repair. The charge was $95. I told him to call his dispatcher to bill the company.

***

For a month, I ran day patrols checking apartment complexes around the city. I'd go through these properties twice during the day. After the second run, I'd get back to the office between about 4:30 p.m. and gas and oil the cars for the night crew. By clock out I'd end up having driven 140 miles in a day.

***

One night that Vanderbilt University had its football homecoming, everything went crazy. I don't know what school they were playing, but by 11 p.m. you couldn't move on any of the streets in the neighborhood.

Lieutenant Williams called all the drivers off our routes for an emergency, except Officer Murray on the hotel route because the hotels were the most important customers.

Sergeant Alford came from wherever, Sergeant Susan came from the Hooters on Second Avenue, and I and a trainee, Officer Jeffery, came from Sheffield. I sped about 115 miles an hour. If you received a call to assist an officer in trouble, you drove as fast as you could. If you passed a highway patrolman or police officer, you didn't stop, you kept going and dragged the police officer and as many of his friends as you could get because if there was trouble, you'd want as many people as you could get. But if you stopped and tried to explain to the police officer, you'd receive a speeding ticket or go to jail.

Due to the traffic congestion, we had to park the car a good distance away, in the front parking area of a Truck Stop of America, on Woodland Street, and walk a mile over the bridge and up the hill to Second Avenue then left to Hooters. While we were walking to Hooters, we realized why we were called: the congestion was preventing police from getting to an area where someone fired a shot, somewhere around Fifth and Main, by the time the police arrived the person would have moved far enough to fire a shot at First and Broadway. The person was likely on a bike because vehicle traffic was bumper to bumper.

Further complicating the situation was that there was a new after-hours bar that was supposed to open when the other bars shut down at 2 a.m., but the police decided not to let it open that night because of the crowds.

It was about a half a block past Hooters. At least one guard would regularly stop at Hooter's at closing time to walk the waitresses to their cars to keep any drunks from harassing them.

The new club had barricades set up to contain the lines of people waiting to get in. It was set for two lines of people to enter the club, but there were ten lines of people waiting thirty minutes before the club was to open.

When Metro announced that the club wasn't opening and the crowd should break up and go to their cars, the crowd wasn't happy. Metro had us security guards move the end barricades while three horse-mounted police started pushing the lines to disperse the crowd.

We finally left down town at 5 a.m.

The only other time all of us were called to the same place for an emergency was at Atwood Apartments.

Two Mexicans had beat up two women, and the women called Metro, but it was just before shift change and the police wouldn't respond until after shift change.

The men were seen going into an upstairs apartment. Our officers would knock on the door, but a woman would answer and there was nobody there but her. We could see into the patio doors into the apartment, and knew something fishy was going on. After about two hours two Metro police arrived. They listened to the women and told them if the two men came out of the apartment and if the women pointed the two men out then the women would have to go downtown and press charges.

Metro said that since the women didn't know the men's names, they couldn't get a search warrant to go into the apartment.

What we did was we borrowed a couple of gas canisters and sprayed them under the front door. Four or five people came out and the women identified the two men. Metro arrested them, and the women went to press charges.

It was about three hours before we returned to our routes.

A month later, Atwood Apartments had more excitement. The guard there called me about two officers from Metro who'd spotted a car of someone nine unpaid parking tickets.

The officers intended to put a boot on the car. I was about two miles away, and went over there. The car owner and his clan were outside by the car when I arrived. One of the Metro officers told me the owner owed $150 in unpaid parking tickets, and if he placed the boot on the car it'd cost $90 more to remove the boot.

"Will you back me up if I put on the boot?" the officer asked me.

"No, it's none of our business," I said.

Then the owner asked me if I was going to stop Metro from placing the boot on his car.

I said no. "If you don't want the boot on your car and pay $240 then pay the man the $150," I told the car owner.

I tell my guard to continue his patrol. He was young and thinking that since he had an armed security license that he could make arrests like Metro.

I told him security guards don't have the authority of the police and can't make arrests.

Chapter Twenty-Six

Small World

By May 2010, I'd worked for SecurityWise for about five years. Paydays shifted from Mondays to Wednesdays to Thursdays, and then there was the issue cashing checks quickly before they bounced.

It became apparent the boss hadn't been paying Uncle Sam his taxes when Uncle Sam shut him down in Nashville, Chattanooga and Atlanta.

I went to file for unemployment and the unemployment office told me that according to their records I hadn't been working, and without documentation like my taxes or pay stubs I wouldn't get unemployment.

I made a copy of my pay stubs for the year and took it to them. A couple of weeks later I received a letter allowing me to draw unemployment for sixteen months at $240 a week. Out of a company of 120 people, I think only six or seven people were able to draw unemployment.

Around this time a very big rain storm had flooded part of Nashville, and among the damaged buildings was the Opryland Hotel. It took over six months to remodel the basement.

So it wasn't just SecurityWise employees who were under water at the time.

In the suburb of Madison, where my house was, was Madison Square Mall. My bank was there and I did a lot of shopping there. I happened to notice that also in there was the office of Hayes Security.

I spoke to one of the Hayes officers at the mall, and showed him my license and cards. He had me fill out an application and a W-2 form, and told me to come back in a couple hours to sign for some uniforms. It sounded like I'd been hired on the spot.

I signed for my uniforms and was told to be at the office at 10 a.m. to receive my assignment. My first post with Hayes was a small private air field named for Rosa L. Parks, in the bend of the Cumberland River.

I drive down Gallatin Pike to Shelby Bottom Road, stopping at Mapco to pick up chips and coffee. I arrived, checked that the gate was locked, and read my Mack Bolan book. All I had to do was check that people coming up were on the list; if not, they had to leave. I was off at 7 a.m. No one came in till 6.30 a.m., so the next two nights I took my Chihuahua with me to make her a guard dog.

Shortly after I started, I found out that the lieutenant that hired me had an argument with owner Billy Hayes and either quit or was fired. With Billy, either one could have happened.

When I first went on patrol there were three routes. Each patrol car was equipped with a computer and a printer. Billy's idea was you type up your report then print two copies. One stays on the property and the second one goes to Hayes.

My only previous experience with a computer was turning it on, getting to the games section, playing solitaire and turning the computer off. I went to the office for a couple hours so they could show me how to hook up the computer and find the patrol forms. Officer Brian told me all I had to do was type a sentence, hit enter and go to the next line. My work week was Thursday, Friday, Saturday, Sunday and Monday. Billy gave you eight hours to run your route and you only got paid for eight hours.

I arrived at work one day and Billy told me I couldn't hand-write my report, I had to use the computer.

I took the computer, went to the car to check the oil, gas, tires, and the hubcaps. Billy fined guards $20 for each lost hubcap, so we wired them to the wheels.

I started the car, plugged in the computer, pulled up the patrol report forms. Everything was a go. I turned right on Gallatin Road, went three blocks to Due

West Road, turned left, went one block and arrived at the first property, Falcon View. We patrolled this property four times a day.

I got out go check the laundry room. It was fine. At 6 p.m. I chased everybody out of the pool and locked the gate, drove to the office, checked that the doors were locked then I started to type my report.

DATE: August 2

TIME: 18OO hours

NAME: Russell Babcock

Then I go to the first line. I type, "Arrive on property, check laundry room OK, lock pool, check office doors locked." I hit the enter key to go to the next line and the computer erases everything.

I'm no speed demon on a computer. I type with one finger and hunt and peck, I stayed there about forty-five minutes retyping until the computer left the two or three lines alone. I went to the top left corner of the report form, hit the file button and hit save.

I drove to my next property, Heritage Apartments. I checked the pool and office doors, drove through the property. I patrolled this property once before and once after midnight. On the computer, I started typing, hit enter – it was erased. Type, hit enter – it was erased. When the computer didn't erase my typing, I saved the file and went to the next property.

This property had two big sections: Graycroft Manor and Graybrook Apartments. There was one office, two pools, two gyms, and two laundry rooms to check and lock.

Over and over I left Madison for Hermitage, hit Aramark then the Elm Hill complex then to Brentwood and Woodlawn Apartments, all of which I'd patrolled for SecurityWise.

It was 4:30 in the morning and I three more rounds to do so I started writing reports instead of using the computer. The next day when I saw Officer Brian, I told him what happened. He showed me how to block the line on the forms. I'd start to get things going along but then be off two days and I'd return and have to hunt thirty minutes to find reports. Once in a while I'd unknowingly hit the down arrow and end up with 64,000 pages or be unable get the printer to work and had to have one of the other guards meet and get fix it.

I decided to buy my own computer to use. I take it to the office and had the younger people download the different tabs, blank report forms, incident report forms, blank time sheets, and set up the programs so that I could either use the Canon printer or the Hewlett-Packard printer that were in the cars.

***

Tish, my pretty young wife, and I had split up by this time.

She had had lived at Brinkhaven Apartments around two years, since we divorced. Her bathtub there was old and scratched up so the office had somebody use an enamel paint to supposedly make it look new, but they made a mess and Tish wanted a new tub.

Anyhow Tish and the apartment office got to arguing, and Tish didn't pay rent for a month or two. The office took Tish to court. The judge told Tish to pay the back rent. She said no. The judge sentenced Tish to ten days in county jail.

The phone Tish used to call me had a bad connection and she was garbled, but I understood she was in jail and her car was parked in public parking. Around midnight I went to Tish's apartment and took her kitty to my home. I put her in an empty bedroom so my dogs Chloe and Poppy wouldn't bother her.

The next morning I had Tammy, my girlfriend Nancy's brother, go with me to get Tish's car. I paid the extra parking fees. Tammy drove it home for me.

In going to the jail to see Tish, I bought her a jail debit card for $20 so she could have a snack.

Her apartment complex was also evicting her for non-payment so I packed and placed her belongings from the apartment in storage. At the end of her ten-day sentence, I picked her up and took her to my house. Her stay lasted about four days, and then she and Nancy got into such a fight that I had to pull them apart.

I had Tish pack what things she had and drove her to a hotel.

***

Around 5:30 one morning, I arrived at my last property of the route. I made my walkthrough and was getting ready to type my report when I noticed the car's temperature light was on. I turned off the car and looked at the fan belt: broken.

I tried calling the other patrolmen, but no answer. I filled my radiator and two one gallon water jugs for backup, and drove the seven miles to the office. When I arrived, I turned in my paperwork and left a big, big note on Billy's door that the fan-belt broke.

Around 3 p.m. Billy called. "Get to the office," he said. When I got there, he started yelling, "You could've burnt up the engine!"

He suspended me for three days. On the bright side, I went home with the night off.

The next afternoon, he called me back to the office. He was short a driver the next two days. "You're going to work those two days, but you won't get paid for them," he said.

I did work those two days.

There was a woman who wanted to be on patrol. I started training her on our shortest route, Falcon View. We locked the pool at 6 p.m. West End Mall check guard, down Ellington Pike. Patrol Hilltop Apartments, lock that pool at 9 p.m. Elm Hill Business Park, Aramark, up Massman Drive to Maplewood Apartments and Appleton Apartments, which were owned by the same management company. Massman Apartments were around the bend on the right. Tremont Apartments. We hit all these four times a night.

This woman trainee would get lost in this area, and go down instead of up, right for left, and it would take her twelve hours to run an eight-hour shift. She argued with Billy about getting paid the extra four hours so he fired her.

Another change was that Billy started transitioning from the old security guard buttons we hat to push while doing the routes. He issued cell phones and placed bar codes along the routes that we had to scan with the phones. Bar code on office door, bar code on Building C laundry-room, Building D second-floor emergency light, bar code lock pool at 9 p.m.

One night I received a disturbance call at Massman Apartments. I arrived and the firetruck, ambulance, and Metro were all there. A drunken taxi driver had wedged his car in the stairwell. The back of the car was on ground floor and the front of the car at the top of the stairs.

There was a night I'd locked the pools at Royal Arms. I was making my second round and I caught about fifteen men and women in the pool. I opened the gate to go in and talk to them. None of them lived there. As I took my phone out to call the police, they jumped over the fence and disappeared.

Another night on my patrol I was at Elm Hill Business Park. I was driving between the buildings and I saw a car parked next to the loading dock and a truck. I walked over and shone my flashlight in the window, and there was a man and woman nude. I went back to my car and in five minutes they were gone.

***

My roommate Nancy and I moved from a house on Duling Avenue to a two-bedroom apartment in Orchard Park, a front downstairs apartment in Building C.

I negotiated for Tish to move into the Rothwood Apartments on Neely Bend Road. It was an apartment on the back side of the building, on the top floor so there was nobody overhead she could hear walking, and there were no occupied apartments to the left or right side to hear noise, just a little old lady in the front apartment.

Tish said I could move in with her and her kitty, and I could keep my dog Chloe on the balcony.

I told her to stop smoking her loco weed.

A couple months later I was running the south guard route. I started in Madison, going first to Falcon View, and then DuPont, hopped on Briley Pike, Gallop to Charlotte Road, turned left, drove a mile to Rolling Hills Apartments and Hanover Ridge Apartments, back down Charlotte, across Briley, three miles to a new subdivision. They were still building new apartments there. It had been the apartment complex where Officer Holmes handcuffed the elderly lady for picking some flowers. I hit I-40 South six more miles to Bellevue, then eight miles to Sheffield. This time instead of checking the pool, we did a full patrol.

Around 1 a.m. a disturbance call came through at Rolling Hills Apartments. I arrived and knocked on the door. There didn't seem to be any disturbance. As I was getting in my car, I heard a car spin out. I walked through an archway to see two men fighting.

I broke up the fight. I was wearing my black guard uniform, black cap, gold security badge on left shirt pocket, black pistol belt with 9mm pistol in holster, baton, and can of pepper spray. The white guy was falling down drunk. He was the only one who didn't recognize me as a security officer.

I'd been standing there ten minutes. I told the couple with him to get him in the apartment and keep him there. They gave me a false apartment number. The white guy yelled at the black guy and started fighting again. I pulled my pepper spray and sprayed the white guy. A supervisor arrived and we got the black guy's name. It took me two hours to type the incident report.

The next morning the apartment manager called Billy complaining about me spraying the resident without identifying myself as a security officer.

Billy fired me over it. I turned in my uniforms. I'd lost a hubcap from my last pay-check so I paid Billy $20 for the hubcap.

"You don't have to pay for the hubcap," Billy said.

"I'm not letting you have the chance to tell people I left owing you money," I said.

***

For a couple of months I lay around the house twiddling my toes and reading my Mack Bolan books. It was during this time I came up with the idea of writing a book about my life.

I felt like there were people with lives more boring than mine who'd written books. Maybe future generations of my family would want to know what my life was like. "Why did Russell join the Army twice?" I could hear them asking.

Within a couple months, I'd made good progress. On a Sunday, I was typing on my book, somewhere around page 150, and my phone rang.

"Can you run a route tonight?" the man asked. I didn't catch his name at first, but it was Billy's son Gary. I thought it was just one of the supervisors.

"You know that I was fired?" I asked.

"That's been cleared up," Gary said. "Now, can you work tonight?"

I went back to work. Billy made me a staff sergeant, and I worked for Billy another few years, but I watched other people getting promoted. One day I told Shannon, the major in charge of the security officers, that I was tired of being passed over. I trained a person and then in two or three months that person was promoted to lieutenant and couple months later they quit or were fired. Shannon promoted me, and I got a fifty-cent raise.

I took off a week to spend Christmas with my daughter Tammy in Savannah, Georgia. Before I left, Billy said he'd text me instructions.

"Text away, I'll call you with the answer," I said. "Babcock don't text."

In early January, Billy's son Gary told me the company was short of drivers and needed to schedule me more than usual. He worked me fifteen days straight, eight hours a day, for a total of 120 hours.

Then I found out that most of the other drivers only worked forty hours a week. The next day I told Major Shannon and Billy that I wasn't going to work that many days again and they could give those hours to the other drivers.

A couple of weeks later on a Sunday night my daughter Tammy called me to say her son Brandon's dad's grandfather had died and that his dad's grandmother had died the week before. Brandon's dad John took Brandon's brother to the great-grandmother's funeral, but couldn't take Brandon to the great-grandfather's. I had enough money in the bank to make the trip so I told Tammy that I'd be there the next day to take Brandon to the funeral in Ponca City, Oklahoma.

I called Major Shannon and left a message not to schedule me because I had a funeral in Oklahoma. I finished my route at 7 a.m., rested until 11 a.m. I got up, got in the car, withdrew $200 from the bank, gassed up at Exxon and bought a twelve-pack of green tea, cup of coffee, and a couple egg sandwiches. Road ready, I took Briley to I-24 East to Chattanooga then south on I-75 to Macon, Georgia, and across I-16 to Savannah.

I arrived around 7 p.m., picked up Brandon and headed back to Nashville. As we were getting onto I-16, I stopped and had Brandon, who was about fifteen, get behind the wheel because I needed a nap. I told him to adjust the seat till he was comfortable, adjust the mirrors so he could see out, and when there were no cars coming, I told him to put the car in Drive and ease onto the highway. He got up to sixty miles an hour. I watched him for about ten miles.

"Are you comfortable?" I asked him.

"Yes," he said.

"That's the cruise control," I said, pointing to the button under the wheel. "Get up to eighty and set it. If you start getting too close to the car ahead, touch the brake a bit to cut the cruise control. When we get to Macon, wake me."

He did fine. I took over driving at Macon until we were above Atlanta. With a stop for gas and McDonald's, I had him take the wheel on I-75 to Chattanooga. I drove through Chattanooga, on I-24, at the foot of Monteagle, that treacherous place I used to drive a big rig. I drove over Monteagle then Brandon drove to the edge of Nashville. The next morning we ate at McDonald's, filled up the gas at Exxon and hopped on I-40 South to Memphis.

As I cruised into Memphis at seventy-five miles per hour, the highway patrol stopped me for cruising too fast. The speed limit was sixty-five. The officer had me show him my driver's license, insurance, and registration. He had me step out of the car.

"Who do you have with you and where are you going so fast?" he asked. I tell him "That's my grandson Brandon," I said. "I picked him up in Savannah and we're going to Ponca City, Oklahoma."

Another officer stood at the passenger door asking Brandon the same thing. They told me to cruise a little slower, and didn't give me a ticket. It was a good thing Brandon wasn't driving on that stretch of road.

We continued galloping through Little Rock and Fort Smith, from Muskogee to Tulsa. We hummed along with Merle Haggard through Tulsa, herded cattle along the Cimarron Turnpike, and moseyed through Stillwater north to Ponca City.

In Ponca City, Brandon called his dad's parents. Brandon's Grandpa Mike was at the church so we went over there.

It was the second time I met John's parents. John wasn't there, but his brother Steve was. John's dad Mike invited us to go with them to a Mexican restaurant to eat. After we ate, I started to pay for Brandon and me, but Mike insisted on paying for it. We thanked him, and said we needed to find a motel room.

Mike volunteered his son Joe's house for us to stay at. Joe was a banker, and had a big stone house with, I think, three floors and a basement. Out the back door were stairs leading to a small pond with koi fish, and surrounded with bamboo bushes. It was much nicer than a motel.

John's brother Steve and I talked for a while, and Brandon went to bed. The next day Brandon spent time visiting some of his friends, and I got the car's oil changed.

The funeral was the following afternoon. Around 1 p.m. there was a small church service then everyone went out to the cemetery, but they didn't bury him right then because his wife had been buried the previous week and the ground supposedly needed to settle for a few weeks. The next morning we thanked Mike and said goodbye.

We started the return trip in reverse. Instead of going the northern scenic route, we dropped down to Dallas and went across I-20 to Atlanta and Savannah.

When I returned to work, I was nearly there, on the overpass across I-65 when a deer ran in front of my car. He knocked a big hole in the grill and broke a headlight. I called Gary to update him and then I called Metro to have somebody come out to make an accident report. After an hour, a highway patrolman showed up and took the report. He asked

"What happened to the deer?" he asked.

I pointed over to a dentist's office parking lot. The deer was laying there with two broken legs. The office took his shotgun and shot the deer, but it wasn't a clean shot and he had to shoot again. I think the officer took the deer to a homeless shelter. I went on to work.

Billy owed Uncle Sam some money, and in the absence of having that money, he signed over the company to his sister and manager Ron Mackleroy to run. Uncle Sam told Billy he couldn't hang around the office but that didn't stop him. He wanted to expand to other cities. He had dreams of an empire. He tried starting an office in Knoxville, but couldn't get it going.

A few months later, though, they did put Wi-Fi in the office. It worked unless it was storming and raining.

One afternoon Billy told me about a new recruit. "He was a computer whiz who worked for me and quit, but now he wants to come back to work," Billy said. "I'm going make him a captain and you a lieutenant."

The next evening Billy had all the drivers come in to the meet the new captain. It was my former coworker Alford from SecurityWise. Before that company went under he'd made captain and was in charge of a patrol, and now he was a captain again. Billy pinned the captain bars on Alford and lieutenant bars on me.

I told Alford congratulations, but to not try to screw me over like he did at SecurityWise.

The next two nights I showed him all the properties and routes. Billy's idea of Captain Alford's duties was for him to come in around noon, check the wording of the contracts, make sure the day drivers were on patrol, go talk to the managers to see how things were going, gas the vehicles, and run patrols two nights a week.

Captain Alford's idea of his duties was to come in around 10 a.m., read over a few contracts, start changing rules and policies, maybe go talk to a manager, gas vehicles, inspect night drivers, and avoid night work.

Billy fired Alford.

He demoted me back to sergeant since I used short easy-to-spell words in my reports instead of fifty-cent words like, "As I approached the hilltop properties I glanced to my right and observed a sleazy skunk and repulsive opossum fighting over a bag of gum-gums." Billy said I didn't know what a supervisor's duties were.

Billy's son Gary came back to work as a major assisting Major Shannon. Former employees Brian and Bailey came back. Another man started to work named William W. Holiday Jr. III.

We added a few properties on the routes, and we finally had to do ten-hour shifts.

The South Route: 1) Falcon View, 4 hits; 2) DuPont, 4 hits around Briley to Charlotte Pike; 3) Holly Acre, 4 hits; 4) Rolling Hills, 4 hits; 5) Atwood Apartments 4 hits, back across Briley; 6) Pinehurst, 4 hits, down I-40 to Bellevue; 7) Bel Aire, 4 hits, then eight miles through the woods to 8) Sheffield, 4 hits.

Route Two: 1) Madison Square, 2 hits; 2) West End Mall, 2 hits; 3) West End Apartments, 4 hits; 4) Woodbend Apartments, 4 hits; 5) Elm Hill Business Park, 3 hits; 6) Aramark, 4 hits; 7) Holmes Building, 2 hits; 8) Men's Homeless Shelter, 2 hits.

Route Three: 1) Heritage Place, 2 hits; 2) Graycroft, 4 hits; 3) Red Grove, 4 hits; 4) Bell Hollow, 4 hits; 5) Chimney Top, 4 hits; 6) Arbor Crest Apartments wanted 24 hits a day but settled for 12 hits a day; 7) Glenwood, 4 hits.

Route 4: 1) Bellevue Apartments, 2 hits; 2) Hickory Hollow, 4 hits; 3) Royal Arms Apartments, 4 hits; 4) Woodlawn Apartments, 6 hits; two new complexes in Franklin thirty miles down I-24 to 5) Ben Oaks Apartments, 6 hits; 6) Royal Oaks, 6 hits.

Billy had the same six cars he'd had for years: four Ford Crown Victoria V-8 police interceptors and two Chevrolet Impalas. All had over 200,000 miles on them.

Car 501 was a Ford. You'd stomp the gas and hit ninety miles per hour. Car 502 was a Ford. You'd stomp on its gas and there was slight hesitation before reaching ninety. Car 503 was a Ford. It didn't have a car radio, but it had 300,000 miles on the odometer, and the other drivers wouldn't drive it. I drove it for a year, and it was the car that the deer damaged. Many a night I flew around town in it at ninety.

Car 504 was a Ford, and Cars 505 and 506 were Chevrolets.

I was in 503, and it wasn't fueled up, it had half a tank of gas. I was running the south route. It was 5:30 a.m. when I turned on Old Hickory, going to DuPont for the last hit. At Gallatin the car died. I put it in neutral and coasted across Gallatin. I was out of gas; I called Brian to bring me the credit card so I could gas the car.

That evening Billy had a bug in his butt about it. "How can you run out of gas? It gets twenty miles a gallon."

"It may have when it was new," I said, "The car has 300,000 miles, but it does get ten miles a gallon." I let it go at that.

Billy kept talking of his grand plans for the company, his plan to go to Knoxville and get high-paying clients, have five patrol routes and do on-site security then move to Memphis and Chattanooga. All of this was obtainable, but Billy was his own worst enemy. He ran the people away. Gary, Brian, and Bailey worked about two months and quit again. In security there was a high turn-over anyway, but some folks with us left quicker.

When we set up the office Wi-Fi, there was some squabbling going on, so Billy called a meeting of the guards: Billy, Major Shannon, Major Gary (Billy's step son), Lieutenant Brian, Bailey, William W. Holiday Jr III, and me.

"What complaints do we have?" Billy asked.

Some supervisors said, "I tell so and so to do something and he doesn't," "Why can Gary wear a beard and I can't?

Lieutenant Brian said, "I don't like Babcock."

"I don't care if you like me or not, I'm not dating or kissing you," I told the whole crew. "The only person in this room my work has to satisfy is Billy. He pays my salary."

Then Billy started yapping about us not hitting every security checkpoint bar code with our phones. "This shows the customer that we are patrolling his property." Billy went to his office and came back with some printouts. "Bailey, you patrol all your properties, but you miss two bar codes."

"Babcock, on Friday you only hit Royal Arms one time. Saturday you didn't patrol Woodlawn," Billy said. I tell Billy

"Where's that lying phone? I'll shoot it," I said.

"The phones cost $400!"

"I don't care. Where's the lying phone?"

Within two or three months Gary, Brian and Holiday quit. On a Friday night Bailey, Hicks, Oliver, Roberts and I were checking our cars, getting ready for patrol, when Billy told Robert and Bailey, "You guys need to shave." Then Billy started in on Bailey. "The dispatcher called you last night and called you last night and you didn't answer."

"The phone went dead," Bailey said.

"I don't care. When the dispatcher calls, you answer," Billy said.

Bailey took his shirt off and threw it at Billy. "I quit!" he said and walked off.

I didn't have another driver to call in so I divided the route. "Hicks, you hit this, this and this properties. Oliver, you have these properties. Robert, you run these this way and this route is covered."

A man named Benny was hired to be a day driver Monday through Friday. He typed his reports but didn't print them. On Saturday and Sunday to cover the day routes, Hicks and I worked it.

One day I was on Old Hickory going west so that I could start my route at Sheffield. The light at Delaware was green. I was driving the speed limit forty-five, when a woman on my left ran the red light and crossed two lanes of traffic into my lane and I hit her.

I knocked the front of her car toward Gallatin Road and my car spun all the way around, with my back bumper against a light pole. My computer hit the windshield and flew into the back seat. A couple of cars going the other way called the fire department and Metro. I was OK. I got out and stood by the car. I lit a cigarette.

"Are you hurt?" a fireman asked me. "Do you want to go to the hospital?"

"No."

Hicks called our manager, Ron Mackleroy, to tell him I was in a wreck. Ron came out. A Metro police woman asked me what happened. I made a statement and the two people who called Metro said the same thing.

The woman driver wanted to be taken to the hospital. As the medics were getting her out of the car, they saw some pills on the floor. The police woman followed the ambulance to make sure a blood test was done.

Ron took me to the office. I put my things in my car, clocked out then went home, put my pistol in the safe, put up the computer. I changed clothes and went to the hospital to get checked out. My chest was sore from hitting the steering wheel. Ron made Gary run my route that night. I was in one of the Impalas, and it was totaled. The company was going to sue the other driver but she didn't have insurance. Soon after, a new guard totaled the other Impala. It was raining and he was speeding.

A month later I was driving Car 503, a Ford. I stopped to lock the gate at Bell Hollow I started driving to the back, went over a speed bump and heard a noise then bump. From the driver seat, I could see the right front fender was lower than the left. I got out and looked. The upper arm of the right wheel was broken. I called Major Shannon and she said to call Ron. I called Ron and he called a wrecker. A couple of hours later the wrecker showed up, loaded the car, and took me to the office.

A couple months later I was in the same car, on the same property and the left wheel fell apart.

***

A couple new clients we had were Trevecca Nazarene University and ABF Trucking.

Trevecca was manned seven nights a week with twelve-hour shifts from 6 p.m. to 6 a.m. The complex had about eight buildings and a sports field. Four of the buildings had six floors, and one of the buildings housed people older than the students, maybe faculty or graduate students.

Car 501, a Ford, was placed on this property. Around every three weeks I'd go gas it up.

Our two guards who were hired for the post only worked about four months. Those guards quit, and we hired two new guards. One was named Al Rossco, and he was steady, while the other guard was always changing. After a couple of months Al got his armed license and moved to patrol.

Eventually, one of the replacement guards started messing up: Some nights he didn't come to work and on some of the nights he did work, he'd go to sleep. The administration of Trevecca terminated the contract.

ABF Trucking was an old friend to me. I worked it when I worked for Wackenhut.

The guards were there from Friday night to Sunday night. The first guard relieved the ABF dispatcher at 11 p.m. Friday and worked till noon Saturday. The second guard worked noon Saturday to midnight then the first guard returned till noon Sunday and the second works from noon till relieved by the ABF dispatcher around 11 p.m. except for holidays.

This property was all fenced in. Just inside the fence was the dispatch office and a warehouse with around twenty doors on each side, then the trailer parking, which extended across the creek.

There were two guards for ABF. Tom Harding wore his hair like Elvis and actually had a small band. We called him Elvis. Tom Brad was a plain middle-aged man. He didn't get a nickname.

***

Our company started having problems, losing people and contracts. At the start of the year we had around 130 people working and five patrols running. Two months later, paychecks shifted from every Monday to Wednesday then Friday. It ended up that we were two weeks behind getting paid, with the staff down to only thirty people and one patrol route.

Billy continued being his obnoxious self. One evening I was preparing to go on patrol when Billy sent a mall guard out to tell me to run off a homeless man. He was on the sidewalk by the curb, a public area, selling newspapers for a dollar. He had an ID card so I told the guard to leave the man alone, he could sell papers there.

Ron, the manager, had us driving Car 502, a Ford, and Car 506, a Chevrolet. Ron or Major Shannon would gas the two cars instead of leaving the money for the guards to do it.

If the money was left for the guard, he'd go to Exxon across the street prepay $50, gas the car up to $40 then go in and get the change and a new gas receipt, put the $10 in their pocket and turn in the receipt that said $50.

Ron would leave the money for me, though.

If it was raining when you arrived at work, you didn't take Car 506. The windshield didn't work well. I drove 506 one night when it a light misty rain started. I turned on the wipers. Swish, the blades went up and stayed. The rain came down harder. I was at Royal Arms and started driving to the office at twenty-five miles an hour. I didn't try to get on the interstate because I couldn't see the lanes. If you went out of your lane, you could be hit by a truck. It took me two hours to drive ten miles. When I arrived at the office, I filled out my log sheet, typed my reports and went home.

***

Every once in a while I'd have a sharp pain in my right knee. A couple of times my knee gave out and I fell. I meant to go to the doctor, but kept putting it off.

My roommate Nancy wanted to move out of our apartment. We still had eight months on the lease. She decided on Brinkhaven Apartments. She was on Social Security fixed income so I co-signed on the lease. Nancy and her boyfriend James moved into Brinkhaven and took her dog Poppy.

At the end of September 2013, Tish's lease at Rothwood was up. I turned in a written thirty-day notice that Tish would be moving out.

In the phone book, I found an ad for some fly-by-night furniture movers: any size job they'd do for $150.

I made arrangements for them to move Tish. I rented a twelve-foot U-Haul truck, and bought a bundle of wrapping paper, some medium and large boxes plus a clothes box. I dropped off the boxes and paper at Tish's. The next morning I picked up the truck, the two men showed up and we went to the Rothwood Apartments. I backed up as close to the stairs as possible. I walked up to Tish's apartment. She put the kitty in a carrier. There was a bedroom set, queen bed, headboard, dresser/mirror, chest of draws, night stand, a sofa and easy chair, small kitchen table with two chairs and two chairs not assembled, clothes and a few dishes.

The movers carried the furniture down three flights of stairs. They got everything loaded and we drove about six blocks to my apartment. It was the first time Tish and I had lived in the same apartment since 2004. It was now October 2013.

Chapter Twenty-Seven

Focus on Family

Back in January 2009 my daughter Tammy had called me and wanted to know if I wanted a dog, a Chihuahua puppy.

I said yes.

My roommate Nancy's dog, Old Blue, was twelve years old and in poor health.

My daughter gave me her friend Melissa's number. I called and she sent a picture of the puppy. It was a white Chihuahua puppy that Melissa's daughter said looked like the "Beverly Hills Chihuahua" movie dog, so I called the puppy Chloe. We'd have to drive to get her.

Nancy and I left the house around 5 a.m. I stopped for gas, coffee and egg biscuits. We went across Old Hickory to Interstate 40 east, through Knoxville and the Smoky Mountains. One of the eastbound tunnels had caved in so we had to go around on a two-lane road. We went over Black Mountain to Greensboro, North Carolina, down I-85 to Atlanta. We picked up the dog, and we bonded immediately.

We took I-75 to Chattanooga and I-24 to Nashville. Old Blue rode with us and was doing fine. Chloe had no trouble in the van either. Sometimes I placed Chloe behind my neck on my shoulders and she rode that way.

A couple of months later, Melissa asked if I wanted another Chihuahua.

I said yes, and Nancy and I went to get it, and we took Chloe. She jumped from the middle console up on my shoulders.

The new dog's name was Taylor, and was a sibling of Chloe. Nancy was afraid of Taylor. After seven or eight months, when I was at work Taylor started going to the bathroom on the bed, so I took her back to Melissa. The last seventy miles from Dublin Air Force Base on I-16 to Savannah, Taylor lay on my lap and Chloe sat on my shoulders. I'd packed a few clothes for me and Chloe, and Taylor's harness, her swimsuit, coats and dresses.

My grandson Brandon took me to Melissa's house, and he brought his mom's Chihuahua Te-Te, which was another sibling of Chloe and Taylor. Before we left Taylor, we took Chloe, Te-Te and Taylor to McDonald's for ice cream.

***

Brandon, who was my daughter Tammy's youngest son, joined the Georgia Air National Guard. The week before Thanksgiving 2013 he was graduating from basic training at Lubbock Air Force Base west of Dallas.

I took off a week to go to this event. I pack three or four sets of underwear, socks, three long sleeve shirts, three pairs of pants and a carton of cigarettes. In a garment bag I had my Army dress blue uniform with my full-size medals all set up, ready to wear.

I was driving a 2012 Blue Kia van that I'd ordered from Kia Carnival in Nashville. The salesman had to go Atlanta to get it. When they returned Nashville the van still only had 240 miles on it.

I took my dog Chloe, so I packed her bag of food and puppy pads. She had seizures like epilepsy so I packed her medicine, a sweater and a coat in case it was cold there. When I take her outside I used a harness instead of hooking leash to a collar for two reasons: first, if they want to walk fast, they start pulling the collar tight and choking themselves; second, if you buy a cheap collar that doesn't lock, it'll open up. (As a puppy she was free to run, but when she was around six months old I put the leash on her collar. On night I took her out to go to the bathroom, I had a cheap collar on her and when she ran, it opened and she ran out in the road. I chased her for thirty minutes before I caught her. The next morning I bought a harness.)

On a Tuesday I bought a twelve pack of green tea, I gassed up at Exxon, then I was off and running. I stayed on I-24 through Kentucky into Illinois to I-57, and we spent the night at Mt. Vernon, got up at 5 a.m. and ate. Chloe had a small glass cup that Nancy gave her. The cup was two inches high and an inch around. I made a pot of coffee and poured mine and then poured some in Chloe's cup and added some ice so she wouldn't burn her mouth.

After we ate and Chloe finished her coffee, I had myself another cup and threw the bags in the van, gassed up and proceeded across Missouri and down through Kansas. We met Tammy at her husband Jason's parents' house outside Wichita around 5 p.m.

Around 10 pm. Tammy put her bags and a wire cage in the back for the dogs. We grabbed Chloe and Te-Te and headed to Lubbock. Jason and his folks would head out after Jason got off work.

Tammy and I arrived at the air base. We parked and walked to the gate, and Tammy showed the papers for our reservations at the guest house. The guard gave her some lip, so Tammy got a map of the base and we returned to the van and drove up to the gate. I showed my military ID and the papers for the guest house, and we went in. The main office directed us to the rooms. Tammy had four rooms reserved, and her room was in a section of the building that didn't allow pets. Mine was in a different section that did, so I was the keeper the dogs. My room was on the ground floor, and ten feet from the door were walking lanes for the dogs. We unloaded our luggage and dogs bags and cage. Tammy went back to her room while I walked Chloe and Te-Te.

Around 6 p.m. Tammy's oldest son, A.C., arrived at the base so Tammy drove to the gate and gave him his pass. They parked A.C.'s truck then we went out to eat, after which I went back to my room, watched some TV then went to bed.

Around 4:30 a.m. I woke up, put on a pot of coffee and took out the dogs for their constitutional. Chloe and I drank our cups of coffee. After showering, I put on my Army dress blues. Te-Te and Chloe settled into their cage in the room. I drove over to meet the family for breakfast.

At 7 a.m. the squadron commander addressed the parents at the base operations building to explain the schedule of events for the day. After a slide show and briefing, everyone went outside. Across the courtyard were the bleachers that we'd be seated on while the new airmen received their challenge coins.

As I was walking across the courtyard, one of the drill sergeants sidled up to me and said, "After the troops run by you and you're filing into the bleachers, tell them you're in the VIP section."

People lined up along the street on both sides to see the men run through. I told Tammy and everybody that when we went to the bleachers, we'd be in the VIP section. There were some chairs lined up along the street and I sat down there until the troops ran past us, turned around and ran back by before they went to the barracks, showered, dressed and marched back to the courtyard. While we were waiting, a civilian woman helper walked up to me, took my name and said, "In the morning when you arrive at the operations building, tell the people you're a VIP so the cadre will place you on the buses first to go to the parade field and stands."

Around 8 a.m. the squadron came running through and the parents yelled and whistled. The airmen turned around and came back through to more whistling and yelling, heading to the barracks.

We went back to the bleachers, sitting in the bottom left two rows of seats. I had my cane with me. Ten feet to our left was a section of chairs for the Air Force VIPS. As we sat, a couple of Air Force sergeant majors sat down by me and we started talking. One of them asked if I'd like some coffee. I said yes, and the sergeant major went to Starbucks for us. We sat enjoying our coffee.

Before the troops arrived, an Air Force colonel asked me if I was Colonel So-and-So. I said no. It seemed this colonel wasn't coming, so they invited me to take his chair.

I talked to the squadron commander and sergeant major. The first to arrive were the airmen from the different companies. About twenty airmen were recognized for accomplishments, one making the highest PT score, the highest weapons score etc. Then the full companies marched on. The squadron commander told the unit commanders to open ranks. Each company had its own coin. Brandon's company was the Bulldogs. The commanders went through their companies giving the new airmen their coins.

The squadron commander then told the airmen that they could go anywhere on base but not off base and that they had to be at their barracks by 2100 hours (or 9 p.m.). The bugle sounded retreat so the airmen could join their parents.

Brandon found us and we went to the Post Exchange for Brandon to buy another bag for his clothes. His step-dad Jason wanted a bottle of Crown Royal so I showed my military ID to buy it. We went into the snack bar and got something to eat.

A few new airmen came up and asked if I'd take a picture with them.

We got in cars Jack and Carman wanted to return to the rooms we went there for a while.

Brandon took us on a driving tour, showing us his barrack, PT field, some of the buildings for classes. It was a full day. After dinner, I went to my room for the night.

I woke around 4:30 a.m. and fixed coffee. Chloe liked her coffee black with a little sugar to knock the off bitter taste. I dressed in T-shirt and sweat pants to take out the dogs. As we went out, I left the door ajar. The dog run was just outside so I didn't even put them on leashes. While the dogs did their business, the wind started blowing harder and rain started sprinkling.

I looked back at the door to see the wind had blown it closed. My room key, phone and car keys were locked in the room. The temperature was dropping. I couldn't walk around the corner to the office because I didn't have the dogs on leashes. I considered breaking the window.

A woman cane out of a nearby room, and I asked her to call the desk and have someone bring a key to let me in. About ten minutes later a clerk showed up. At least the coffee was still hot. I fed and caged the dogs. In putting on my uniform, I start thinking I should have brought my Army dress whites for variety.

We had family breakfast and went to the operations building. It was announced that due to rain, each company was having its own graduation ceremony. Tammy and a cousin went to Starbucks for coffee. I sat visiting with a chaplain who was a major.

Before I left Nashville, I thought that I'd packed a set of thermal underwear, but I hadn't. By the time Tammy returned with coffee, the wind had picked up and I was cold and shaking. A man offered me his civilian coat, but I thanked him and declined.

The ceremony finally ended, and the parents could enter the barracks and go to the bays to see how their airmen lived. Their bunks were made with hospital corners, the cover starched so you could bounce a quarter on it, a chore the airmen shared with generations of servicemen before them.

A few more airmen wanted pictures with me. Brandon, his drill instructor and I had a picture taken together.

Festivities over, the new airmen were allowed off base to go downtown. We went to old town, walked around looking in different shops. We met Brandon's stepdad Jason's relatives in a Mexican restaurant. The waiters lined up five tables together for us. One of Brandon's friends and his mom joined us too. I visited with an uncle of Jason's who was an Air Force pilot.

Back at the base, Tammy and I checked if we could extend our stay at the guesthouse, but it was booked. Tammy had a friend staying at a Days Inn just off base, so on her recommendation we went there. We put the dogs up, and returned to base to wrap up. We ordered a packet of graduation photos from the PX's photo shop. I think the packet was about $160. I paid a hundred and A.C. and Brandon split the rest.

As they dropped me off at the motel, a woman with two girls said that her oldest daughter on base had taken a picture with me, so I took a picture with the mother and her younger girls. I walked to Denny's for dinner and returned to the room.

Brandon was to fly out early Sunday morning to Wichita Falls, Texas for advanced training as crew chief on a C-130 aircraft.

Around 10 a.m. Tammy called to say to pack up. A storm front was corning in with snow. We headed back to Jason's family's home near Wichita, arriving around 8:30 p.m. I rested till 11:30 then Chloe and I left going north to Manhattan, Kansas, where I stopped to see Josh, my second grandson. We messed around then I visited his aunt Nora. I stayed the night in Junction City. Chloe and I left early the next morning for Nashville. I drove a while, started to get drowsy, so I stopped and napped then went on.

Around midnight I was on I-24 with around 130 miles to go before home. I called the security office number to converse with someone to keep my eyes open. My coworker Al was on duty, and I talked to him about an hour and a half. We got home around 3:30 a.m. and I crashed. I didn't unload the van until the next morning.

It was two days before Thanksgiving. I went to the Kroger and ordered a small turkey dinner for Tish and me. I asked Tish if she wanted to invite her friend Darla over for dinner, so we shared a good meal. On Friday night I returned to work.

The road trip was rewarding. It was a moving experience for me to watch my grandson find his place in the world, and for that place to be in the armed services defending our country, which was a duty close to my heart.

Chapter Twenty-Eight

Health is a Battle

I continued having problems with leg pain and numbness. I frequently used a cane.

Around mid-December 2012, the VA physical therapist had me come in. They gave me a couple of pages of foot and knee exercises to do with a large rubber band.

The exercises didn't do much. I bought a walker, and told the security company I had to quit.

Tish would run water in the bathtub and had to help me in and out of it. One night I was sitting on the porch smoking when Tish took Chloe out to the sidewalk in the parking lot. Chloe took off running down the parking lot with Tish running behind her, and I couldn't do anything to help. There was serious pain in my right knee.

I went to the emergency room at Skyland Hospital and had them X-ray my knee and told them I wanted to see an orthopedic doctor. On January 3, I had an appointment at 2:30 pm. I arrived at 2 p.m., turned in my paperwork and sat down. Time passed, and it was about 4 p.m. I went to the desk. "Nurse, my appointment was supposed to be at 2:30. When am I going to see the doctor?"

A few minutes later the doctor called me in. "Looking at your X-rays, I see you have arthritis in your knees," he said. "Do you want a shot?"

"I know I have arthritis in my knees," I said. "I also have arthritis in my shoulders. Hell, no, I don't want your shot. I want someone to check the nerve endings in my legs. I had a tumor removed from my spine in 2004."

He said to come in at 11 a.m. January 5, two days later. Tish drove me to the appointment. The doctor tested my legs, said there he didn't see anything wrong, but set an appointment for a MRI for January 7.

Tish didn't drive me. I drove myself. I left the house about an hour before my appointment, stopping at Exxon for coffee. Outside the hospital, I sat drinking my coffee and smoking some cigarettes and read a book. I arrived on time for the appointment. The nurse said to undress down to T-shirt, shorts and socks. I hated boxer shorts so I wore bikini shorts. I put on their gown.

As I was trying to get on the gurney, my feet slipped and I almost fell. The nurse gave me a pair of non-skid socks. After the MRI, I dressed and a nurse put me in a wheelchair up to the doctor's office. This doctor looked over the nerve test, looked at the MRI images and told me I had another tumor on my spine.

"Well, I drove myself and I had no feeling from my waist down," I said.

He left a couple black skid marks on his floor rushing me to the emergency room. "Get this man a room!" he told them.

After I was admitted, I called Tish to say I was in the hospital and to bring me some sweats and underwear, my denture cup and my medicine. When she brought the stuff, she had her friend Darla with her, and Darla was drunk. The next day Tish and Darla picked up my van from the hospital lot to take it home. I had a hard time getting Tish to bring me clean clothes.

I called my daughter Tammy and told her that on January 9 I was having surgery to remove anther tumor from my spine. The morning of the surgery I was doped up, and didn't realize Tammy and my old roommate Nancy had showed up. After five or six hours of surgery I saw them in my room and asked them when they got there.

The neurologist came in and explained he used a fusion method and that I had to quit smoking so as not to destroy the surgery. He put in a couple of screws, a few wires and super glue. I had a neck brace on. A couple days later they put a smaller brace on. Tammy stayed a few days then drove back to Wichita until January 30 when I'd be released and she'd fly to Nashville and drive me to Wichita to recover with her and Jason.

In the meantime, I had Tish take my walker to Walgreen's to buy two wheels for the front legs. She brought my walker back and the physical therapist put the wheels on and wrapped and taped a washcloth on the right handle of the walker. I gave Tish one of my ATM cards to buy food and things.

The nurse moved me from intensive care down to a third-floor room, but left my dentures and walker upstairs. I went up to get them myself. It was good exercise. For a few nights I woke up around 1 a.m. I'd hobble from my room down the hall, past the elevators to the nurses' station. I talked to them for a while and they'd give me some coffee and Jell-O or ice cream. After thirty minutes I hobbled back to my room. The night I slipped and fell in my bathroom was the end of my wandering. I could only get out of bed without a nurse helping me.

They treated my smoking habit with nicotine patches. Monday, Wednesday and Friday I went to the gym to do knee and hand exercises and getting in and out of vehicles. On Tuesday and Thursday the orthopedic nurse helped me take showers. Although I could open and close my right hand, I didn't have any strength in it, and was unable to open sugar packets or put my socks on.

The physical therapist at the hospital placed a rubber band around my ankle then I'd bend or straighten my leg, walk up and down steps with and without the walker, wrap two-pound weights on my ankles and raise and lower them. For my arms, I'd use five-pound weights for arm curls, raising arms overhead, practice getting in and out of a car, stacking Legos.

The orthopedic nurse had me practice moving from the wheelchair to the commode and back, soaping a wash cloth, soaping and using a long-handle brush to wash my back, and moving from the wheelchair to stand up and using the commode.

On January 26 I called Tish. She hung up on me. I called back and left a message, "If you don't bring my van here, I'll have Metro come to the apartment for the van. If you lock the door, I'll authorize them to break down the door."

She brought my van and gave the keys to the desk nurse.

I was finally released January 31, a Friday. Tammy drove the van to the front door. The nurse wheeled me to the van, and I stood up and got in. Tammy put my bag in the back, and we went to McDonald's. Tammy opened my door and placed the walker there. I got out, and we went in successfully. After we ate, I went by the office to pick up my last check. We went to the apartment office and told them I couldn't go up the steps to the apartment, and I'd be leaving to live with my daughter. Tammy went up to get Chloe and her stuff that Tish had packed.

We went to the bank for me to make a deposit, and to change the ATM card number from the one I gave Tish. Tammy and I got a motel room. I called my old roommate Nancy to get her boyfriend James and his friend Ray to help take my things to storage the next day.

After breakfast I called the police to have an officer meet me at Orchard Park Apartments to run interference with Tish while I got things out of the apartment. When the policeman arrived, he went and knocked on the door. Tish let him in and told him the only thing I could get out of the kitchen was the table and four chairs, and I could have everything in the bedroom. Most of the dishes were mine, the microwave was mine, but Tish wouldn't let me take them.

I had a four-cubic-foot ice chest, the sofa and easy chair, too, but I didn't argue. I took the table and chairs and five plastic containers on the porch. In the bedroom Tammy, Nancy and James packed up my clothes, my army blues and whites, my case with all my ribbons and medals, my cowboy hat, my briefcase, pistol. The two duffle bags with other military clothes I threw away. The TV stand, safe, a tall cabinet, my army files and certificates were taken to storage. The bedroom set, thirty-two-inch TV and kitchen table, I gave to Nancy. While James and Ray were taking my things to storage, Tammy carried that heavy TV outside. When James and Ray returned I cussed them for forgetting the TV.

I had Tammy drive to Hermitage to Aaron's rent-to-own store. I told them to pick up Tish's bedroom set. I only had three payments left to pay on it, but was worth not paying to annoy Tish.

Tammy and I return to the motel the next morning we say goodbye to Nancy and hit the road.

After my doctor's appointment in early January, I'd turned in a written notice to the apartment complex that I was moving. They said they required a sixty-day notice, and were going to charge me $875 rent ($ 775 rent for February plus the first five days of March). I called the electric company to turn off the lights February 1, and send my final bill to me in Kansas. I heard that Tish and her friend Darla stayed in the apartment until the end of February, and when she moved, all she took was my dishes and her clothes.

***

Tammy and I arrived back in Wichita about February 4.

Tammy's husband Jason and his son built a ramp to the door so I could get in and out of the house, but I wouldn't have the strength to do it for four or five months.

It snowed around six inches that night we got back. In the morning I had an appointment with a doctor to get a referral to a neurology clinic in Wichita. Tammy found a nursing group that did in-home care. The first one was a male nurse. I didn't like him so I had them send another nurse, a female. She was good, but was pregnant so she eventually had to stop. She'd come by once a week to see that the physical therapists were coming and doing what they were supposed to. There was a woman who came in Tuesday and Thursday to give me a bath.

The last week of March the Neurologist gave me permission to remove the brace when I showered. For my first beard shave in a long time, the woman took scissors and cut the three-inch whiskers then used the trimmer on my electric razor then then the electric razor. Next up was a haircut. She used a pair of clippers on old Shaggy.

I had an appointment with the neurologist set for mid-April, but before I saw him I went to the regular doctor's office for X-rays, and the doctor removed the neck brace for good.

I'd ordered a wheelchair while I was in the hospital in Tennessee. It finally showed up in May, but by then I didn't use it much because I was getting around fairly well with the walker. However, there were two events in May for which the wheelchair came in handy.

The company where Tammy worked had a Saturday breakfast and a 5K run or a 2K walk at Wichita's Riverside Park. The two of us entered the 2K walk. I pushed my wheelchair halfway around the course, but after we crossed the bridge I got in the wheelchair. We completed the walk in forty-eight minutes.

I'd also started going to the local senior center. Every other Saturday night they had country dancing. I hadn't been dancing in thirty years, not since my second wife Charlotte and I used to go dancing.

At my regular doctor's appointment a week after the 2K walk and dance, I told him about my adventures and he had a hard time believing that I went dancing, but he seemed to think a 2K walk was normal after you have a tumor removed from your spine. I was also back to using my cane for short periods.

The second event when the wheelchair came in handy was a Memorial Day parade.

I was beginning to lose my boyish figure, with my thirty-inch waist starting to spread out. I fixed my dress blue uniform with my full-size medals. I put my shirt on no problem, but for my pants I had to lie down and have my son-in-law jump up and down on my stomach while my daughter pulled the zipper up and fasten the pants.

Tammy and I went downtown. We started walking. I pushed my wheelchair three or four blocks until we saw people lining up. I sat down. Some of the VA volunteers brought some wheelchair veterans to be in the parade and they ask me to join them. We ended up having a good time.

***

With my recuperation, I started wearing clothes that were easier to put on.

I'd wear cowboy-style shirts with snap buttons instead of real buttons, colored T-shirts with pockets, different colors of sweat pants. Previously, I wore bikini briefs but now wore form fitting boxers. If I went swimming in Tammy's pool, though, I wore Speedos, and that drove her crazy.

I still had dress shirts and pants and blue jeans, but needed help to button them up. It was the same with lace-up shoes.

Also, I started wearing a veteran's Tet Offensive commemorative ball cap with some of my mini medals pinned to it. The reason I wore my medals on my cap was because Senator John Kerry pissed me off.

That may sound funny, but I got tired of seeing him represent America as secretary of state under President Obama because I felt he was a fraud.

We shared some similarities. I was born in January 1942 and grew up in Delta, Colorado, on the western slope of the Rockies. John Kerry was born in December 1943 in Aurora, a suburb of Denver.

In 1966 he joined the Naval Reserve, and went to Vietnam in 1968 as an officer. He was a river boat commander, and, like me, saw combat and was awarded the Bronze Star, Silver Star and three purple hearts.

The differences start when we came back to America. He joined the anti-war movement and in 1971 said that he'd thrown away his medals. My recollection was that he said, "The medals are worthless, but at least with a dollar I can buy a cup of coffee."

He was out of touch with regular people even then; back then a cup of coffee cost fifty cents.

He became a senator in the 1980s and in 2004 ran for president against George W. Bush. During the election, he touted his combat record and claimed he never actually threw away his medals, completely contradicting his 1970s antiwar statement. In 2004, he claimed the medals he threw away had belonged to a veteran who couldn't attend the rally. So, was he lying in the 1970s or was he lying in 2004?

Vietnam combat veterans haven't always been looked on kindly, but I don't shy away from what I did. I defended my country. Maybe I've disagreed with the courses our government takes, but I've never disowned my nation. I believe the fact of the matter was that those antiwar protesters spent more time indulging in sex and drugs than they did engaging in meaningful ways to end the Vietnam War.

John Kerry might have risen to secretary of state and married an heiress (of the Heinz food fortune), but he's still an A-hole in my book.

***

Over a July 4th weekend, we drive to Wichita Falls, Texas, to visit my grandson Brandon.

He had one more week of training to be the crew chief of a C-130 transport plane. He shows us his barrack, the buildings where he learned how to work on a C-130. We went to the post guest house, met a few of his friends, and went downtown to have a good time.

In June 2014 Tammy and I went to the DMV to get our Kansas driver licenses. A couple of weeks later Jason got his Kansas license, too. Mine had a veteran insignia on it. After so many years of spending time in Kansas here and there, I was finally permanent.

I started driving again, but usually too far. The farthest I'd drive would be to Ponca City a few times.

After the last surgery, I lost the ability to close my right hand, and also lost the sense of feeling on my skin from my right little finger to my elbow. I had to be careful. I could rest my elbow on a hot surface and burn the skin off and not know it.

Chapter Twenty-Nine

I Guess I'm Getting Old

By May 2014, Tammy was taking me to the local senior center on a regular basis.

While I was in Nashville, I'd worked and was on the go all the time and never knew anything about senior centers. The local one in the Wichita suburb of Park City offered events every day. It served lunch every day. Tuesdays and Thursdays were chair exercises. Line dancing and square dancing were each offered once a week. I tried both, but they moved too fast for me.

At my son-in-law Jason's parents' house, I read the newsletter for their suburb's senior center and saw they were offering a class on how to use iPhones, iPods and computers the next Thursday morning. I went. I learned some basic skills, and was glad I did. I felt like I could communicate a little better with my kids and grandkids.

At the Wichita VA hospital, I saw a doctor and took all my medicines with me so he'd know what to order for me. A couple of weeks later I received a letter stating I had an appointment at a spinal cord clinic August 17, and not to eat or drink anything after the middle of the night before. When I arrived, they took blood and urine samples. Then I went to the second floor. A questionnaire asked if I'd ever had any operations, when and for what. 1) Gunshot wound, right front chest, May 1968, Vietnam; 2) Tumor removed from spine, November 2004, VA Nashville; 3) Tumor removed from spine, January 2014, Skyline Hospital, Nashville. I took my records from Skyland and Wichita with me.

The doctor poked me with a pin in the right thumb. "Did you feel it?" he asked.

"Yes, the feeling is at skin level," I said.

He poked my right little finger.

"No."

He poked the top of my forearm.

"Yes, skin level."

He poked the underside of my forearm.

"I know you're doing something, but what, I don't know," I said. The doctor continued poking all over my body. The next test was pushing and pulling my arms and legs. Then I had X-rays. I was there five hours. There was a medicine hot line I could call and reorder some of my pills as needed, like blood pressure and vitamins. For a couple of medicines that I got monthly, I'd have to call my nurse and pick it up the next day.

I met a woman named Sandy at the senior center, and we had a couple of dates then parted company. Dating is tough when you're older.

The week before Thanksgiving 2014, Tammy and I went to College Station, Texas, between Waco and Houston, and home of Texas A&M University. We spent a few days with Tammy's oldest boy, A.C. He went to college there to be a physical therapist.

We returned to Wichita for Thanksgiving dinner at Jason's parents' house.

I no longer helped or got in the way of baking pumpkin pies. The most I made one year was twenty-four pumpkin pies. I'd make the pumpkin pie filling from scratch, but bought the ready-made pie crust. I'd bake four pies at a time. I enjoyed the holidays when I made the rest of the food, too: dressing; a turkey or ham marinated in Andre Champagne; a pan of sweet potatoes with maraschino cherries, chopped pineapple, cinnamon and marsh-mallows.

Nowadays I let other people do the cooking and add my two cents by eating.

A few days before Christmas, Tammy's youngest son, Brandon, came in from Georgia, where he was attending school when he wasn't on Air National

Guard duty. About three inches of snow fell, and the family bought a plastic sled and pulled it around with a four-wheeler.

For the afternoon of New Year's Day 2015, we went to Jason's parents' house for a while. The next morning we took Brandon to the airport, so he could get back for school. A couple weeks later, Tammy and Jason gave me a small birthday party. I got a new western shirt and a pair of blue jeans.

In April, Tammy, Jason and I went to Waco, Texas, for A.C.'s wedding. We stopped in Ponca City to pick up a longtime friend of Tammy's, Jean. In Waco around 5 p.m., Tammy and Jason went to the rehearsal and supper, while Jean and I went to what we thought looked like the only decent restaurant in town.

Just as Jean and I finished eating, A.C. and his wedding party walked in. We all said hello, and I met his fiancé. I didn't recognize A.C.'s father John or John's brother; it'd been so long since I'd seen them.

We stayed in cabins at a small resort with a lake. One of Jason's cousins from San Antonio brought his boat, and we tooled around a bit during the trip.

The wedding was outside. Tammy and Jason sat in the front row with the bride's parents, and I sat in the right section, second row, with A.C.'s dad John and John's brother Steve and his family. That time I recognized them.

It was one of the best weddings I'd been to, much bigger than any of my own four.

***

For Memorial Day weekend, I didn't go to any parades or dress up, but I did go to a local American Legion and VFW Post and have a couple of drinks and talk to other veterans for a while.

It was around this time Tammy asked me about something every family deals with whether they want to or not: What were my plans for when I die?

With my health problems and the death of my sister Donna, it was something I'd thought about. I'd already gone to the JAG lawyers at Wichita's

McConnell Air Force Base to make a new will. Tammy had been made executor of my estate, and was given power of attorney.

I drove to the military cemetery in Winfield, Kansas, south of Wichita, to reserve a plot.

Tammy and I went to the funeral home in the suburb of Derby and picked out the casket and made arrangements for an honor guard, and transportation to the cemetery. I'd be buried in a uniform, my dress green uniform. I go to G.I. Jane's military store to pick out the jacket and pants, then had her sew the 25th patch, E-7 stripes, ten stripes on the left sleeve (for thirty years of service), five stripes on the right sleeve (for two-and-a-half years of combat duty). I bought new collar brass that had the lacquer to stay shiny. I bought new EIB and CIB medals, all new ribbons: eighteen for the left side and five for the right side, and a new infantry rope.

My grandson Brandon would receive my Army dress blues with my full-size medals. My grandson A.C. would receive my Army dress white uniform with my miniature medals.

Since my waist had spread out from thirty inches to thirty-six inches, I'd had to replace both the dress blue pants and black pants for the dress white uniform. Then I could get into the pants without my son-in-law jumping up and down on my stomach.

Off and on during the summer, Tammy and Jason went to Ponca City to work on a relative's house. They were there for the July 4 weekend so I drove down and rented a room. I brought Chloe and Te-Te with me. We went to someone else's house with an in-ground pool. There were some water guns, and Tammy squirted Jason's parents and me.

I didn't have any swimming trunks, but I set my watch and wallet on a table, and jumped in the pool anyway, in my clothes. I dunked Tammy.

***

August marked my first annual checkup since my last surgery. I had them do an MRI to see if they'd removed the whole tumor, and there was no sign of it.

I planned on having a MRI done every two or three years. I didn't want to let another tumor get as big as that last one was.

***

That same month, Jason's son Logan joined me on a drive to Nashville. I was going to pick up my ex-roommate Nancy and bring her to Kansas for a month.

As we went through Clarksville, Tennessee, I pulled off Interstate 24 to Fort Campbell.

We pulled on post, and I stopped at the museum. I showed Logan around the exhibits. In the gift shop, my good friend Rosie wasn't working but would be there the next day. A lady named Ashley was working. I asked her about Colonel David, Colonel Jones, and Colonel Loachner. Unfortunately, David and Jones had died.

Logan and I got back on the road to Nashville. We still had seventy miles to go to Nashville. Once in town, we got a hotel room. We stopped at the old security office and visited a while.

In April I'd received divorce papers from Tish and I'd told her lawyer that we were already divorced. I recalled the lawyer saying that Tish was working at an Enterprise car rental, so I drove to three or four agencies on Gallatin Road up to Goodlettsville to see if I could find her. She wasn't at any of the places that I checked.

I drove back to Old Hickory Boulevard and found Nancy's house. Her puppy growled at me but a little later he wanted me to pet him. I told Nancy we'd pick her up at 9 a.m.

We go to Shute Lane and into Hermitage to my favorite Exxon station. One of the ladies who worked that I always talked to, Bridget, was on duty and when she saw me, she howled, "Where the hell have you been?"

"I live in Kansas now with the Wizard of Oz," I said. I ask her about her co-worker Jim. She said he'd a stroke. Jim was a couple years older than me and grew up in a little town near my hometown of Delta, Colorado.

After we talked to Bridget for a while, I showed Logan a few places I patrolled. I showed a spot where a woman climbed over the fence and stole some aluminum air conditioner cores and electrical wiring. We stopped at McDonald's and I talked to one of the old clerks I knew.

We picked up Nancy and drove downtown to show Logan Tootsie's Bar, the old Ryman Auditorium, the football stadium, and the Ramada Inn in front of the stadium that has a guitar-shaped pool in the basement.

We went back through Clarksville and Fort Campbell. At the Museum I showed Nancy and Logan around the pavilion, and we talked to Rosie. It was great to see her again. She told us there were a couple of halls in Division's new headquarter building that had displays. We took a look. One display had a five-foot wood pole that Lincoln was carried on, and another included some papers for Audie Murphy's leadership completion.

We hit the road again, stopping in Mt. Vernon for food and motel. The motel was packed full because the next day was the first day of deer season.

We drove across Missouri, and at Kansas City took I-35 into Wichita. Around 4 p.m. we dropped Logan at his home and then we went to Tammy and Jason's house. While Nancy was in Wichita, I showed her several parks, the zoo, things like that.

We decided to go to the Halloween dance at the senior center. The costume that Nancy picked out at the costume store surprised me because Nancy didn't wear dresses that often, and a dress that short I'd never seen her in. We found her some matching shoes and a wand at Wal-Mart.

We had fun at the dance. Not everybody dressed up for Halloween, but one couple dressed as chefs with big floppy chef hats and white aprons. One man was a security guard, another couple dressed as clowns. Around 8 p.m. the dancing stopped for thirty minutes to eat and have a raffle, and then back to dancing.

For Veterans Day I put on my dress white uniform and we went to downtown Wichita for a parade. We went to the end where the floats would park. There was a helicopter, a tank and truck from Fort Riley. I talked to the troops there a few minutes then we found a curb to sit on and waited for the parade. Afterward we went to a VFW post for drinks and then home.

A few days before Thanksgiving, Logan and I drove Nancy back to Nashville.

Somewhere between O'Fallon and Mt. Vernon, Logan hadn't watched the gas gauge and we were close to fumes. It was late but we found an open gas station and I had Logan put in $10, enough to get to Mt. Vernon. We stayed at the same motel as before.

In Nashville around 12:30 p.m., I decided to look for Tish again at a few more Enterprise offices. Tish wasn't working at any of them. I went all the way to Gallatin, and still didn't find her. We dropped off Nancy at home, visited a bit. When Logan and I left, we stopped back at the Exxon to see Bridget for a few minutes.

Then I drove from Hermitage to Fesslers Lane and Murfreesboro Road, where the Drake Motel was. They had a sign that said "DRAKE MOTEL, WHERE THE STARS STAY." That might have been true when it was first built. In the lobby, they had photos of a lot of actors and singers like Dolly Parton. A room was $50 a night, the carpets were grungy, the furniture was scratched, and everything had cigarette burns. If any stars stayed there anymore, they were on the downhill slide.

But, we still took a room there. We went next door to eat at Sonic. It was still only 8 p.m. on a Saturday, so I told Logan, "Come on, we're going into town."

At Mapco around the corner, we hit the doughnut shop. Sure enough, one of the old bakers I knew from my guard rounds was working. He told me he'd worked six months and quit, and then about eight months later they hired him back.

I looked for Tish some more. We stopped back in at the Hayes Security office and I talked to the manager, Ron, and Major Shannon. They said they didn't have any patrol routes. They'd lost most of the properties. I didn't ask but I figured they may have had ten people working, including themselves.

I took Logan downtown. We parked in the underground parking lot next to the old Ryman Auditorium, the original home of the Grand Ole Opry. As we passed I heard someone say Merle Haggard was playing, but if you hadn't gotten a ticket in advance you weren't getting in.

We walked to Broadway. Around the corner three doors down was Tootsie's Bar, a real honky tonk. We went in and it was packed. A band was on stage on the right side of the door. We fought our way through the crowd and up to the second floor, where there were two bands playing. I ordered Logan a beer and myself a rum and Coke. I went to the restroom on the third floor, and when I returned Logan had accidently spilled my drink so I went to the bar and ordered another. A man standing at the bar noticed my cap with the medals. He bought my drink, and I thanked him.

A table came open so we sat. Pretty soon two young women wanted to sit with us. I let them. They wanted to buy me a drink but this time I ordered a plain Coke because I didn't want to get drunk and take advantage of those gals. After an hour, we went back down to the first floor. I ordered another beer for Logan and another Coke for me. A man at the bar noticed us and told the waitress that he'd pay for the drinks.

Logan couldn't believe that everybody was buying me drinks. After fifteen minutes I told Logan we'd leave for some other shops and bars. As I was starting out the door, one of the guitarists stopped me to ask about my cap.

"Don't go anywhere because we're going to play a song for you," he said. He bought me a drink too. He told the crowd I was a Vietnam veteran, and the band played me a song.

When I finally got outside Logan was standing next to an Elvis impersonator. I had them take a picture.

We went in a couple of western clothing stores. You could buy a cowboy hat, but if you wanted a Stetson brand hat, you'd better have some money; the price started around $175 and went up. The cowboy boots usually started around $90 and the shirts and pants ran between $30 and $80.

Now, if you wanted a suit with rhinestones like little Jimmy Dickens or Porter Wagoner, you'd pay around $1,000.

We entered an Earnest Tubb Record Shop then we started in another bar but couldn't get in because Logan left his driver's license at the motel. We wandered up and down the street with everybody else.

There were horse-and-buggy rides and limo rides too, but traffic was at a crawl. We returned to our room around 2 a.m.

The next morning we headed back to Wichita. This time when we went through Clarksville I decided to show Logan the train caboose downtown. I stopped at a Dollar General store for directions to the old train depot.

The depot museum wasn't open on Sundays, but the guide was there. A man and his sons had stopped there at the same time we did so the guide gave us a tour anyway. I told the guide how the museum got hold of it.

In the spring of 1997 we took an old caboose that had been at Fort Campbell in WWII, and had some volunteers repaint it.

It was kind of an inconvenience for me because wherever the volunteers poured paint thinner on the ground, the base EPA agent made me dig up a two-foot round hole by two-feet deep, place it in a plastic bag then place the bag inside a five-gallon can with the lid on and sealed and take the cans to a hazardous material collection point.

After we'd finished painting the caboose, we put it on two semi-trucks and took it down to the Clarksville train depot and placed it on the tracks behind a train engine that was there. The guide unlocked the caboose and let us inside.

***

Back in Wichita for Thanksgiving Day, everybody came to Tammy and Jason's house for dinner.

A couple of weeks before Christmas, Brandon came home for a month.

On New Year's Day, Jason wanted to go to a military store and look around. We went to the Alpha 1 Drop Zone in west Wichita, but when we got there we discovered it was closed for the holiday. On Monday, Brandon and I went back.

We only figured on staying ten or fifteen minutes, but I started talking to the owner, Steve Gonzales, and he started telling me about different events he'd planned for 2016, and he asked if I'd come to these functions.

March 14-18 was the Week of Heroes at the downtown Museum of World Treasures. On Monday I sported my Army dress blue uniform with full-size medals. I visited with people and passed out some fliers.

School kids completed various tasks and received prizes like military-style dog tags with their names on them.

On Tuesday morning, I joined a panel of Vietnam veterans and we each talked for ten minutes about what we did in the Vietnam War. We had two helicopter pilots, a B-52 pilot, a combat photographer who sent photos to intelligence, and a guy who worked in intelligence. As a regular soldier, a grunt, in the middle of combat, I required from six to ten people like these guys supporting me. The intelligence person would give me information where the enemy was, and I would give him information. Troops, bullets and beans all came via helicopter and plane.

The Week of the Heroes was capped off that Saturday, March 19, at Alpha 1 Drop Zone, when Steve hosted a meet-and-greet for women veterans. There were some American Legion and VFW club members who formed two lines of honor guards for the women veterans to walk through into the building.

One woman had been a Marine recruiter during the Vietnam War, another was a WWII WAC (Women's Army Corps) member, and there were others.

I met Wichita's Rosie the Riveter, a lady named Connie Palacioz, who worked in the local Boeing Aircraft factory during WWII. If it weren't for gallant and determined women in all American cities and factories, we wouldn't have won WWII with Germany and Japan blowing up four planes and five tanks a week. All our Rosie the Riveters would build seven planes and eight tanks a week to offset and gain on the losses.

That day was the highlight of the week for me, but that morning as I was getting ready to go to it, a button popped off my dress blue jacket. I put it in my pocket and stopped for some gas station coffee. As I was getting back in my van, another button popped off. I raced to GI Jane's for a quick repair. She happened to be open, and moved all four buttons a bit to the left so it looked like nothing was wrong. I was saved.

It was an honor meeting Ms. Palacioz. She had another moment in the sun in 2017 when a B-29 bomber she had helped build was restored in Wichita and took to the skies again. The TV news stations kept her busy with interviews when that happened.

It was also great connecting with Steve Gonzalez of Alpha 1 Drop Zone. He is an Air Force Vietnam veteran who earned the Silver Star, Bronze Star and three Purple Hearts. His customers know he cares about the military community. He celebrated twenty-five years in business in April 2016.

Helping with his events have given me motivation to get out and about on more than a few days.

***

For Jason's fiftieth birthday party in October 2015, his parents rented a hall, and someone made a birthday card telling the different events throughout his life using different brands of candy bars: Baby Ruth, Zero, Butterfinger.

The next month, after Thanksgiving dinner, we went to the nearby Wal-Mart to stake out the Black Friday starting at 8 p.m. They handed out wristbands for items in limited stock. I was interested in a new laptop computer for $200 and Jason and Tammy wanted a big-screen TV and a few other items. Ten minutes before 9 Jason wheels me to electronics where the laptops were being sold, but we found out the clerks had already passed out all the wristbands for the laptops.

The next day Tammy started putting up Christmas things: the tree, outside lights, the Christmas socks. Everyone had a sock: Jason, Tammy, A.C., Brandon, me, Te-Te, Chloe and Jason's big dog Duke.

Early Christmas morning we opened presents, but the dogs were the winners. Duke got a 12 inch bone to gnaw on, and Chloe and Te-Te each got a small bag of doggie treats and a small toy bone. Later, Jason's folks, sister and brother came over for dinner.

In June 2016 Tammy, Jason and I went to Junction City to celebrate my ex-wife Mary's birthday. Normally, Mary and I couldn't be in the same area more than ten minutes without arguing, but we were there almost six hours without arguing.

Maybe Mary and I didn't get along and didn't have a wonderful marriage, but our kids turned out to be a great legacy, and they have kids of their own, some of whom have already started families.

Nora had one boy and a girl

Loretta had one boy

Alvin had one boy

Nancy had three boys and one girl

Tammy had two boys

Ella had two boys and one girl

Total: ten boys and three girls

As for great-grandchildren:

Nora's daughter Jenna had one boy

Loretta's son Josh had one boy and one girl

Ella's son Anthony had one boy and one girl

Ella's son Jonathon had one boy and one girl

Total: four boys and three girls.

At an event honoring women veterans at Wichita's Alpha 1 Drop Zone military store, I met Connie Palacioz, who worked as a riveter on B-29 bombers at Boeing Aircraft during WWII.

Chapter Thirty

Wrapping It Up

I spent most of 2016 and 2017 writing down my memories so my family and maybe other readers would know what I experienced as a boy on a farm, as a soldier at war, and as a man in regular life.

Maybe you'll have identified with my experiences or learned a few things. Maybe you'll say thank you to a veteran after getting an idea of what they go through to keep America safe.

Sometimes we veterans keep paying the price of our service over a period of years, both psychologically and physically. In my case, maybe I would be healthier if I hadn't suffered battle wounds and exposure to chemical agents like Agent Orange in Vietnam. But, if I could do it again, would I still fight for my country's freedom? Yes.

With new generations of American soldiers returning to civilian life after serving in Afghanistan, Iraq and elsewhere, it's important to contact our senators and representatives on a regular basis to make sure the government maintains health care for the people who preserve our freedoms.

***

In writing down your own story, it can be hard coming up with an ending. I think I have a good one, though.

In May 2017, as I was wrapping up this project, a letter reached me saying I'd been invited on one of the charity Honor Flights that take veterans to visit the memorials in Washington, D.C.

I submitted a request for the trip in 2014. Priority is given to older and ill veterans of World War II then Korea and Vietnam. The Honor Flight Network transported more than 20,500 veterans just in 2016.

The trip lasted three days in early June 2017.

My daughter Tammy flew out with me early on a Tuesday, and we arrived in Washington, D.C., in early afternoon and were taken to Fort McHenry in Baltimore, where the 1812 siege inspired Francis Scott Key to write "The Star Spangled Banner."

The next day we visited the monuments on the National Mall: the Washington Monument, Lincoln Memorial, Martin Luther King Jr. Memorial, and the National WWII Memorial. Tammy got a real workout pushing me in a wheelchair.

Last, we visited the Vietnam Veterans Memorial Wall.

I had previously seen the traveling Vietnam Memorial, and at that time, in the 1990s, I couldn't bring myself to get close enough to touch it. This time was different. I have come to terms with what the monument represents, the friends and cohorts I lost, and the experiences I had.

I touched the memorial wall. I found a few names. It was one of the most profound moments of my life. Most of the day went by quickly, but I'll hold that memory at the wall.

I'd encourage every veteran to make the journey. In Kansas, Mike and Connie VanCampen and their team do a tremendous job of organizing and leading these Honor Flight trips.

We left Washington early the next morning, Thursday, and we were greeted in Wichita by a firehose salute from the airport fire department. After getting off the plane, we walked toward the front doors to leave, and there was a crowd to welcome us back with cheers and signs saying, "Thank you."

I like to wear my Tet Offensive commemorative ball cap. On one side I pinned my mini Legion of Merit and three mini Purple Hearts and on the other side my mini Silver Star and my mini Bronze Star for personal valor and the two additional meritorious Bronze Stars awarded to units I was in.

ACKNOWLEDGMENTS

I want to thank fellow Vietnam veteran Steve Gonzalez, owner of Alpha 1 Drop Zone in Wichita, Kansas, for his encouragement and fellowship.

Ron Adams, a Vietnam veteran, and U.L. "Rip" Gooch, a WWII veteran, retired Kansas state senator and aviator, gave me information and encouragement. They also taught by example through their memoirs.

Thanks also to cover designer Crystal Gibbon and my collaborator Glen Sharp for making my words fit for print. He also co-authored Rip Gooch's memoir, *Black Horizons: One Aviator's Experience in the Post-Tuskegee Era.*

If you have comments about this book, you can send them to us directly by emailing TwiceASoldier1961@gmail.com. You are invited to find our *Twice a Soldier* book page on Facebook, and to leave a review on Amazon.com.

Additional copies

of this book

may be purchased on

Amazon.com

or in bulk

at a discount

from the author at

twiceasoldier1961@gmail.com

92830899R00222

Made in the USA
Lexington, KY
09 July 2018